Fast strategy

How strategic agility will help you stay ahead of the game

Yves Doz and Mikko Kosonen

Ideas.Action.Impact.
Wharton School Publishing

An imprint of Pearson Education

Harlow, England • London • New York • Boston • San Francisco • Toronto • Sydney • Singapore • Hong Kong
Tokyo • Seoul • Taipei • New Delhi • Cape Town • Madrid • Mexico City • Amsterdam • Munich • Paris • Milan

PEARSON EDUCATION LIMITED

Edinburgh Gate
Harlow CM20 2JE
Tel: +44 (0)1279 623623
Fax: +44 (0)1279 431059
Website: www.pearsoned.co.uk

First published in Great Britain in 2008

ISBN: 978-0-273-71244-2

British Library Cataloguing-in-Publication Data
A catalogue record for this book is available from the British Library

Library of Congress Cataloging-in-Publication Data
Doz, Yves L.
   Fast strategy : how strategic agility will help you stay ahead of the game / Yves Doz and
Mikko. Kosonen.
        p. cm.
   Includes index.
   ISBN 978-0-273-71244-2
   1.   Strategic planning. I. Kosonen, Mikko. II. Title.
   HD30.28.D696 2008
   658.4'012—dc22

2007039097

10 9 8 7 6 5 4 3 2
11 10 09 08

Typeset in 9pt Stone Serif by 3
Printed in Great Britain by Henry Ling Limited, at the Dorest Press, Dorchester, DT1 1HD

The publisher's policy is to use paper manufactured from sustainble forests.

Praise for *Fast Strategy*

"This book addresses in a fresh way, one of today's key leadership challenges: how to transform your core business without losing momentum. The authors provide stimulating food for thought on strategic agility."

Henning Kagermann, Chief Executive Officer, SAP.

"Strategic agility is perhaps the strategic imperative facing senior leaders and their teams. *Fast Strategy* cogently presents a set of provocative and fresh ideas that are rooted in current research as well as practice. Doz and Kosonen's researcher/practitioner collaboration is one of those rare managerial books that is rigorous as well as relevant. I found of particular interest their call for balance between managerial passion and analytics in the shaping of strategic agility."

Michael L. Tushman, Professor of Business Administration, Harvard Business School

"Most companies fall victims to the curse of success, very few show the strategic agility needed for sustaining outstanding performance. Doz and Kosonen provide practical and compelling advice on how CEOs and their teams can achieve strategic agility."

Gary Hamel, Visiting Professor at the London Business School, and Director of the Management Innovation Lab

"Yves Doz and Mikko Kosonen provide tremendous insight into one of the most relevant issues in business today: how does a company balance the need for stability and operational efficiency with the need to renew itself? This book will help every executive and manager understand their own company better and, ultimately, to make it more competitive."

Olli-Pekka Kallasvuo, President and CEO, Nokia

"It has long been a dilemma – how do companies reinvent themselves? The *Fast Strategy* findings are an important contribution – being attentive to the evolving environment and developing the capacity within a leadership team for 'collective commitment' resonates powerfully with my own experience. A thought-provoking contribution for those seeking to renew their own business."

Vivienne Cox, Chief Executive – Gas, Power & Renewables, BP plc

"In *Fast Strategy*, Doz and Kosonen have done a great job passing the challenges that all top managements are facing as the pace of strategic change accelerates. They have inventoried the myriad problems that are prevalent in large, established companies; prescribed tools to move them consistently toward more strategic agility; and provided a taxonomy of situations companies start from which suggest various orderly ways to apply them. I found their treatment of the subject very useful."

Craig Mundie, Chief Research and Strategy Officer, Microsoft

"In today's fast-paced global economy, an organization's ability to innovate and continuously re-invent itself hinges on fast, decisive action and open collaboration in the marketplace.   It is not enough to talk about change — you need to take bold risks and affect change through your actions. Yves and Mikko offer a compelling blueprint that guides and challenges every business leader to embrace this imperative."

Nick Donofrio, Executive Vice President, Innovation and Technology, IBM

To our families,
in appreciation for their support

Contents

Acknowledgments

Our warmest thanks go to the two people without whom this book would not have been written. The authors' collaboration on this project stems from a series of exchanges and dialogues on the Advisory Board of the Center for Knowledge and Innovation Research (CKIR) at the Helsinki School of Economics. Seija Kulkki, CKIR's Director, was a catalyst in getting our project started. Without Muriel Larvaron, who cheerfully and tirelessly acted as project manager, research assistant, and sounding board and kept us going in good and in difficult times, *Fast Strategy* would never have been completed. We thank both of them very warmly.

Many others contributed to make this book possible. Jorma Ollila, the Chairman, and Olli-Pekka Kallasvuo, the CEO of Nokia, allowed Mikko Kosonen to devote his full time and energy to our research and writing for over a year. Landis Gabel and Anil Gaba provided support, encouragement and funding for Yves' work, as colleagues and in their roles as R&D Deans at INSEAD.

A few executives played a decisive role in making our field research possible in their companies, in particular, Karthik Krishnamurthy at Cisco, Debbie Brackeen at Hewlett Packard, Claudia Woody at IBM, Martin Curley at Intel, Ted Sapountzis at SAP. We are very grateful for their support. We are also deeply grateful to the nearly 150 executives, in many different companies, who generously gave us their time for interviews, openly shared their experience and their insights, and encouraged us with our research.

Obviously, the work of many researchers stimulated our thoughts as we were trying to build inductively a model of strategic agility. In particular, the research of Joseph Bower, Robert Burgelman, Kathy Eisenhardt, Sumantra Ghoshal, Quy Huy and C. K. Prahalad was a source of guidance and inspiration in our efforts.

Colleagues gave us very valuable feedback at various points in our work: Sari Baldauf, Matti Alahuhta, Pekka Ala-Pietilä and Hallstein Moerk in

Finland; and Joseph Bower, Dominique Héau, José Santos, Gabriel Szulanski and Keeley Wilson, among others. INSEAD MBA participants, executives and academics in conferences and seminars where we presented our work also made very helpful suggestions and added to our understanding of a complex phenomenon.

We also want to express our deep appreciation to Olli-Pekka Kallasvuo not only for his continuous interest and support, but also for applying the findings from our research in the company he leads. We could not expect a greater show of commitment and confidence.

Finally we thank Tim Moore, Jerry Wind, and Liz Gooster, our editor, for their enthusiasm for publishing a book on strategic agility and their support for our work, and Jennifer Mair for helping us edit the text. Their support and commitment were precious.

Despite the help, advice, and encouragement we received from so many quarters in this project, its failings and limitations remain entirely ours.

Yves Doz and Mikko Kosonen
Fontainebleau and Helsinki
September 2007

Introduction

What allows companies to be strategic and agile? Usually being fast evokes images of nimbleness and flexibility, while being strategic evokes images of being strong but ponderous, and hence slow. Where does speed in strategic decisions and commitments come from?

Why are some companies able to thrive on disruptions, and catch the waves of technology or market discontinuities to outrun and beat their competitors, when others falter or fall into oblivion?

Why did Digital Equipment, unable to commit to a new strategy and a new business model in time, disappear? Why, and how, was IBM reborn, like a phoenix, as a solution, service, and software provider, from the ashes of computer hardware? How is Nokia transforming itself to capitalize on internet mobility services? What challenges does SAP face in changing its business model to open platforms, mid-market development and indirect distribution? Was Carly Fiorina right at HP, but not given the time to succeed by an overly impatient board? How did Canon renew itself? Why do Cisco and Intel keep succeeding?

Strategically agile companies not only learn to make fast turns and transform themselves without losing momentum but their CEOs and top teams also have higher ambitions: to make their companies permanently, regularly, able to take advantage of change and disruption. They want their organizations to learn to thrive on continuous waves of change, not to periodically and painfully adjust to change, in an alternation of periods of stability and moments of upheaval. Put differently, they want their companies to learn a new competitive game: the fast strategy game – a game where nothing can be taken for granted, where no competitive edge may last, where innovation and the constant development of new capabilities are the only sources of advantage.

What separates winners from losers in the fast strategy game? How differently are the winners led? How are they organized? How do they make decisions? These are the questions we set out to answer in this book.

In our research, we saw that winning at the fast strategy game hinges on a few deciding differences. One such difference is high strategic sensitivity: the early awareness of incipient trends and converging forces, the acute perceptions of their importance, and the intense sense-making and reflective efforts they trigger. Winners have sharp emergent insights on strategic situations, as they develop and evolve, and are ready to pounce, like the leopard jumps and strikes its prey.

Winners of the fast strategy game are also prepared to take key decisions, and make real commitments fast. In many companies decisions of major importance are usually stuck in individual hesitancy – and fear – and mired in bureaucratic politics. But, with the fast strategy approach, the collective commitment of the management allows firm decisions to be reached at lightning speed once a strategic situation is understood, and the choices it opens or closes intellectually are grasped. Commitments are not delayed by personal insecurities and political stalemates at the top.

Commitments, though, are only as good as the resources put behind them. Resource mobilization, and fluidity in their deployment or redeployment, provide the underpinning – a necessary but not sufficient enabler – to fast strategies. Together,

- strategic sensitivity
- collective commitments and
- resource fluidity

allow CEOs and their management teams to perceive early, decide quickly, and strike with strength and speed.

In this book you will see how these three elements comprise the capability for an organization's fast strategy, providing a consistent and effective pattern of resource allocation over time, but one that can be adjusted and evolve fast in response to strategic opportunities. Of course, you could argue that there are other specific mechanisms – such as corporate venturing and processes, such as organizational learning – that are part and parcel of strategic agility. These mechanisms and processes, however, all contribute to the three dimensions of our focus, which are the essence of strategic agility, the key to fast strategies.

Where is strategic agility needed most?

How to achieve strategic agility has been an age-old dilemma since the beginnings of strategic management. We believe that strategic agility is even more solely needed today than in the past. More and more companies are exposed to fast and complex changes. Of course, though, strategic agility is needed to respond to these changes. Some companies have been able, at least for now, to shelter themselves from the demands for strategic agility. In some cases, change was slow, and simple, predictable and linear. In others, change was slow, or some form of corporate entrepreneurship was sufficient to address fast changes.

For about a century the basic architecture of the car as a product has not changed and, since Ford introduced the "Model T" and assembly lines a century ago, its manufacturing process has not changed much either, notwithstanding the diffusion of Japanese lean manufacturing, allowing more efficient, higher quality production. The automobile industry has not been exposed to rapid change – it has so far negotiated fuel emission standards that were compatible with slow adaptation – nor has it faced huge convergence and complexity increases, despite the growing importance of electronics in the car. Ultimately operational capabilities – efficiency, quality, supply chain management – control the business. Style and design matter too, but operational deficiencies are unforgiving. The better companies – Toyota, Honda, Volkswagen – win, while the weaker ones disappear (Rover) or suffer agonies (Ford). Hybrids may change the popularity of one brand or another, depending on the price of oil and the timing of product introductions, and now give a further advantage to Toyota, but they do not fundamentally transform the nature of the competitive game.

Industries which go through complex but slow change can rely on conventional strategic planning. Weapons and military intelligence and control systems, for instance, are increasingly complex, with the convergence of many technological and strong disruptions (Al Qaeda being a more inventive and less predictable enemy than the Soviet Union) but they change slowly. It is not unheard of for a young engineer fresh from school to start on the predevelopment of a particular weapon system and retire, 30-odd years later, still working on the same system! It's not a coincidence that strategic planning emerged from Lockheed in the 1960s, popularized by Igor Ansoff and his followers.[1] Nuclear proliferation and global (rather than localized) terrorism have the potential to increase dramatically the need for strategic agility in weapons systems firms and their customers, but this is hardly starting yet.

Medical equipment and healthcare company Johnson & Johnson (J&J) has been very successful across a broad range of medical devices, from contact lenses to stents, as well as a range of consumables from wound treatments to injection needles and, of course, pharmaceuticals. Some of these areas do go through a lot of change fast, with the development of new radical procedures, changes in regulation, genetics, etc. But J&J's opportunities are relatively separate and independent from one another. J&J can pursue each as an entrepreneurial business opportunity, in a distinct business unit. The overall logic of the company is based on entrepreneurship. Many other, mostly American, success stories – such as HP in test instruments and medical instruments, or 3M in chemical applications – are based on a similar logic: entrepreneurial proliferation of distinct products and small business units.

More and more companies, though, are facing the real challenge of speed and complexity (see upper right corner of Figure I.1): interdependent opportunities in the world of convergence and fuzzy industry boundaries, and of rapid emergent systemic change in environment. This is the most difficult position: companies are facing both very complex emergent systemic strategic situations, and situations that develop fast, and where the fast strategy game is such that winners and losers may be decided very early, without anyone even noticing.[2] Obviously, because of speed and the fact that causes and consequences are not always clear, we are not quite in a situation similar to the proverbial chaos theory of a butterfly wing-flap triggering a storm at the other end of the world, but almost.

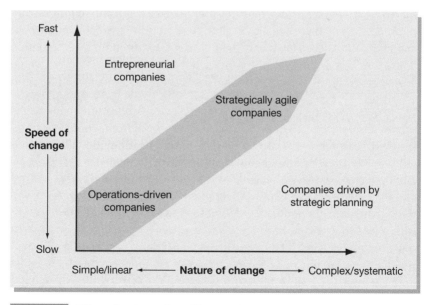

figure I.1   **Where is strategic agility needed most?**

A report from the (b)leading edge

To search for fast strategies and strategic agility we went to the ICT (information and communication technology) industry, looking for the leading edge of the phenomenon. Contrary to the simpler or more stable industries just mentioned, ICT has been facing the twin challenges of speed of emergence and of the erosion of industry boundaries. In fact, the word "convergence" (eroding industry boundaries) had been coined first with reference to that between computers, home entertainment, and communication services. The ICT industry has gone through many technological and market disruptions over the past few years, from the shift from centralized mainframe computer architectures to decentralized client–server ones, through the disruptive advent of the internet, opening the gate to all kinds of new information service and interactive business models and ecosystems.

In a way, we went to the ICT industry in the same way as geneticists go to fruit flies because they reproduce and mutate fast. It's an industry characterized by fast change, and also by complex systemic interactions. However, it would have been too easy to go to the "new flies", the bevy of entrepreneurial firms that spring up all the time in one corner or another of the ICT industry. This would have taken us to the entrepreneurial renewal argument. Instead of going to the newborns, we went to the long-term survivors, these companies that not only survived, but thrived on disruptions. So, rather than Google or eBay, and swarms of small firms whose names are mostly unknown, we went to the household brands: Accenture (known as Andersen Consulting until not too long ago), Canon (which started as provider of reconnaissance cameras to the Japanese military in World War II), Cisco (still a youngster, but not exactly new), HP, IBM, Intel, Nokia, SAP, STMicroelectronics, and others.

For each of these companies we collected extensive background information (annual reports, books, case studies, press coverage, analysts' reports, etc.) and performed between one and twenty interviews (depending on interest and access) for a total of about 150 interviews, each lasting between one and three hours. We also held small group feedback and discussion workshops with several of the most intensely researched companies, and kept an ongoing intellectual exchange with several of their key executives, as sparring partners. We researched in greater depth the more complex companies in our sample (e.g., HP, IBM) and those going through significant strategic agility challenges (e.g., Nokia, SAP), and companies with the most innovative management practices (e.g., Cisco, Intel, and IBM).

The need for strategic agility did not affect the strategy process of all these companies in the same way. How the need for strategic agility interacts with the nature of the strategy process depends on the diversity and scope of a company's strategic opportunity horizon.

An opportunity horizon made of many diverse and small opportunities calls for an emergent internal opportunity discovery and creation process, with decentralized entrepreneurship and a corporate strategic filtering – or retention – process, selecting from many opportunities the areas most important to corporate success, in a coherent way.[3] Others are culled early, sold, spun out as stand-alone companies. So, as a corporation builds or preserves strategic agility, it selectively incorporates features of typical entrepreneurial conglomerates. Corporate ventures are paving the way and opening up the strategic development of its core business.

Conversely, a few very big – "bet the company" – opportunities will necessarily result in a top-down centralized process. You can hardly imagine Microsoft deciding on a new operating system, or even an improved Windows version – like Vista – in a decentralized entrepreneurial way, creating multiple alternatives, backing some, and cutting some. Similarly, Boeing would not launch a major program, such as the 787 Dreamliner, as a result of decentralized entrepreneurship.

The companies we researched in the ICT industry were in a middle ground, but most challenging, position: to a varying extent diverse, but neither adopting an entrepreneurial conglomerate nor a single core business logic. Some, such as HP, were diverse but in search of a corporate value creation logic. Their top management also encouraged and favored cross-business units, and cross-business strategic integration efforts. Others still, like IBM, were developing an increasingly integrated corporate value creation logic, and using it as a filter not only to select among opportunities but also to shed existing product lines and business units.

We focussed our research effort on companies most exposed to the challenge of speed and complexity. Some were relatively diverse companies trying to exploit interdependencies and opportunities for strategic integration, and build an integrated value creation logic at the corporate level, such as HP and IBM. Others were companies that had been relatively unitary, but strove to balance the need for strategic integration across highly independent businesses with the need to exploit the wider strategic scope available to them. Nokia, SAP, or Cisco are examples of this second group.

Although the ICT industry has perhaps been at the (b)leading edge of speed and complexity challenges in strategy we see the same forces affecting many other industries. Healthcare, for instance, is going through a major transformation, driven by new scientific knowledge (e.g. decoding the human genome) and by the search for more efficient delivery economics. On a less grand scale, nutrition, over-the-counter pharmaceuticals, fitness training, and related industries converge into a wellness and "aging gracefully" market with the graying of the population in developed countries. The energy industry is also likely to go through radical transformation. The search for energy efficiency cuts across a great many hitherto separate industries and growing public awareness and worries about global warming are adding an increasing sense of urgency. Related to oil prices and global warming, the auto industry may well soon face a strategic agility challenge of some magnitude. Not only are hybrid cars likely to gain ground with every increase in the price of oil, but new CO^2 emission regulations may force a massive reorientation of the European industry toward smaller, fuel-efficient cars. These may call not only for different product designs, but also for different concepts of ground transportation systems.

In other words, although the ICT business is perhaps where the fast strategy game has originated, it is spreading fast to other industries. Furthermore, even in the absence of industry-wide change, companies that gain strategic agility, such as Procter & Gamble in its "Connect and Develop" model of open innovation,[4] can gain strategic advantage in traditional industries and create or transform markets.

In sum, strategic agility is not needed only from companies that are in the maelstroms of complex and rapid change. Companies in mature industries that develop superior strategic agility can leave their competitors behind, create new markets, rejuvenate their business models, and renew the way they compete.

Organization of the book: a guide to the reader

In Part 1, Being strategically agile, the first chapter provides an introduction to the fast strategy game, and explains why the need for strategic agility is greater now than in the past.

Chapter 2 outlines the key dimensions of strategic agility – strategic sensitivity, collective commitment, and resource fluidity – and summarizes how strategic agility differs from usual strategic planning, and calls for different capabilities.

Chapter 3 paints an unlikely portrait: how IBM today has become (to borrow ex-CEO Lou Gerstner's phrase), "a dancing elephant". Among the companies we researched, IBM perhaps faced the greatest strategic agility challenge and addressed it most effectively.

Part 2, Fostering strategic agility, delves into the specific management practices and tools that sustain each dimension of strategic agility. Chapter 4 considers the fact that strategic sensitivity hinges on extensive external and intensive internal dialogues around strategy.

Chapter 5 argues that collective commitment results from strategic and structural choices that make collaboration among the top team a must.

Chapter 6 explores the way that resource fluidity is critically dependent on flexible capital resource utilization and reallocation, as well as people and knowledge mobility.

Part 3, Rebuilding strategic agility, focuses on the management tools and leadership behaviors that enable companies to regain strategic agility once they have lost it, either because they have gained excessive momentum down a strategic trajectory that may take them into a dead end, or because stagnation has crept in, and the company has stalled strategically.

Chapter 7 explores the challenges that confront companies once they have lost strategic agility, and outlines a leadership agenda to regain agility.

Chapters 8, 9, 10 and 11 respectively analyse in detail the CEO's leadership agenda for mobilizing minds, re-energizing people, flexing and depoliticizing the organization.

Chapter 8 highlights the importance of bringing new thinking to an organization to have it broaden its course of action and consider a wider and more distant opportunity horizon. It focuses on what Andy Grove called an "inflection point",[5] i.e., how to redirect the company from momentum, before stagnation and rigidity have set in. Nokia's recent challenge of moving from voice communication to multimedia, and from operator-based to more diverse business models, is an example of strategy facing such an inflection point. SAP's recent redirection toward integrated open platforms supporting a range of application suites is a strategic renewal triggered by an inflection point.

Chapter 9, in contrast, focuses on how to re-energize the company after stagnation has set in. IBM's and HP's efforts to regain strategic agility provide interesting examples of multibusiness companies facing this challenge. It shows that the main additional challenge companies stricken by stagnation face is that of rekindling commitment, and that such rekindling is an emotional process where values and leadership play a determining role.

Chapter 10 focuses on the more usual dimensions of organizational change, arguing that, when implemented correctly, and supported by appropriate tools, processes, and leadership behaviors, a multidimensional organization (with, for instance, customer groups, product lines, core processes, and technology platforms all reflected in the organizational structure) can be enormously effective. It also shows why, without the right tools, processes, and behaviors, it can lead to paralysis rather than agility.

Chapter 11 stresses the importance of depoliticizing the decision-making processes in the strategically agile company, to allow leadership unity and collective commitments.

Chapter 12 summarizes and compares the different renewal paths identified in chapters 8 to 11. The sequence of renewal actions depends on your starting point and destination. It also depends on your perspective, whether you look at strategic agility from a multibusiness-corporate or business-unit perspective.

References

[1] Ansoff, H. Igor, *Corporate Strategy: An Analytic Approach to Business Policy for Growth and Expansion*, McGraw-Hill, 1965; Penguin Books, 1968.

[2] In the case of the ICT industry, obviously, increasing returns to adoption (the value of a good, or a service, to a customer depends on how many other users there are already) and the dynamics of network effect mean that many competitive battles are fought quite early around the adoption of standards, and competitive outcomes are thus played out early in the game.

[3] Burgelman, Robert A., *Strategy is Destiny: How Strategy-Making Shapes a Company's Future*, Free Press, 2002.

[4] Huston, Larry and Sakkab, Nabil, "Connect and Develop", *Harvard Business Review*, March 2006, Vol. 84 Issue 3.

[5] Grove, Andrew S., *Only the Paranoid Survive: How to Exploit the Crisis Points That Challenge Every Company*, Currency, 1996.

Being strategically agile

Chapter 1 analyses why strategic agility is needed today more than ever, with complex forces of change buffeting companies, and corporate leaders facing increasing demands for charting and following a steady course of growth and renewal.

Chapter 2 introduces, defines, and develops the three key dimensions of strategic agility:

1 strategic sensitivity (both the sharpness of perception and the intensity of awareness and attention);

2 collective commitment (the ability of the top team to make bold decisions – fast, without being bogged down in "win-lose" politics at the top);

3 resource fluidity (the internal capability to reconfigure business systems and redeploy resources rapidly).

Chapter 3 explores how a company once famous for its staid culture and rigid bureaucracy, IBM, is now a strategically agile leader. We selected IBM as an extended introductory example rather than Nokia because it was the most unlikely agile company we observed in our research.

1

The fast strategy game

Nokia: strategic agility in action

Nokia's success in mobile telephony (who would have expected a rubber boot company springing from the barren fringes of northern Europe would come to lead the global mobile phone revolution?) was based on strategic agility.

As compared to most industry players, and to its direct competitors, Nokia developed a higher strategic sensitivity. When everyone saw mobile telephony as a professional service, Nokia's leadership saw mobile phones as consumer – almost fashion – products. Rather than predict five or ten percent maximum penetration rate, Nokia quickly imagined everyone in the world having one – or why not several? – mobile phones for personal as well as professional use. Deregulation and the licensing of new mobile service operators in many countries provided the market discontinuity that Nokia could thrive on. Where others saw mobile phones as a niche tool for mobile emergency workers – perhaps extending to taxi-drivers and fishermen – Nokia saw them as a mass consumer product. Nokia also escaped the dependence on traditional fixed network (monopoly) operators to foster and support the development of newly licensed entrepreneurial mobile service providers. As Jorma Ollila, now Nokia's Chairman, who led that development at the time, said:

The "planetary alignment" was right, a unique combination of trends and changes created a massive opportunity, but no one else saw it, or was able to capitalize on it.

Nokia's success in mobile telephony moved from imagination to reality through:

- an organizational flexibility that yields resource fluidity;
- a combination of a global approach to business building, bypassing the conventional wisdom of needing large national subsidiaries for international expansion;
- an emphasis on globally integrated business processes that provided the underpinnings for Nokia's accelerated growth in the late 1990s.

Nokia's executive team in the early 1990s was a bunch of young men and women with a lot of innovative potential, and their backs to the wall. They had to succeed. They had just lost a huge "captive" market with the fall of the Soviet Union. Survival instincts, combined with the thrill of building the first truly global company from Finland, drove them into becoming a tightly knit team capable of bold, fast, collective decisions.

Nokia's two major incumbent competitors, Ericsson and Motorola, were caught wrong-footed, victims of their own orthodoxies and organizations.

Ericsson's approach to the mobile opportunity was largely shaped by its core business of fixed networks. It saw mobile networks and telephones as an extension of its core business. It was dependent on established postal and telecom authorities, which had been its core customers for a century.[1] To serve them best, when they were national monopolies in closed markets, it had established a vast network of national subsidiaries, each with its own manufacturing division and often its own R&D, and Ericsson had tried to handle globalization by more recently connecting these subsidiaries into an integrated network.[2] These subsidiaries each held considerable resources and wielded much influence on their own, and, as a result, global integration had been slow. Decisions were made in complex negotiation and bargaining sessions among members of the top team and of the various subsidiary groups and did not always lead to swift action. So, on all three key dimensions of strategic agility – strategic sensitivity, collective commitments and resource fluidity – Ericsson was outmaneuvered by Nokia when it came to the mobile communication opportunity.

Motorola was different from Ericsson, but did not have an easier time. Its strategic sensitivity was shaped by its experience of serving professional markets, such as the police, the military, or fire departments, and by its fear of Japanese competition. Its attention was not on Nokia. Where Ericsson was geographically fragmented and very focussed on the telecom business, Motorola was worldwide but focussed on the US and Japan, with a rather diversified electronics group.

In both cases, the ability to make fast, bold, collective commitments was hampered, and resources were hard to redeploy. Table 1.1 summarizes these differences.

To reduce the above story to the cliché of entrepreneurial companies displacing dinosaurs would not be entirely accurate.[3] Nokia itself was a century-old conglomerate in forest products, cable, rubber products, chemicals, and consumer electronics. Thanks to the "neutral" status of Finland in Europe, Nokia had for long enjoyed a lucrative and protected

table 1.1   Nokia *vs.* Ericsson and Motorola in the early 1990s

	Nokia	*Ericsson*	*Motorola*
Strategic sensitivity	▓ Mobile phones seen as a separate consumer-driven opportunity ▓ A huge new opportunity to change the rules of the game ▓ New operators	▓ Infrastructure focus, "terminals as extensions" ▓ Success of "AXE" switch to be protected and nurtured ▓ Incumbent telco customers	▓ Military/ professional mobile radio heritage ▓ "Technical excellence" ▓ Focus on Japanese competition
Resource fluidity	▓ Little legacy, focus on new operators ▓ "Born global" (for the new global business opportunity) ▓ Cross-functional process organization with product programs	▓ Locally rooted multi-domestic management structure ▓ Focus of sales and support on traditional telcos	▓ Public sector customers ▓ US-driven autonomous business units ▓ Diversified electronics group
Collective commitment	▓ Integrated business ▓ Young, tightly knit top team ▓ Survival instinct (USSR crisis)	▓ Subunit advocacy ▓ Senior, very experienced top team	▓ Subunit advocacy ▓ Senior, very experienced top team

position as a leading "gateway" in the technology and raw material trade between the Soviet Union and the West. It had been in mobile telephony since the 1970s, and bet on GSM digital systems and handsets only in the early 1990s. Ericsson was a technology powerhouse, with an unbeatable market presence around the world. But where Nokia created a new business model – offering turnkey "end-to-end" solutions to new, specialized mobile service providers – Ericsson responded (mainly) through its existing business model: mobility services as an additional niche offering for the traditional fixed network operators that its many national subsidiaries served so well, and mobile "terminals" as an appendage to their networks.

" strategic agility is about the capability to think and act differently "

Strategic agility is not about the vitality of small new entrepreneurial firms challenging tired incumbents, but about the capability to think and act differently, leading to new business model innovations: How well do incumbent companies change their business models? How fast? How do mature companies, like Nokia in the 1980s, invent new businesses and imagine new business models? How do companies such as Ericsson or Motorola, leading companies, the strategic agility of which would naturally deteriorate with maturity and industry leadership, maintain or regain strategic agility?

From agility to rigidity

The questions are relevant because companies naturally become victims of their own success: as they grow and become successful they lose some of their adaptive capacity. The search for efficiency drives flexibility out. Success dulls strategic sensitivity. The legitimate short-term challenges of scaling up, and of managing fast, profitable growth from quarter to quarter, reaping economies of scale in the process, lead to a narrow focus on core growth businesses, a mix of tunnel vision and strategic myopia. Ericsson's remarkable success with the AXE digital switch in the 1970s and 1980s led to such difficulties; so did Motorola's focus on professional mobile radio. Existing core businesses – such as fixed line networks in Ericsson's case – become prisms or filters, through which new opportunities are seen by a top management team whose experience is mainly with the core business. Such experience leads to good snap judgments in the existing businesses, and justified self-confidence, but may not provide reliable guidance in new fields.

Resource fluidity also deteriorates over time. The structuring of functions, subsidiaries, business units, and product divisions naturally traps resources. Business models and activity systems are optimized, or adjusted to fit current conditions, and become more tightly defined and strongly structured.[4] Efficiency gains over flexibility, for good reasons. The lock-in of close relationships with key customers – in both Ericsson's and Motorola's cases – hid key market environment changes, and the hubris of their successes led them to discount the possibility of disruptions.[5] Close collaboration with suppliers and partners also turn into "ties that bind", not so much contractually as with a company's perceptions. Customers, suppliers, and partners drive what top management perceives, and crowds out – from busy agendas and spans of attention – new trends and potential disruptions. Companies can lock in on a sense of who the competition is as well. While focussed on Japan as a competitor, Motorola – the major early innovator in mobile telephony – let Nokia grow, seeing it as an ally in a common cause, only to discover later it had let the genie out of the bottle.

Collective commitments – the implicit agreement of people in the same company to work together toward a common end – also become more difficult with success. First, new challenges may not offer the same thrill as the company's initial success. "What to do for an encore?" is all too real a question for tired heroes. Second, growth, success, and formal structures lead to specialization: experts of different functions, areas, product groups, defer to each other about decisions. As a company grows, and perhaps recruits seasoned executives from the outside, its managers grow by "being in charge", a pattern often carried all the way to one-on-one relationships with the CEO. Collective commitments are replaced by individualized negotiations. Lieutenants turn into barons.

The Appendices provides a detailed assessment grid, and more specific descriptions and analyses of the toxic side-effects of growth and success. Let it suffice here to say that strategic agility should never be taken for granted; it all too easily turns into rigidity.

Indeed, most companies fall prey to the toxic side-effects of growth, success, and industry leadership. Once these have set in, change and renewal become difficult, painful, and periodic exercises. These tend not only to be disruptions at the top (to introduce change, the board hires a new CEO, who brings in a new executive team), but also throughout the organization. Because change takes place in response to a felt crisis, usually characterized by deteriorating performance, it most often results in restructuring and lay-offs and in the dispersal and squandering of key competencies and capabilities. Over time, such changes breed growing cynicism and skepticism in middle management ranks and an increasingly serious weakening of the corporation's renewal capabilities.

Strategic agility – as an ongoing capability for real-time strategic sensitivity, quick collective commitments, and fast and strong resource redeployment – is an antidote to the pain of repeated sequences of success, slowdown and rigidity, crises, and renewals.

The very phrase "strategic agility", or for that matter "fast strategy", may be seen as an oxymoron, a contradiction in terms. The idea of strategy formulation followed by implementation, feeding periods of calm continuous effort, punctuated by episodes of soul searching and upheavals is more common. As will be seen, strategic agility results from a mix of stability in processes and people, in values and aspirations, and of sensitivity and flexibility in perception, fluidity in resource deployment, and leadership unity in making collective commitments.

The cost of such cycles of success, rigidity, crisis, and renewal is simply no longer affordable. It is not affordable at the top; CEOs cannot and should not live in fear of the shareholders and the board abruptly ending their tenure. The cost of induced short-term thinking is enormous. It is not affordable throughout the organization; fears of lay-offs and giving one's best to an organization don't go well together. Thriving at work calls for development, trust, and medium-term learning. Major companies are also repositories of critical skills and capabilities, particularly in R&D, that need sustained nurturing. Alternations of periods of feast and famine simply don't allow these skills to flourish, or even to survive.

❝ strategic agility is needed today first and foremost by the most knowledge-intensive companies ❞

To avoid the pain and cost of these changes, strategic agility is needed today more than ever, and first and foremost by the most knowledge-intensive companies. Let's see why.

Strategy – as we knew it – is dead: welcome to the fast strategy game

Olli-Pekka Kallasvuo, Nokia's new CEO, commented on the nature of strategy as follows:

Five to ten years ago you would set your vision and strategy and then start following it. That does not work any more. Now you have to be alert every day, week and month to renew your strategy.[6]

Steve Steinhilber, Corporate Vice President Strategic Alliances at Cisco, another company we researched, paints a more vivid picture of the same reality:

Think of it like competing for an Olympic gold medal. It used to be you would pick a race that fit your innate skills – say [the] 400 meter race – you would train for years, compete, make it to the final ... and you could train again for four years, punctuated by world championships and other races, and perhaps win the medal. And it was likely that for a dozen years you would compete more or less against the same few competitors. Today you enter a race which you believe fits you, but after the first lap you are told this is not 400 meters but 5000 meters, and you go out of the stadium ... and you find someone new racing alongside, who just tells you: "It looked like an interesting race going by, so I just joined". Everything is unpredictable ... five years ago could Nokia really have expected Apple to be the main threat to their high end phone business?

Strategy, as we knew it, was based on foresight, on anticipation, the chess master's ability to see many moves ahead, where his lesser opponent sees only a few. But foresight is only as good as an ability to understand and map out an environment and anticipate its evolution. In fact, traditional strategy making assumed a detailed understanding and some control of the corporation's environment. Some companies today in the ICT industry are perhaps still in this position.

But, in fact, among the companies we researched, only one jumps to mind: Intel. And Intel is a special case. Intel is perhaps unique in its ability to guide the co-evolution of its offerings and of its customers'.[7] Intel has, for two decades, relentlessly driven the evolution of computing power down a very predictable trajectory of semiconductor density increase, cost reduction, and performance improvement. It coined and followed the now famous "Moore's Law": The power of microprocessor technology doubles and its costs of production fall by half every 18 months. A unique combination of R&D skills, of product architecture and process efficiency, plant ramp-up skills (to bring yields to profitable levels quickly), willingness and ability to commit massive investment resources to new plants, and, more recently, thoughtful attention to ecosystem development, earned Intel the sustained ability to lead the microprocessor industry, and to set the pace of personal computers' evolution. AMD, originally an Intel licensee that then pursued its own product and process development efforts, challenged Intel on several occasions, but did not succeed in wrestling leadership from it.

Massive investments, long development cycle times (Intel has to anticipate "usage models" years and years in advance), and growing technical challenges (e.g., with higher and higher circuit density, cooling and power consumption became big issues) call for Intel to retain an ability to plan reliably and, hence, to influence its environment. So, strategy as we know it still largely applies for Intel. Not so for others.

Very few companies indeed are in Intel's privileged position. Few can rely on something as predictable as Moore's Law, and even fewer can deploy massive resources to follow it. Fewer still can exercise the level of control on or purposeful co-evolution with its environment as Intel does. Most are in Cisco's position: entering undefined races, over unpredictable terrain, against unknown competitors, toward no arrival line.

In this new fast strategy game, strategic planning – and the comfort of "scenarios" on which to anchor plans – no longer works. In fact, planning scenarios are downright misleading. Insight needs to replace foresight. The game you play appears only over time, as when you assemble the kind of puzzle where how a piece fits is slowly discovered as more related pieces are found, and assembled. In these emerging strategic situations, fast pattern recognition, rather than accurate strategic scenarios, becomes key. The world around us keeps emerging, and our perception of it keeps reshaping itself as we play. Some of our pieces will fit the puzzle, other won't. If you are fast in fitting pieces, the overall structure of the puzzle will evolve your way: you create your own future and shape the markets and the competitive landscape to your advantage. It is not just specific opportunities that are emerging, propelled by the learning from new ventures and special projects, but the overall structure of where and how they might fit together. We need a new way to strategize, both more opportunistic and more strategic, the more and the faster changes take place.

Industry boundaries – as we knew them – are dead: usher in the era of convergence

Major destabilizing forces have been at work in the last few years; they have eroded industry boundaries in unprecedented ways.

Digitalization

This has affected not only the information, communication and entertainment industries, but also the way companies in all industries manage supply chains, sales, marketing, distribution, and logistics. In many cases, digitalization of

❝major destabilizing forces have eroded industry boundaries in unprecedented ways❞ information has completely redefined the asset and capability mix that companies need to have in order to compete in their industries, thereby eliminating long-standing barriers to entry and allowing companies from hitherto quite separate industries to compete. The music industry is a case in point. For decades, the dominant players were EMI and RCA, and more recently Sony Music, which had built up the assets and capabilities needed for recording, manufacturing, and distributing vinyl records and cassettes. In today's digital world, however, companies like Apple, which have none of the traditional music industry capabilities, are becoming leading players. Business models of incumbent music firms become obsolete almost overnight.

Globalization

Competencies and competition are increasingly distributed around the globe.[8] Accenture and IBM face the emergence of new major, and very fast-growing competitors, who create new business models to exploit dispersion and globalization, like Infosys' Global Delivery Model for large system engineering software, which not only provides lower cost but also higher quality. After years of efforts to transform itself, IBM finds the benefits of successful transformation eroded by new competition. Infosys, Wipro, Tata Consulting Services, and a bevy of Indian followers may win out.

Deregulation

Public policy-makers were often watchdogs of industry boundaries. In the US, for instance, banks could not participate in other financial services, nor be investors; or long-distance communication service providers had to be distinct from local telecommunication companies; and there were endless numbers of other examples. In many countries, the allocation – or auction – of radio frequencies constrained the path of mobile communication development. The world was full of protective regulations. Geographic protection was also rampant, from airline ownership in the US to the imposition of joint venture partners in China. A number of international bodies, from the World Trade Organization to the European Commission, have tirelessly been chipping away at these. Many governments have also recognized the virtues of deregulation and abandoned their protective armory.

Taken together, and they often interplay with and reinforce each other, these three major forces – digitalization, globalization, and deregulation – widen strategic arenas.

Wider playing fields, players focussed on core business

Within these expanded spaces in which to compete, companies are buffeted by contradictory forces that drive them to focus more sharply: ecosystems and alliances, shareholders, and the limits to their own competencies conspired to force focus on core businesses.

The ecosystems revolution

In a rapidly growing number of industries, customers are not interested in a given product *per se*, but in a solution to a problem, or in an experience. IBM's business customers, for example, buy complete "business improvement solutions". Purchasers of Nokia's phones aren't particularly interested in the phone as a device but rather in the experiences it can afford them – the ability to take and send a picture spontaneously or to speak to a loved one at any time and place they want to.

In a paradoxical way, the needs of customers for integrated solutions led companies to realize they could not meet these fundamentally different expectations on their own. This, in particular, has prompted the recent wave of alliance formation and the currency of ecosystem thinking. In turn, this allows individual firms to see themselves increasingly as providers of a particular piece of a complete ecosystem, and to focus on delivering that piece outstandingly well.

The shareholder revolution

Shareholders' interests, and investments, are increasingly represented by fund managers. Not only do they put more demands for performance on management – after all, their heads are on the block too – they also prefer the simpler valuation of "pure play", and the allure of growth stocks. This means that companies need to be more focussed, and their leaders need a good growth story to tell. The combination leads CEOs to concentrate on core business growth.

For companies involved in multiple businesses, a good model for value-creating interdependencies across businesses, and a compelling logic for how corporate management adds value by keeping all its businesses "under one roof", become essential.

In other words, CEOs and corporate management teams have to worry about two layers of value creation and develop a very articulate and compelling rationale for both:

■ the quality of the business model for each of the businesses within their company;

■ the value creation logic of the corporation as a whole, i.e., what value does belonging to a common corporate group add to the value that each business can create individually? This may involve operational integration of certain common activities, such as logistics and manufacturing; the exploitation of shared intangible assets, such as corporate brand and the reputation that goes with it; and opportunities for coordinated strategic action and integrated approaches to common customers.

For instance, during its period of fast growth, through the 1990s, STMicroelectronics had a robust corporate value creation logic: to develop its expertise in "system on a chip" design of integrated circuits. It brought diverse technologies to difficult-to-develop chips combining digital signals (the way computers work) and analog signals (the way human beings work). It became a lead supplier to companies, ranging from Seagate in disk drives, to Nokia in mobile phone modules, and to Hewlett Packard in inkjet printers' cartridges. Each of these applications benefited greatly from the competencies and the reputation built in pursuing other innovations. STMicroelectronics' value creation logic added nearly $12 billion to shareholders' wealth. It was entirely built on lateral exchanges, such as cross-learning and shared capacity management between business areas.

Short of developing such a compelling integrated corporate value creation logic, CEOs and their business group heads will face growing pressure from shareholders and private equity investors to split their companies.

The core competence revolution

First articulated explicitly and popularized over a decade ago by C.K. Prahalad and Gary Hamel,[9] core competence thinking has since gained increasing currency among corporate leaders. In short, core competence thinking stresses that companies should focus on a few distinctive competencies[10] that can be redeployed and leveraged from business to business and provide for dynamism in market entry and exit by reducing the cost of resource redeployment. The classic example among the companies we researched is Canon. Its core competencies were first confined to optics and the micromechanics needed for cameras. But they quickly expanded to imaging, electronics, printing, and other related areas of technology, as well as to channel management and indirect distribution systems. This allowed Canon to create new businesses – such as small-office personal copiers – and to gain leadership in business after business, from photocopiers and fax machines to microlithography. Core competence thinking has led firms to focus on a few related business areas, and seek a corporate value creating logic that leverages these precious few competence areas as widely as possible, but avoids straying too far from them into businesses where they would not apply.

Taken together, the two sets of forces create strategic tensions. Digitalization, globalization, and deregulation triggered wider strategic discontinuities, did away with defined strategic arenas, widened the playing field and opened the game, creating the unpredictable races, the shifting rules Steve Steinhilber worries about. On the other side, customer focus, the allure of "pure play" companies (focussed on a narrow market segment), and the concentration on core competencies drive companies toward narrower core business focus.

❝ while the field of battle is wider and wider, the need for focus and integration is greater and greater ❞

In other words, while the field of battle is wider and wider, with the fall of industry boundaries, the need for focus and integration in the deployment of one's efforts is greater and greater. Customers demand integrated solutions, not disparate product assortments; shareholders call for a compelling integrated corporate value creation logic that justifies keeping the firm's assets together (rather than breaking it up) and its leadership in unified command. Core competence thinking provides an attractive framework for that leadership to address shareholders' and customers' demands.

So, strategic agility can no longer be achieved by what has historically been its simplest form, or mean: dynamic business portfolio management. It used to be a really simple game: reposition the company by buying and selling businesses, and bring management quality and discipline to the management of each separate business unit. This, after all, was at the heart of Jack Welch's success at General Electric. Leading the diversified multidivisional company could largely be done from the CEO's office, with the support of good dealmakers, strategists, lawyers, and investment bankers. Management selection, development, and succession received great attention from the top, as did the development of management tools, but other areas were largely delegated to business unit leaders. These were submitted to periodic business reviews and personal assessments.

Today's true test of strategic agility is not portfolio restructuring but rather continuous redirection and/or reinvention of the core business without losing momentum. The conventional wisdom supported by a lot of management literature suggests that separate corporate venturing or evolving into so-called ambidextrous organizations would provide us a solution for this challenge. The key argument in both of these approaches is to let new businesses develop on their own conditions. The corporate value added in these approaches comes from high-level financial and management support. At best, top management can shift resources from one unit to another and speed up the development of new opportunities. However, the challenge with both of these approaches is that they negate the core strength of large companies: capability to leverage massive resources for a breakthrough. Bringing Silicon Valley inside the firm[11] sounds good but represents only half of the truth. Fragmentation into smaller entrepreneurial units improves agility but it gives up strategic strength. This is particularly problematic for large incumbent companies whose new businesses need to scale up fast to have a noticeable impact at the corporate level.

So, the paradox of strategic agility – insight replacing foresight, and integrated corporate value creation logics substituting for decentralized management — creates higher order demands on corporate leadership. The strategically agile company at the same time needs to be fast and integrated. How to address these demands is the heart of this book.

References

[1]　Meurling, John and Jeans, Richard, *The Ericsson Chronicle: 125 Years in Telecommunications*, Informationsforlaget, June 2001.

[2]　Doz, Yves, *Government Control and Multinational Management: Power Systems and Telecommunications Equipment*, Praeger Publishers, 1979.

[3]　Schumpeter, Joseph A., *The Theory of Economic Development*, Harvard University Press, 1934 (first published in German, 1912).

[4]　Siggelkow, Nicolaj, "Evolution Toward Fit", *Administrative Science Quarterly*, March 2002, Vol. 47 Issue 1.

[5]　Christensen, Clayton M., *The Innovator's Dilemma: When New Technologies Cause Great Firms to Fail*, Harvard Business School Press, 1997.

[6]　Olli-Pekka Kallasvuo, Chief Executive Officer, Nokia, *Financial Times*, 4 December 2006.

[7]　Burgelman, Robert A., "Strategy as Vector and the Inertia of Coevolutionary Lock-in", *Administrative Science Quarterly*, June 2002, Vol. 47 Issue 2.

[8]　Doz, Yves, Santos, José and Williamson, Peter, *From Global to Metanational:*

How Companies Win in the Knowledge Economy, Harvard Business School Press, October 2001.

[9] Hamel, Gary and Prahalad, C. K., *Competing for the Future*, Harvard Business School Press, 1996 and "Competing for the Future", *Harvard Business Review*, July/August 1994, Vol. 72 Issue 4; Prahalad, C. K. and Hamel, Gary, "The Core Competence of the Corporation", *Harvard Business Review*, May/June 1989, Vol. 67 Issue 3.

[10] Selznick, Philippe, *Leadership in Administration: A Sociological Interpretation*, Harper & Row, 1957.

[11] Hamel, Gary, "Bringing Silicon Valley Inside", *Harvard Business Review*, September/October 1999, Vol. 77 Issue 5.

2

Strategic agility: the challenge

Strategic agility is most needed in markets characterized by fast changes and growing systemic interdependencies. In such rapidly changing and complex conditions, the usual recipes for sustained advantage do not apply. Scale and scope, or traditional concepts of competitive advantage – such as bargaining power and relative concentration between customers and suppliers at various stages of a value chain – do not last. Competitive advantage is constantly being challenged by the irruption of new technology, the imagination of new business models, and the clash of competitors from different origins, bringing with them diverse business patterns and corporate value creation logics. In such an environment, advantage is always precarious, and most often only transient. It needs to be constantly renewed, and regained, through innovation. Value creation and capture come from being first with innovative propositions, and from the business-building expertise required to turn ideas into reality fast.

More lasting value may come from identifying areas where complex, evolving, shifting interdependencies are likely to endure, and where markets are not going to be efficient. Microsoft in operating systems and networking, SAP in internet-based business process platforms, or Nokia (via Symbian, a mobile data communication software platform joint venture) in data mobility platforms are trying to establish lasting advantage based on that logic. But even in these cases, substantive new contributions are needed all the time.

Strategic sensitivity

In these fast changing and complex conditions, a strategic mindset is required more than ever. However, what is needed is not the traditional way of thinking about strategy. Strategy is normally based on superior foresight, a better way to anticipate key trends and changes, and to see further into the future than competitors, customers, suppliers, and partners. This is still needed, but as turbulence increases it needs to be complemented with strong strategic insight.

Strategic foresight: still important

❝ acquiring and maintaining foresight is difficult due to multiple time-frames ❞

The value of foresight does not disappear in the fast strategy game, but acquiring and maintaining foresight is more difficult due to multiple time-frames, some very long term, some nearly instantaneous. From scientific invention, or discovery, to innovation – the building of a business incorporating knowledge from that invention or discovery – the elapsed time is often of the order of 20 years. Science-based innovation takes time. Innovation lead times may be considerable – producing complacency or the dismissal of the innovation opportunity – but decision times may be very short. Companies may be caught wrong-footed, having for instance invested too much, too early, and finding themselves in a cutback divestment mode when the market finally takes off. In the 1990s, this type of behavior separated winners and losers among US regional telecom operators entering the mobile communication field.[1] It may pay to be first, but the game is still played slowly. Latecomers with better insight can beat true innovators: Google, for instance, did not invent the search engine advertising-revenue-based industry. Overture did, but Google won. The game accelerated abruptly. The adoption of a standard, the authorization to commercialize a new drug, or any regulatory decision may have almost instantaneous consequences. The internet, by making distribution easier and faster, and by allowing "word-of-mouth" reputations to be built, or destroyed, fast, further accelerates that process. Critical mass effects – the need both to achieve fast market growth and to capture a leading share of that market particularly in an industry where standardization matters – are stronger, and tipping points come sooner. This does not take away the value of foresight, even if, somehow, lock-in commitments are made early in the game. It is useful to know what is coming ahead of time, even if you can no longer change it.

Acquisitions, consolidations, and alliances may also have consequences that are felt very quickly: for instance, Oracle goes on an acquisition spree, and the whole software products industry feels the heat.

The critical issue here is that the rhythm of strategizing may shift suddenly, abruptly. There may be long periods of calm, where a high level of strategic attentiveness and of sensitivity is required but no action follows, and then a sudden burst of action, during which missing a beat leads to failure. That makes agility essential.

So, the conventional approach of identifying key trends and disruptions before everyone sees them still pays off, even in the fast strategy game. Identifying key technologies and their holders early, and, more critically, understanding why and how these technologies are going to matter is key. Gaining early insight into emerging lead markets and innovation "hotspots" is also of paramount importance – and more difficult. Matsushita, for instance, developed video compression and decompression technology in Singapore, partly in order to participate, first hand, in video-on-demand experiments that local broadcaster and communication companies were entering into earlier than their counterparts in Japan, or elsewhere. In the 1990s, Motorola located part of its mobile phone development effort in the Old Town of Stockholm, in order for its engineers to "see" local users of new services and new phones. Novartis recently located its US research center in the middle of MIT. Anticipating roadblocks and diffusion traps (e.g., the fact that hydrogen or bio fuel cars will need a massive investment in distribution systems to reconfigure, or complement, traditional gas stations) and the difficulties of bringing all the pieces of a new complex ecosystem into play at the same time over the same territory, in a value creation logic that provides viable business models for all ecosystem participants, matters too. In fact, business models embedded in complex ecosystems, in which multiple contributors have to come into play at the same time, makes identifying trends and assessing the speed at which they unfold all the more critical.

Understanding one's own binding and creeping commitments is also important. Early, and perhaps seemingly innocuous and unimportant standardization choices (on emerging technologies whose potential is not yet grasped) need to be addressed carefully; they are obviously part of the fast strategy game. Similarly, intellectual property rights need to be tracked and followed closely, and attention paid to how to protect one's own intellectual property. Beyond the famous examples of Intel letting AMD independently pursue the further development of Intel-based microprocessors, or of IBM leaving the intellectual property of PC operating systems to Microsoft – then a small development subcontractor – stories abound of failures to consider intellectual property rights (IPRs) in a strategic perspective, because of lack of proper anticipation. Seemingly minor, unimportant product design choices made way upstream have similar consequences. Nokia's response to Motorola's introduction of clamshell (folding) designs in mobile phones was hampered, and seriously delayed, by its reliance on a particular circuit design for a key handset subsystem that happened to be too thick to fit a clamshell design and could not be redesigned easily, partly because of mass-production process constraints. A different design choice could have been made years earlier, but component thinness did not look so important at the time.[2]

In sum, strategic foresight remains important. It remains important to anticipate the consequences of key trends, to identify disruptions and discontinuities early, and either affect them to one's advantage, or have the lead time to adjust to them effectively and in a timely fashion. Foresight may also allow you to anticipate defining moments in a fast strategic game, around, for instance, the adoption of standards or key regulatory rulings. Foresight is also critical to put your own long lead time early commitments – such as product architectures of critical component choices – in a proper strategic context, rather than have such decisions made in ignorance of their strategic consequences. Foresight is an antidote to unnoticed creeping commitments that become strategically binding over time.

> **❝foresight is an antidote to unnoticed creeping commitments that become strategically binding over time❞**

Strategic insight: now critical

Yet, where change is fast, complex, and systemic, and stable sources of strategic advantage short-lived, strategic foresight needs to be strongly complemented by strategic insight: an ability to perceive, analyse and make sense of complex strategic situations as they develop, and to be ready to take advantage of them. Heightened strategic sensitivity is required.

Most critical here is the quality and intensity of external sensing: being exposed, being in touch, being connected. Strategic insight is not an armchair exercise to be performed in the corporate "war room". The quality of information and the acquisition of intelligence – of understanding and sense making – drive the quality of sensing. Some insight may result from intense personal awareness and conviction, such as Pekka Ala-Pietilä at Nokia being an avid Mac user and seeing the potential for Nokia to turn mobile phones into mass market consumer goods the way Apple was doing for personal computers. Some may result from serendipitous institutional and organizational similarities, such as Nokia's experience in serving small local telecom operators in Finland – which despite its small size had a number of local fixed line operators – providing a useful precedent for understanding the needs of newly licensed small mobile operators. Beyond the advantage of metaphors, analogies, and precedents, insight may also result from more systematic processes, such as Procter & Gamble's "Future Works", which systematically explores emerging trends in consumer behavior. Opening the strategy process widely to external influences, maximizing the knowledge exchange surface with the outside world, and becoming or staying connected with different, unusual sources of information, as well as borrowing the insight of others – strategic partners for instance – are key ingredients of gaining insight.

To gain insight, casting the intelligence net wide enough is a challenge. First, we tend to associate with and like those we resemble, and hence to narrow down the range of contacts we maintain. Second, as they climb corporate ladders and become CEOs, executives are increasingly isolated. Of course, their networks may seem wider and their Rolodex thicker, but the opportunities for genuine, disinterested, open, and frank brainstorming discussions become fewer, both inside their company (power, sheer busyness, status, and fear usually get in the way) and outside (communication has to be more guarded, more purposeful, others pursue their own agenda). So senior executives are often more isolated, and lonely, than they look, and opportunities from the broad-based sensing that yields new insight is more limited than one would hope.

Third, like the proverbial man looking for his keys under the street lamp not because that's where he had lost them, but because that was the spot where there was enough light to see them, we tend to sense where the going is the easiest. In corporate settings this usually means proximate sensing and search: close to where we are, close to our operations, together with our most important and most trusted customers and suppliers. Such proximate sensing may give a false sense of comfort: we are externally oriented, open to the outside, but where we look will only reinforce, rather than challenge, our existing information and convictions. Rather than be future and disruption oriented, we are past and continuity oriented. We reinforce yesterday's strengths. Combined with the psychological bias to select confirmatory evidence and discount dissonant evidence – to see what we believe, rather than believe what we see – proximate sensing can be devastating. In order to combat such risks, the CEO of a very large global company told us that he always travelled alone internationally, with no assistants, local managers, body guards. He saw being on his own as essential to hearing the truth, internally – from his company's own units – and externally – from the rest of the world. He could also blend into the local environment easily on his own, something he stressed could not be done as a delegation. He was able to gain first-hand insight in a way many CEOs don't.

Beyond overcoming the risks inherent to a CEO who loses touch with the outside, we saw companies develop multilayered approaches to staying intensely connected with the outside, involving a wide cross-section of executives, experts, and staffs in various interface roles. The next chapters describe, in particular, Cisco's and IBM's approach to external sensing.

Staying connected does not always suffice though. First-hand experience may be required to gain insight. Unless one is a player figuring out how the fast strategy game is played, this is impossible. Experiencing rather than hypothesizing is required; thought experiments need to give way to true experiments. This will allow a thoughtful use of venturing and new business building processes, as experimental procedures are required to gain and sustain insight.

Simple adaptation rules: when all else fails

When uncertainty is extreme, and the complexity of the environment cannot be gauged, conventional strategy making and decision models no longer apply. Even developing insight becomes impossible. Simple rules of variation and selection may work better in these situations.[3] Rather than making sense by seeking to create insight, instead multidirectional, almost random, exploration may work best, with simple decision rules. To borrow a military analogy, a breakthrough can be achieved in at least two ways. One is superior intelligence, finding the enemy's deployment plans, the articulations, and potential gaps between armies' marching plans, or positions, the bottlenecks in the logistics, etc. This is foresight, planning ahead, in anticipation of the enemy's future moves; insight if done in the middle of the action, in reaction to the enemy's movement. But in the absence of enough foresight yielding intelligence, and in the face of fast, complex changes, a breakthrough can also be achieved by just probing randomly at the enemy's positions along a broad frontline, and having the simple rule to concentrate one's forces and attack where the enemy's reactions to exploratory probes are the weakest. No great decision-making intelligence is required here, but in the face of very high uncertainty, trying is better than guessing! In other words, at the extreme of speed, uncertainty and systemic complexity, rather than attempting to develop a comprehensive understanding of a strategic situation simply devising action rules, such as allocation of sales force attention to new accounts, or simple plant utilization optimization rules, may well be all what can be done, and yield much better results than a late or wrong attempt at making overall sense of the environment.

From sensing to making sense

Internal connectivity

Sensitive nerve cells exposed to external stimuli, however, are useless unless they are well connected internally, unless all synapses are active. A strong active internal dialogue around key strategic commitments is essential. People of different sensitivities, areas of expertise, cultural origins, age, gender, and types of intelligence need to be brought together in a structured, purposeful dialogue. This dialogue, as opposed to debate, means a conversation where participants share assumptions and explain the logic of their thought, rather than affirm conclusions and present arguments. This, of course, is not easy in a corporate context. We are used to and trained for oratory tournaments, where the most forceful argument – not always grounded in the most thoughtful considerations – wins. Expressing difference or dissent in a corporate hierarchy is often difficult, and potentially costly, yet it is essential to strategic sensitivity. If divergent, different views are suppressed without being examined, or self-censored before they are even expressed, valuable perspectives are silenced, and sources of insight lost.

> **❝ strong active internal dialogue around key strategic commitments is essential ❞**

A way to help foster such a dialogue, rather than a narrow self-interested debate where people always "stand where they sit", is to help people see their organization as a whole, as an integrated body, as if standing outside of it, some distance away, and being able to examine it from different perspectives, to model it. Of course, taking some distance is not easy; we tend to see the world only from within our own cave, and to be hostages of the organizational context in which we are stuck: job definition, routine roles and responsibilities, action registers that fit these roles and our personal skills and psychological idiosyncrasies, externally imposed measurement and reward systems (rather than internal compasses), and the comfort of continuity. We are creatures of habits and routines. Strategic sensitivity is impossible to obtain from a collection of cave-dwellers caught in the narrow confine of their own contexts.

Intelligence

A working nervous system is useless unless it connects to a clear mind. Corporate intelligence – brainpower – is important. Think of strategy as a theory. A theory of how to compete, how to create and capture value, and developing strategy requires theory-building skills. Like scientists, executives build theory. To the CEO, strategy is a theory of the future applied to an all-important sample of one – their own firm – and its likely validity, before it's implemented, can only be assessed based on the quality of the process that generates it. In other words, the quality of the strategy-making process is fundamental, yet it often receives little attention from top management as compared to more easily measurable issues, perhaps with less important consequences than the quality of the strategy-creation process. Underlying and conditioning strategic agility lies the quality of the strategy-making process (how foresight, insight, and probing rules drive the way in which choice alternatives are created and decisions made).

Beyond an impressionistic but real "smell of the place" assessment, we can apply to strategy making the tests scientists and researchers sometimes apply to how they generate theories, before they can verify them. Let's review the criteria they use.[4]

Imagination is needed to define problems and opportunities, and carry out thought experiments. To sustain thought experiments, developing and challenging working hypotheses help. Discipline in logical thinking when developing a strategic commitment, and systematic attention to a detailed "How plausible is this really?" question, help improve the quality of choices. Making sure that truly separate, different possibilities are reviewed and analysed is also important. In unfamiliar territories the evaluation of process quality on more formal grounds makes sense. Generating true alternatives, independent from each other, and considering formal criteria of development of each alternative provide a healthy discipline to the process.

In some cases a single visionary CEO, perhaps Steve Jobs at Apple, or a founder change agent, perhaps Hasso Plattner at SAP, can personally play a determining role. More often than not, though, distributed intelligence, when well harnessed, is superior to the power of a single mind. All the companies we researched did compete for best minds. Google's recent job advertising campaign, with mathematical puzzles on roadside posters and a "Call us with the solution to apply for a job" sign, is perhaps an extreme form of that approach. The quality of the team at the top, and more than anything else, the quality of its working as a team, are essential.

Collective commitment

Difficult decisions

Fast-changing, complex environments tax the usual strategic commitment processes of incumbent firms. Where strategic agility is needed most is also where traditional companies find it difficult to tread. What makes decisions difficult? First, in fast-changing, complex environments, decisions need to be made under conditions of very high uncertainty, with a set of risks not well understood and hard to specify. Of course, real option models, and sequencing learning and commitment stages can help. Nonetheless, the thoughtful strategic decision-making process outlined above is unlikely to be widely practiced. In familiar territory it is not really needed – action and faster, well-informed judgment suffice. In newer, less familiar, fast-changing environments, building foresight and gaining insight are key steps. In extremely uncertain environments, rules for adaptive responses are perhaps as well as one can do. In sum, different levels of uncertainty in the fast strategy game call for different approaches to making strategic commitment. Discriminating between situations and adapting the very nature of the commitment process is the first challenge faced in fast-changing environments.

❝ choices are very interdependent – another dimension of complexity ❞

A second challenge is that choices are very interdependent – another dimension of complexity. Each commitment is part of a sequence, and the very search for a corporate integrated value-creation logic between businesses – where they support each other strategically, and share core competencies and key corporate resources – intensifies the interdependencies between decisions. Decisions about one business cannot be made without the whole company in mind and without considering potential strategic and operational impacts on other businesses. This means that centralization of choices, as a way to respond to interdependencies, would overload the top and probably result in ill-informed choices, and that delegation would result in fragmented, disjointed decision-making, leading to overall inconsistency in the sequence of interdependent choices.

Choices, therefore, need to consider multiple levels of analysis, from individual products and businesses to an overall corporate integration perspective in framing the alternatives. This also needs to involve decision makers at multiple levels within the organization, from subunit executives to the top team and the CEO. But corporate integration cannot become an excuse for individual units' weaknesses. In interdependent decisions, in the context of a corporate value creation logic, each business that makes a contribution needs to be strong, as an individual player, as if the rest of the team did not exist. Yet, collaborative, joint commitments need to be made, sometimes in ways that individual business unit heads may see as detrimental to their own individual performance and capabilities. Such trade-offs between working as a team and strengthening oneself as an individual player are extremely hard to make individually. Self-interest cannot freely prevail, nor can unrecognized self-effacing altruism. In other words, both the strength of individual businesses and their contribution to the corporate value creation logic need to be recognized and rewarded.

The fear of disruption may make decisions even more difficult. Timing key choices requires vision and courage. Disruption challenges mean that one has to be prepared to start to cannibalize one's own business, in favor of what initially looks like a worse – and certainly not technologically equally respectable – alternative. Pride in an emotional attachment to the existing business and its products may undermine the ability to make the decisions needed in response to a disruption. This is, of course, particularly true of executives who built the success of current products. And it is always possible to justify postponing a response to disruption based on an economic logic, since disruption undermines the existing business model of the firm and is likely to replace it with something intrinsically less profitable.[5] For instance, among telecom service providers, the convergence of fixed and mobile communication terminals and subscriptions today is starting to destroy the value creation logic of mobile operators – built partly around roaming fees – and they will need to respond to this issue.

Captains *vs.* architects

Not only are key executives reluctant to make the fast, thoughtful, uncertain, and interdependent decisions strategic agility requires, they may also be ill-prepared to implement such decisions successfully. In an incumbent leading company, most senior executives are first and foremost used to growing and running the existing business, and to refining its business model. Most often, this implies being focussed on products, technologies, channels, and successful day-to-day execution. As the company grows, so does specialization of roles and responsibilities internally, and executives increasingly focus on the success of their subunits. Execution drives successful outcomes. Managing growth without crisis is hard enough. There is always something important requiring urgent attention. Beyond scale-up, and the fit of the business model and activity system to the strategy they currently pursue, executives seldom take the time, or perhaps do not have the skills, to reflect on new ecosystems and industry structures, or new business models and activity systems' architectures. In other words, they are unlikely to implement the management process and activity system innovations that being strategically agile calls for. Being the designer or architect of a new system calls for very different skills from being the successful operator – or even builder – of an already designed business system. Key executives who are not organizational architects tend to shy away from new business model and activity system design.

Barons *vs.* courtiers

Lastly, strategic agility is also a challenge to the usual delegation and one-to-one reporting models typical of today's decentralized firms. The rather Darwinian selection process on the corporate ladder at most firms favors independent types with a deep need for power and autonomy. In the absence of a strong value system and a collaborative culture to temper this need, such people will naturally tend to carve out territories in which they can enjoy a high degree of autonomy and clear accountability. They generally favor having direct reports in specialized roles who meet with them one-on-one. This is simpler for them and, on the old principle of divide and rule, enables them to protect their power base. As they rise through the corporate hierarchy, they carry the preference with them and reinforce it; as unit chiefs they are used to having the CEO deal with them as the individuals responsible for their particular units. Their communications with the CEO are conducted privately. Of all the executives on the top team, the CEO has perhaps the greatest adjustment to make in striking a new deal. Authoritative CEOs find it particularly difficult, because the new deal requires them to accept openly – even encourage – challenges to their thinking.

In sum, the need for strategic agility taxes the leadership capabilities of the CEO and key executives of many incumbent companies in three major ways:

1 decisions need to be fast, but they face high uncertainty and interdependency;

2 strategic agility calls for the design and development of new ecosystems, business models, and activity systems, which key executives in incumbent companies are often ill-prepared to undertake;

3 the usual one-to-one, king to baron-like interaction models between a CEO and members of the executive team do not mobilize the top team's energy toward collective commitments.

The need for collective commitments

❝collective decisions are likely to be less conservative and more self-confident than individual decisions❞

Strategic agility, however, calls for collective commitments, made in a unified fashion, by the top team. First, this helps the intrinsic quality of decisions. Cognitive diversity, fuelled and sustained by maximizing and diversifying knowledge exchanges with the outside, and reconciled through active, thoughtful dialogue internally, allows multiple well-informed, well-thought-through perspectives to be brought to bear on critical decisions. This allows informal checks and balances against managerial conservatism and excessive self-confidence and hubris. In other words, collective decisions are likely to be less conservative and more self-confident than individual decisions made by executives who have more to lose by being wrong for the first time than to gain by being right one more time. Collective decisions are a safeguard against a bias toward the status quo and non-commitment in major companies. Occasionally, collective decisions can also be a safeguard against the opposite difficulty: excessive and potentially reckless commitments made single-handedly by an individual executive. Such commitments are likely particularly in the case of uncertain risky decisions which face negative early feedback: rather than question the wisdom of their decision, faced with such a situation human beings have a tendency to redouble efforts in the face of growing adversity, leading to absurd and dangerous escalation situations.[6]

Collective commitments are also required for the difficult trade-offs between the individual players and their whole team, and the balance between individual successes and contribution to the collective success. The key point here is that a corporate value creation logic is seldom set once and for all and cast in concrete. It is constantly reinvented, rediscovered. Opportunities for cross-business unit or corporate-wide value creation are not given. At Hewlett Packard, for instance, turning broad corporate value creation themes – such as "rich digital media" – into concrete business development opportunities calls for intensive dialogues across different business divisions. Like other forms of innovation, they result from the constructive and purposeful exchange among senior executives, exploring and analysing opportunities to create value by working together.

Making collective commitments also has obvious mobilizing and energizing advantages. Not only do the various executives feel personally committed to "being right" – i.e., making their decision successful – they also feel mutually obligated. To borrow a popular image "they are all in the same boat". If the quality of the decision-making process is good enough – in particular with differences and dissent being allowed to be openly expressed, articulated, and cleared – the fact that executives will agree on the decisions provides a strong bond between them. Rather than blaming each other, or the CEO, once a decision has in principle been made, but its implementation not addressed, they all wholeheartedly dedicate themselves to collective success, and successful implementation. As we will see in subsequent chapters, SAP's top management commitment to a new platform strategy greatly benefited from a collective decision process.

Resource fluidity

Strategic sensitivity and collective commitments are of little value without resource fluidity, the ability to redeploy resources quickly toward strategic opportunities as they develop. Fast decisions in complex environments call for rapid resource deployment for their implementation. Since choices and commitments cannot be decided and planned well ahead of time, reactivity is needed: resource commitments need to be sudden and vigorous, the same way as exploiting military breakthroughs requires pouring resources into the opening in the front line that a breakthrough creates.

Imprisoned resources

For most established companies, rapid changes in resource allocation patterns are difficult to achieve. There are several reasons for this. First, resources in incumbent companies are often locked in support of existing activity systems, leaving very little leeway for redeployment. Continuous resource constraints and creeping doubts about the fairness of corporate-level resource allocation lead business-level executives to hoard resources within their units. The more successful and the more powerful and autonomous the business units grow, the more this becomes a problem. The heads of the biggest, fastest growing and most successful groups end up virtually taking the top management hostage. As a result, resources are trapped into subunits resulting in a risk of over-funding established legacy businesses and under-committing to new strategic opportunities.

For instance, in a desire to enhance accountability and focus, decrease management complexity, impose tougher performance demands, and face lean, more specialized competition in a focussed way, John Akers, IBM's CEO until 1993, decentralized management responsibility in IBM to a series of business division heads in the late 1980s. As a result, the autonomy of IBM's business groups grew and its resources were trapped in units fighting for the "limelight". Corporate-wide resource allocation to new promising opportunities, and dealing with IBM as an integrated supplier of IT systems and solutions, became increasingly difficult.

Secondly, resource allocation choices are typically made in relatively long planning and budgetary cycles, and amounts that can be reallocated on short notice are limited. Sudden opportunities disrupt resource allocation plans. Ironically, conventional planning systems and budgeting practices only deepen resource imprisonment in many companies. Formal bureaucratic management processes leave little room for adjustment and change. Instead of challenging, they protect the interests of core businesses by seldom questioning the history and existence of the legacy.

Further, companies do not always achieve an effective separation of performance measurement (P/L) and of investment, letting the mature, most profitable businesses over-invest in their future development and maintenance, but starving corporate management from the resources needed to nurture new opportunities. Also, because core business stakes are large, visible, and well understood by the whole top management team, resource allocation may also favor the core business, to the detriment of new initiatives in wider, more uncertain, playing fields.

Deep and long-lasting customer and partner relations do not make resource allocation to new business opportunities any easier. Letting customers drive allocation provides impetus only for commitments to existing markets. In fact, the resource allocation processes of many companies deny resources to technologies and investments stemming from emerging, less well-known, new areas and customers. The company's resources are hostage to serving existing customers.

Some resources are more fluid than others

Not all resources are so difficult to reallocate as funding and investments. Although when we speak of corporate resources our minds jump to the allocation of funds and budgeting games, framed in a win-lose mode, many corporate resources need not be allocated at all. On the contrary, they are resources that not only can be shared, used by one business without depriving another from their use, but also which increase in value the more widely and intensely they are used within the firm. Take a corporate brand, like IBM or Nokia. Provided it is used responsibly and wisely, it gains in value the more it is used by all business units within the firm, rather than each unit promoting its own brand. A portfolio of patents provides similar advantages. Some resources, such as competencies, raise a more complex challenge: in principle the more they are used, the more they gain in value, like, say, wing aerodynamics for British Aerospace (which is the leading wing designer in the world and reinforces its leadership the more types of wings it designs and the more frequently it designs new wings). In reality, though, resources may be both scarce and "sticky". The competence resides with a relatively small cadre of key experts who can only work on a few projects at a time, or risk spreading themselves too thin. To grow that group is possible, but takes time and would risk deteriorating the quality of the

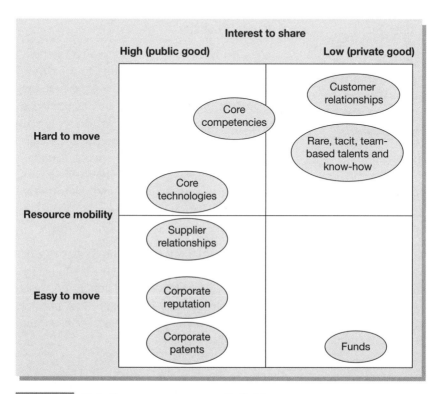

figure 2.1   Not all resources are equally fluid

work, no matter what. To train new people, to move part of the capabilities elsewhere would require effort, and take time. In other words, competencies are sticky both in location (they cannot be moved easily) and in time (they cannot be grown or even redeployed fast) – they are not a fluid resource. Figure 2.1 positions the relative fluidity of various types of corporate resources, based on two criteria: (1) whether they can be shared or need to be allocated, and (2) how embedded and sticky, *vs.* easily movable they are.

The importance of modularity

Beyond the administrative inertia of resource allocation patterns, and the lesser mobility of some resources, we observed a third challenge in fostering resource fluidity: the risk of a "one size fits all" approach to the packaging, sharing, and provision of scarce resources. This concern affects, in particular, shared corporate services, common business processes, and IT, which all face an inherent tension between the economies of scale and scope, and the flexibility and fluidity corporate uniformity and central allocation bring, on the one hand, and the need to best fit to specific business unit characteristics and circumstances on the other. Business unit managers understandably fear that "common" resources will be provided in a form that does not fit their needs, and that their availability will be conditioned on complex interfaces and negotiated priorities that will hamper rather than foster agility.

❛❛ decentralized entrepreneurship is inefficient and potentially dangerous; compatibility may become a straitjacket ❜❜

In a wider context, proprietary product architectures with strong backward and forward compatibility requirements across generations of products provide a similar architectural challenge to resource fluidity. Without smartly crafted modular product architectures, breaking out of these "customer and partner lock-ins" over time is difficult. Agility loses out to compatibility and uniformity. Here it's a matter of balance: decentralized entrepreneurship is inefficient and potentially dangerous; compatibility may become a straitjacket.

Organizations benefit from modularity in a similar manner to that of products. An organizational design consisting of modular business processes and IT systems enables greater variety and higher redeployment potential, in the same way as with products. In practice this means that business process modules designed to a specific activity can be reused in another business configuration having the same activity.

Dissociating strategic direction from organizational structure

The more resource allocation is dissociated from day-to-day operations, the better for resource fluidity. The challenge is not so much one of budgeting, planning, and accounting systems. That can be taken care of by planning processes that allocate resources more dynamically and strategically.[7] The challenge is mostly cognitive, and political, more than procedural. In other words, what counts is that executives in the top team take perspectives, in the strategic dialogue they entertain, that are not exclusively aligned with their operational roles. Creating a multidimensional organization into which multiple perspectives are structurally embedded is a way to foster such diversity of perspective and break the blind alignments of the strategic on the operational. Combining customer facing and channel management organizations, product groups, platforms for areas of technology, core competencies, standards, etc., provides a way to embed multiple perspectives that have to be reconciled, and organizational units that have to work harmoniously together to bring results. An integrated corporate strategy consisting of distinct but interdependent businesses needs, and should be executed via, a multidimensional organization, not via independent business groups. A multidimensional organization is a vehicle not only to enhance strategic sensitivity and top team collaboration but also to force greater resource fluidity. It "unlocks" resources from organizational "silos" by separating business management and results from resource ownership.

Summary

This chapter started to explore how playing the fast strategy game taxes the capabilities of most incumbent firms (see Figure 2.2 overleaf, from strategic management to strategic agility). Strategic agility calls for three fundamental shifts in the emphasis of top management, in how they steer the firm. First, it requires a shift from foresight-driven strategic planning to insight-based strategic sensitivity, putting more emphasis on making sense of current situations as they develop than on the anticipation of future strategic interactions. Second, strategic agility calls for a very deep change in the way the top team works, and in how its members relate to the CEO, from usually one-on-one relationships to collective commitments. This calls for a new deal at the top, from individual independent responsibilities to interdependent collective commitments. Third, strategic agility needs a mindset and behavior shift from resource allocation and "ownership", to resource sharing and leverage, and from a focus on budgetary games and tournaments around capital allocation to a commitment to sharing and exchange around intangible resources like brands and competencies.

This is not an easy shift. To many business unit and business group leaders strategic agility looks Janus-faced: they are afraid that strategic agility at the corporate level will slow them down. An integrated corporate value-creation logic may not be easy to articulate; and it may not bring much value, in particular if the corporation's activities are diverse, and the stronger businesses can succeed on their own. Such logic may be seen, and lived, as a constraint, justifying ill-guided and ill-informed corporate intervention in subunit strategies. Common "fluid" resources may not be as fluid as they should be. Depending on "accessing" corporate resources or "sharing" those of other units laterally fuels a latent fear, and a primal desire to "own" key resources at the subunit level. Fear of the "one size fits all" syndrome is also quite significant – and very real. Corporate solutions do not always fit specific units needs, and the costs of a poor fit are not always assessed and weighted appropriately. Collective commitments may be seen as slowing down decisions, and leaving less room for compelling

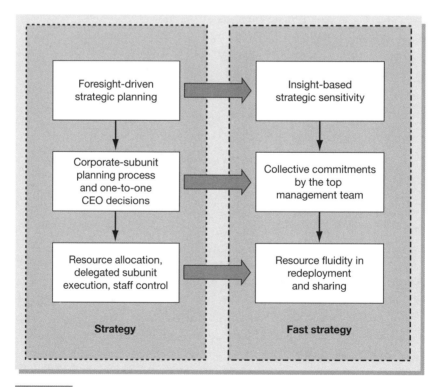

figure 2.2 **From strategic management to strategic agility**

arguments to win the day than one-on-one interactions and more formal meetings. Strategic agility, therefore, is not simple to achieve. It demands more from senior executives, mid-level managers, and CEOs than more traditional approaches to strategy formulation and implementation.

Fast strategy is needed in a market and competitive context different from that in which the more traditional approach to strategy was developed. Strategic planning relying on foresight needs to be complemented (or replaced) by strategic sensitivity based on insight. Traditional patterns of subunit delegation, autonomy and one-on-one commitments need to be replaced by collective commitments made by a united leadership team working as a single integrated body. Stable, long-term patterns of resource commitments need to become more fluid, more able to change rapidly. That's the strategic agility challenge.

References

[1]   Noda, Tomo and Bower, Joseph L., "Strategy Making as Iterated Processes of Resource Allocation, *Strategic Management Journal*, Summer 1996 Special Issue, Vol. 17 Issue 7.

[2]   Authors' interview, Pekka Ala-Pietilä, former President of Nokia, 13 February 2007.

[3]   Eisenhardt, Kathleen and Sull, Donald, "Strategy as Simple Rules", *Harvard Business Review*, January 2001, Vol. 79 Issue 1.

[4]   Weick, Karl E., "Theory Construction as Disciplined Imagination", *Academy of Management Review*, October 1989, Vol. 14 Issue 4.

[5]   Christensen, Clayton M., *The Innovator's Dilemma*, Harvard Business School Press, 1997.

[6]   Staw, Barry and Ross, Jerry, "Knowing When to Pull the Plug", *Harvard Business Review*, March/April 1987, Vol. 65 Issue 2.

[7]   The issue of how to make management system and resource allocation processes more strategic has been well researched and well documented over time, from Bower's seminal contribution (*Managing the Resource Allocation Process*, Harvard Business School Division of Research, 1970) to a series of further developments (Haspeslagh, Philippe, "Portfolio Planning: Uses and Limits", *Harvard Business Review*, January/February 1982, Vol. 60 Issue 1; Chakravarthy, Balaji S. and Lorange, Peter, "Adapting Strategic Planning to the Changing Needs of a Business", *Journal of Organizational Change Management*, 1991, Vol. 4 Issue 2; Hamermesh, Richard G. (ed.), *Strategic Management*, John Wiley & Sons, 1983), some of which was summarized in Bower, J. and Gilbert, C. (eds), *From Resource Allocation to Strategy*, Oxford University Press, 2006).

3

The dancing elephant

One company that has tackled the strategic agility challenge head-on is IBM. After being given up for almost dead in the late 1980s by observers and analysts, and, indeed, flirting with bankruptcy, it was nearly taken apart by its management into separate companies around each major product group, as a measure of last resort. From this "near death" experience, as IBMers now recall it, it has renewed itself very deeply. By the mid-2000s, a most unlikely candidate for achieving strategic agility had become a large, diverse, strategically agile company, with an integrated corporate value creation logic focussed on services and solutions.

This chapter reviews the management systems and processes, the leadership behaviors, and the organizational architecture that contribute to strategic sensitivity, to the making of collective commitments and to fast, fluid resource redeployment, and which thus make IBM strategically agile. The pages that follow paint a surprising portrait: perhaps, indeed, there are dancing elephants.

Strategic sensitivity

From its ivory tower of "splendid isolation" of the late 1980s, when it had lost the capability to be in touch with the outside world, and even with its closest customers, IBM has now built many different channels, processes, and arenas to stimulate and heighten its strategic sensitivity, maximizing the knowledge exchange surface with the outside. It is intensely connected with customers, partners, scientists and engineers, specialized experts, public policy-makers, NGOs ... They all provide insight, and allow IBM to be fast. IBM has also created and honed a process for new business development and venture experiments, as a way to renew businesses and gain experiential "learning from trying" insight. Both contribute to strategic sensitivity.

Being connected to the world

❝for decades the company had led the development of the computer industry, and it simply believed "it knew better"❞

In fact, IBM's strategic sensitivity development started with the "survival crisis" of 1993. As a longtime IBM customer, Lou Gerstner, the new CEO and Chairman of IBM, came in with a personal conviction that IBM needed to reconnect with its customers and the outside world in a deeper and broader manner than ever. For decades the company had led the development of the computer industry, and shaped it around its mainframe integrated system offering, and it simply believed "it knew better". In the summer of 1993, after having been in the job only a few weeks (in a desperate move the board had appointed him in April) and visiting many customers himself, Gerstner sent each of his top 50 executives to visit a customer's CEO to learn about customer needs. This "Operation Bear Hug" as he humorosly dubbed it, marked the beginning of a more open strategy process at IBM. Active collaboration with and learning from existing and potential customers has featured high in IBM's priorities ever since. In an attempt to seek new growth IBM has since the early 2000s developed many new channels and mechanisms to connect with multiple external stakeholders more broadly and deeply on an intellectual and experiential level. All these mechanisms give a stronger voice to the outside in IBM's strategic deliberations. Some strengthen foresight, by providing future-oriented "outlooks"; most foster insight, by enabling better real-time information and ongoing dialogues. Let's review them.

Amplifying the voice of the customer

Already back in 1993, through IBM's "Operation Bear Hug", Lou Gerstner and senior IBMers understood that the company could do much more for customers than it was doing at that time. There was clearly a need for more system integration and services among IBM core customers to counterbalance the excesses of the client-server decentralization of IT systems,[1] and the company still had a lot of the integration knowledge which it was not using fully – and risked losing for good if it didn't use it.

Dennie Welsh, then head of IBM's Integrated Systems Services Corporation in the US, also sensed the move to services to be an important one, not just a support activity for the sale of mainframe computers, as services had been seen at IBM in the past. According to Gerstner:

He [Dennie Welsh] envisioned a company that would literally take over and act on behalf of the customers in all aspects of information technology – from building systems to defining architectures to actually managing the computers and running them for the customers.[2]

Since Gerstner's appointment as CEO, services have provided enduring and steadily implemented corporate value creation logic for IBM. One major step towards expertise in the business of services took place with IBM's acquisition of PwC Consulting in 2002. IBM created a new global business unit, IBM Business Consulting Services, transferring 30,000 PwC consultants to IBM.

Picking the brains of leading customers

The importance given to the customer now goes far beyond providing services. IBM understood that the most natural and obvious co-strategizing partners were its best current customers. In this context, "best" refers to providing learning opportunities, not necessarily contract size. For instance, IBM has for years systematically used its leading customers to provide foresight on future needs. This practice of "picking the brains" of others has its origins in Gerstner's personal experiences as an IBM customer, which convinced him to push IBM towards higher integration in the early 1990s. If he had been able to foresee the most valuable future for IBM, from the outside as a customer, why would other leading customers not be able to do the same? One was A.J. Lafley, the head of Procter & Gamble: he helped IBM understand the huge business opportunity of outsourcing and, later, of "On Demand" business. On Demand Innovation Services were launched in 2002 to provide customers with a small team of researchers specializing in high-end business transformation and technology consulting. It enabled faster communication with companies and thus facilitated a fast reaction to change. "On Demand" became the motto for IBM's faster strategy. Lafley, for instance, helped Palmisano, the CEO of IBM, shape IBM's On Demand strategy by saying that much more of P&G's business could be run by a company such as IBM. The order of magnitude difference between Palmisano's own modest view of IBM's potential and that of P&G's CEO made Palmisano realize the full potential of On Demand.[3] Many other new growth ideas and opportunities can be traced back to customer interactions, including IBM's hugely successful life science business, which happened thanks to a chance conversation between a Mayo Clinic scientist and an IBM supercomputer developer in Minneapolis.

Tapping substance experts and futurologists

Collaborating with customers to identify new growth opportunities is not enough. IBM wants to cast its sensing net wider and further into the future, rather than run the risk of proximate learning. IBM also needs to understand the key trends and challenges of the broader society in order to develop and position its own value offering correctly over the longer term. This requires active intellectual exchanges around strategic issues with multiple stakeholders beyond mere business firms. For example, IBM's Global Innovation Outlooks aim at connecting the company with the world's thought leaders well beyond conventional customers. IBM organizes on an annual basis Global Innovation Outlook (GIO) sessions in each main region of the world. The main purpose of these events is to identify and address major societal challenges together with the world's leading thinkers from the corporate, university, and public sectors. As a result, IBM not only learns more broadly from the world but is able to mobilize different stakeholders to innovate and work on the same themes. As examples, the themes of the 2004 Innovation Outlook were Healthcare, Government and its Citizens, and The Business of Work and Life. IBM has also extended its cooperation to broader societal issues, such as working with *National Geographic* to trace and report the evolution and migration of human being from our origins.

Bringing together external partners, customers' researchers and internal innovators

To complement the GIO sessions IBM has more recently started to organize "Innovation Jams"[4] (a brainpower mobilization process it had piloted internally around the development of its own values) to support collective innovation around key themes with various internal and external parties. The Innovation Jams provide all IBMers and its ecosystem partners (around 70 companies participated in 2006) with a virtual shared web-enabled innovation environment for 72 hours. During this time all participants are encouraged to share everything they know and to come up with new innovative ideas (technologies, business models, processes, etc.) in selected themes (identified for instance in the Innovation Outlooks). The Innovation Jams help IBM to innovate new businesses and ways of working with all employees and key partners worldwide.

This collective innovation process is facilitated by a network of voluntary (high potential) moderators from different parts of IBM who guide and synthesize the web-based discussion towards actionable outcomes. In addition,

IBMs most senior executives stay "online" to encourage the participants and provide sponsorship for the most valuable ideas. Advanced text mining techniques are also used to link similar ideas to each other and to identify common themes and patterns across the thousands of ideas. Participants are also asked to vote for the best ideas, which will be funded by a special $100 million fund.

ff many companies have assigned dedicated functional experts to key stakeholder relationships ""

Another connectivity process, the Engineering and Technology Services, helps IBMers win the "hearts and minds" of their customers' R&D engineers and learn about new technologies and solutions – in addition to selling services. Many companies have assigned dedicated functional experts to key stakeholder relationships, but IBM has institutionalized this practice even further. Substance matter expert networks enable deep learning at an individual and team level. It has established an independent Engineering and Technology Services (ETS) unit for directly interfacing with R&D people in different companies across industries and helping them solve their problems through more innovative use of IT. Through this process IBM co-innovates with customers' scientists and engineers. It has redirected its research organization to support its services and solutions business more directly by assigning scientists and researchers to solve practical and important customer problems together with the rest of the organization. As IBM's CEO Sam Palmisano states:

Our researchers understand that the business problems we are trying to solve for customers are not elementary stuff … it's hard, hard, hard … Technical leaders want to make an impact, which means seeing their work make a difference in the real world. Sure, they thrive on publishing and going to conferences. But they understand there's no better way to do that than by working with real live customers.[5]

Strategic partners and open innovations

Open business approaches are another important mechanism for heightened strategic sensitivity at IBM. It realized the value of more open business definitions in the late 1990s in connection with its server business crisis. It had to lose most of its market share before it understood that its server business was better off with horizontal core platforms managed by another unit inside IBM. In fact both businesses, the vertical server business and horizontal "open platforms" business, had more room to grow within the new organizational set-up.[6] Since then, IBM has become an active proponent of and contributor to open source movements such as Linux. It also has released to the public domain a whole range of patents and proprietary IPR (intellectual property rights) material to foster collective application development and innovation and to give an incentive to others to co-innovate with IBM. IBM has moved rapidly to an intensely partnered and open development process.

Business development experiments and corporate venturing

At the end of 1999, IBM launched a new business building process called Emerging Business Opportunities (EBO) in order to experiment with new businesses on a continuous manner, enter new emerging application areas and technologies, and rekindle growth. The main targets were:

▦ to open up new growth avenues and create new applications areas for sustaining core businesses and leveraging their competencies into new areas;

▦ to put a real emphasis in resource allocation to longer-term, more distant horizon businesses, with true "game changing" opportunities for new and core businesses;

▦ to accelerate the development of core businesses by making new technologies, and pioneering market experiments widely available within IBM, across a broad range of applications, and business groups and divisions;

▦ to renew specific core businesses by providing a vehicle for experimentation, and for new developments, and for migration to new value creation logics and business systems.[7]

The main purpose of the EBO process is to promote new experiments and business development in a systematic manner. New business in IBM meant not only independent new business opportunities but also renewal of the core business. As a result, EBOs in IBM could reside in any place, in connection to existing core businesses, and report to business groups, or separately as part of completely new growth platform initiatives under corporate strategy staffs. Regardless of their organizational home base, all EBOs in IBM are overseen by corporate strategy and reviewed regularly as a corporate-wide effort by top management. According to Rod Adkins, Senior Vice President, Development and Manufacturing, IBM Systems Technology Group:

The key to EBOs' success is to allocate independent funding that separates EBOs from existing core businesses, and to do the same for people, in fact to dedicate our best people from traditional businesses to EBOs. You need separate resource allocation and the engagement of the best and most credible leaders from our traditional businesses.[8]

In parallel to EBOs, IBM differentiated business processes according to three different time horizons. Each time horizon had a different target setting, different review processes: more learning oriented for more distant Horizon 3 business opportunities, more customer acquisition driven in Horizon 2, and more performance oriented for current, ongoing Horizon 1 businesses. All of them were followed up separately on a corporate-wide basis to ensure that investments were allocated in a balanced way to opportunities in different time horizons. As they matured, EBO ventures were reviewed and managed increasingly like usual business units to facilitate their reintegration in the existing organization.

The EBO process has developed into a well-established core strategic agility process for IBM with encouraging results. In 2005, IBM generated no less than $19 billion of new revenue stemming from EBOs. The EBO process gave IBM the flexibility to enter new domains, such as life sciences; to bring new innovations and issues, such as mobility, to existing established businesses; and to bolster the position of existing businesses via new related ventures, such as client-server computing. Beyond its direct business building and renewal contribution, it is a way to generate experiential insight, complementary to the informational insight other approaches bring.

Being connected among IBMers

Internal connectivity is equally as essential as external connectivity. Beyond putting very different people on the same team on client projects — like ex-PwC senior consultants and IBM Labs scientists working together on customer R&D problems — IBM has also developed internal connection channels. An open strategy process provides not only a "platform" for IBMers to stay connected with the external world but it also heightens IBM's strategic alertness and encourages active internal dialogue. IBM has further boosted its strategic alertness by ambitious and broad goals communicated via its values. Values such as "dedication to every client's success", "innovation that matters – for our company and for the world", and "trust and personal responsibility in all relationships" provide ambitious direction setting for people across the company. The values also embody the importance of external connectivity and relevance to the outside world. IBM sees itself as creating value for society.

IBM has paid a lot of attention to improving its internal dialogue. Otherwise it would be difficult for it to reap the benefits from an open strategy process and heightened strategic alertness, as collective commitments require collective sense-making. In addition to the Jams concept (where practically all IBMers and various partners participate in a facilitated web-enabled dialogue) IBM has been actively developing its meeting structures, including the top team. The team-based top management governance mechanism, which selectively includes non-executive participants, encourages active and substantive dialogue. A multi-perspective organization at the top, with interdependent complementary responsibilities assigned to various top team members, also forces the top team and the whole organization into an active continuous dialogue.

This strategic dialogue is not confined to the top team but extended in various ways to promising minds throughout the organization. IBM is assigning additional strategic roles for high-potential people such as the Innovation Jams moderators, who voluntarily play an additional strategy role. IBM also appoints high-potential leaders as "semi-permanent" members to its top management teams. After six months as CEO, Sam Palmisano abolished the company's Corporate Executive Committee[9] and replaced it with three teams, one for strategy, one for operations, and one for technology matters. Each of these three teams focuses IBM-wide on their own areas of interest with a composition most suitable for each of the substance areas. In addition to the top-line executives, roughly half of the members of each team are "hand-picked" by Palmisano to the team as full mandated decision-makers for a year or more. These high-potential people are expected to bring additional factual and conceptual richness, given the range of their backgrounds and the depth of their experience, as well as cognitive diversity, to the top management dialogue. For instance, an executive who grew up in India can significantly contribute to an effort to better penetrate markets there with products that embrace the local styles and customs.

> **" high potential peole are expected to bring additional factual and conceptual richness, as well as cognitive diversity, to the top management dialogue 』 』**

Fundamentally, for IBM the new team-based management system is a way to engage a number of the best brains *vis-à-vis* specific issues in strategizing and technology management for a limited but long enough duration (one year) in an intense way, on an ongoing basis, rather than rely on specialized permanent staffs or on members of the top team exclusively. IBM's new top management meeting structure also constantly exposes and invites the highest executives, including the CEO, into an open dialogue with the most demanding senior middle managers and experts. As a result, the collective understanding and commitment of the whole organization increase.

In addition to cognitive diversity, IBM's extended and specialized management team structure allows more time and expertise to be allocated to key cross-company decisions. The strategy team focuses on long-term business development, the technology team on the various technology issues, and the operating team on the ongoing business concerns with financial focus.[10] Depending on who is selected to these teams by Palmisano, specific new perspectives and new insights can be brought to bear on the issues.

In sum, IBM has systematically developed its strategic sensitivity through a combination of external connectivity channels and activities that provide both foresight and insight; through more open innovation and business building networks; through a thoughtfully structured corporate venturing process that provides for differentiation and integration; and through a series of approaches that widen and sustain a high-quality strategy dialogue within the organization.

Collective commitment

One of the root causes of IBM's strategic paralysis in the early 1990s was management divergence resulting from business line autonomy. The end of the mainframe integrated system era meant that IBM was increasingly facing focussed, "best of breed", specialist competitors. Rather than delegating integration to IBM, customers were buying a mixed bag of "plug compatible" equipment from multiple sources. The old mainframe-based corporate value creation logic was breaking down. Business unit heads, and analysts, started to see belonging to IBM as being trapped in a value destruction logic: why incur high group overheads when competitors did not? By focusing on services and solutions, rather than individual businesses, Gerstner was able to reinvent a corporate value creation logic, a rationale for keeping IBM together, and an organizational integration justification. Product lines that did not contribute to that logic, because they were commodity products (disk drives) or were increasingly serving individual consumer-like markets (PCs) would be divested when the opportunity arose. So it was more than natural for Lou Gerstner to put high priority in changing how IBM's top team members interacted with each other, to reflect the need for corporate integration in the implementation of the new value creation logic. Gerstner completely changed the charter of IBM's Corporate Executive Committee. Only IBM-wide matters were allowed to be discussed in the top team. Gerstner also introduced an interdependent organization right after taking over in 1993. This forced the IBM top team members to collaborate on a much deeper level than before. The top team members also assumed responsibilities of various corporate-wide development programs in addition to their line responsibility.

Today IBM's new management team meeting practice also allows Sam Palmisano to play multiple roles. He participates as a team member in each team on a "first among equals" principle. As a member, not chairman, of any of the three teams, he can challenge the status quo in a different manner than as chair. Assigning different roles to the regular or temporary members of the top team allows the CEO more freedom to play multiple roles. He can concentrate, for instance, on new opportunity identification and theme shaping, while maintaining the authority to revert to the traditional authoritative CEO role when necessary. The CFO can in this case play the role of the demanding authority for the business results, and the head of the CEO office can chair the discussion concerning, for instance, a new strategic project or organizational design project.

The use of teams also forced IBM's senior executives to break the traditional one-on-one reporting and commitment-making processes found in most companies. By working together on a shared agenda, with interdependent roles and tasks, senior executives could no longer behave as barons defending their fiefdoms. IBM's use of teams constantly exposes and invites the highest executives, including the CEO, into an open dialogue with the most demanding senior middle managers, and provides for greater cognitive diversity. As Sam Palmisano said, learning to play according to these new rules and roles has been difficult for everybody, including himself.[11] It is also intellectually, socially, and emotionally very demanding because personal strengths and weaknesses become much more visible in this approach. But the benefits of this practice are clear: more cognitive diversity, more depth and breadth in substantive dialogue, and, most importantly, more leadership unity across the top team and the whole organization.

IBM's systematic job rotation principle supports constructive top team dialogue. Anyone reaching the top team has covered several roles and gained multiple perspectives in the company before his or her current role. "Having been there before" with first-hand experiences allows substantive discussion and provides legitimacy for anybody to challenge anybody else in the top team. It also provides each member more of an overall perspective on the company as a system, and allows them to play a role in architectural decisions, around organization and management systems, not just to be a skillful operator or seasoned captain. In this kind of an environment, conflict and dialogue leads to collective commitment via genuine and visible personal dissent (instead of public agreement and private dissent via invisible personal disagreement). The quality of the team at the top depends on its composition. IBM's "NextGens" program is devoted to the acceleration of high-potential talents.

In essence, IBM's ability to make collective commitments and leadership unity is built on collective responsibility stemming from high interdependency in responsibilities and tasks at the top, supported by additional corporate roles and shared strategic agenda and incentives. This provides the foundation for strong collaboration, made easier by overlapping areas of expertise and a CEO acting as "first among equals".

Resource fluidity

The company has also moved a very long way from the independent product lines and the geographic fiefdoms of the early 1990s. Where these units had been driving resource allocation, a much more flexible process is now in place, freeing strategy and resource allocation from structural lines.

Freeing strategy from structure

As with strategic sensitivity, IBM's resource fluidity development started with the transformation journey initiated in 1993. By shifting the power balance in the organization from geographies to global business units, IBM created a truly multidimensional organization capable of freeing strategic direction from organizational structure. Suddenly, the contribution of all the dimensions in the organization was needed for creating IBM's strategy and implementing any major business decision. At the same time, IBM harmonized and globalized its business processes and shared services to reintegrate the company and improve efficiency. This organizational change dissociated business results from resource ownership, as an increasing amount of resources did not anymore reside "under the thumb" of geographical business managers, product line executives, or any other single business dimension. Parallel to creating common business processes and shared services, IBM had to renew its global management system to provide multidimensional transparency to all of its operations.

IBM realized the benefit of modularity of processes and IT systems when implementing common processes and systems to all businesses. The

❝modular processes and systems also enabled IBM to lower its "center of gravity" in decision-making❞ various IBM businesses and geographical needs could simply not be met with "one size fit all" processes and systems. Modularity of business procedures and systems, with relatively small process modules that could be combined in various ways, and adaptability provided more variety and versatility for common processes and services. Modular processes and systems also enabled IBM to lower its "center of gravity" in decision-making closer to customers: a complete virtual global IBM structure can now be found any place on earth. Increasingly modular common processes and systems also enabled IBM to develop a sophisticated role and task-specific global work environment IBM calls "On Demand Workplace", for global knowledge workers on top of its global systems. This has enabled IBM to lower local hierarchies, as people's work can now be structured and followed up from anywhere in the world.

Making it easier for individuals to assume new roles and tasks

IBM's internal "On Demand Workplace" is a new work environment with encouraging results. The main target of the "On Demand Workplace" is to enhance IBM employees' productivity and innovativeness. This virtual work environment provides each employee (and IBM's closest partners) with up-to-date, role-based and context-specific knowledge of their work on a need basis. This helps the whole company and its partner network to improve productivity by "freeing" work from the constraints of time and place. As a result, over 40 percent of IBM employees were truly mobile in 2006. They do not need an office as they can do their work anywhere – increasingly at the customer premises – at any time. At the same time, as managers can lead their projects and people from anywhere, a lot of local hierarchies and reporting layers have become obsolete. The organization structure is getting flatter and flatter.[12] (Flat companies are the opposite of the pyramidal structures of organizations that most companies have used ever since the industrial revolution.)

On top of more productive management of routine work flows, IBM's "On Demand Workplace" has recently become a major "innovation platform" as individuals and various communities of practice (across IBM and its partners) have started to share their ideas and insights on it.

Modularity in processes and systems has also enhanced knowledge sharing and people mobility in IBM. However, the main mechanisms for these have been institutionalized job rotation principles, normative control via values and fairness, and transparency of evaluation. Moving people in and out from the core business to new business opportunities in a systematic manner has decreased the natural politics related to moving from "high powered" core business leadership jobs to risky new business development organizations.

Institutionalizing mobility in and out of core businesses

Business unit "silos" are natural holders for strong opinions and personal loyalty, which may become harmful. They breed cave-dwellers. In addition to multidimensionality, a systematic practice for moving people in and out of the core business is an efficient vehicle for increasing cognitive diversity in the organization. Moving senior leaders in and out from the core business by actively encouraging them to run the Emerging Business Opportunities (EBOs) not only sends out a strong signal that renewal is important but also encourages "old dogs to learn new tricks" by forcing senior executives out of their comfort zones. At the same time this practice makes sure that new business opportunities have the most credible and experienced leadership in place. In the same manner, IBM systematically moves people from EBOs back to core businesses and in this way imports new thinking patterns and entrepreneurial experience into core businesses.

One of the main benefits of this practice is that it allows IBM to over-differentiate the business management processes while under-differentiating people management. By over-differentiating management processes the company avoids stifling entrepreneurial ventures under the weight of corporate bureaucracies. Yet, at the same time, by under-differentiating people management, it neutralizes the "personal loss or gain" related to the change and smoothens the reintegration process of a venture into a mainstream business.

Lowering the "center of gravity" of the organization

Agility stems from decentralized initiatives, in particular in a service and solutions company which co-innovates with its clients. Strategic strength stems from the ability to mobilize quickly and deploy significant resources against the opportunities identified from decentralized initiatives. Modular subunit structures can be used for creating and replicating multiple small units of a large multidimensional organization, allowing each to undertake its own initiatives, without losing the benefits of global transparency and economies of scale. Small customer-facing organizations – down to the size of a key account team of a few people – become the "center of gravity" of the organization, i.e., for help they pull in resources from various global back-office support functions. These small customer-facing organizations are similar, and can be redeployed, recombined, and rearranged relatively flexibly depending on the evolution of customer needs and specific contracts. The back-office resources are provided to them via some form of internal market. The profitability of doing business with a customer becomes a resource allocation rule, subject to exceptions, decided by management: resources and attention are allocated to the most profitable customers.

In order to improve its responsiveness to local customer needs and encourage decentralized innovative initiatives, in 2005 IBM consolidated its European country and regional organizations (including IBM headquarters in Europe) into two Integrated Operating Teams (IOTs) bringing together all key dimensions of IBM's global organization. According to Palmisano, this way the company is "lowering the center of gravity" closer to customers. Each of the IOTs has further organized its operations into key customer accounts run by a managing director responsible for all IBM operations globally for the customer in question, and into geographical teams responsible for smaller customers. A transparent modular organization allows the local business leader to run a virtual IBM consisting of all the required competences and guidelines needed for fast decision making and execution. The main task of the two European IOT teams is to dynamically allocate scarce global resources across the various customer interfacing teams, depending on the market demand.[13] At the same time, IBM has moved all the back-office work to global service centers in countries like India. As a result, the modular and transparent organizational design has helped IBM to improve its local responsiveness and cost at the same time. Yet, obviously, the more decentralized the organization, and the smaller the modular units, the more difficult control and direction become. Smaller entrepreneurial units easily diverge.

Management through values

According to Liz Smith, General Manager, Infrastructure Access Services, IBM Global Technology Services, values provide a strong normative control mechanism for internal and external collaboration among smaller units, and also throughout the organization. According to her, if and when IBM employees can create trust among each other and partners, they can also gather together the right people and resolve conflicts faster and closer to the customer.[14] In other words, the main target of IBM's values is to make people across the organization more "self-directed". More broadly, shared values emphasizing active collaboration, and management systems evaluating each manager's "values-based behavior", have encouraged people all over the organization to share resources and knowledge, and move around tasks and projects. According to Sam Palmisano, values are just about the only means to manage a complex multidimensional organization:

If there is no way to optimize IBM through organization or management dictate ... you've got to create a management system that empowers people and provides a basis of decision-making consistent with who we are at IBM. Values inject balance in the management system – balance between the short-term transaction and long-term relationship, balance between the interests of shareholders, employees, and clients. Values help you make those decisions in a way that is consistent with who you are as a company.[15]

The emphasis on values, therefore, and their very strong role in providing meaning and strategic direction, allowed the management process of IBM to shift from the tight control and discipline process put in place by Gerstner to a more autonomous, delegated, customer-facing process, controlled by values and norms, rather than a top-down hierarchical process. Both approaches served a purpose. The first was needed for transforming IBM and the second for institutionalizing strategic agility.

Linda Sanford, SVP of "On Demand" transformation in IBM, emphasized also the role of values in fostering collaboration and encouraging reciprocity:

Our values very clearly say that people are expected to share their knowledge and resources with their colleagues if they are asked to do so. Of course people have sometimes good reasons not to share, but then these are also easy to understand by colleagues. If you explain to your colleague why you can't right now share your resources, your colleague understands it and might even appreciate it. As a result, you might get a good score for "collaborativeness". It is the behavior, not individual act, that we measure. Do you give an impression of being open and sincere as opposed to driving your own agenda?[16]

❝Do you give an impression of being open and sincere as opposed to driving your own agenda?❞

This "help and share" attitude and behavior are carefully measured as part of IBM's regular performance reviews. A bad score in this core value is today seen very negatively in the company.

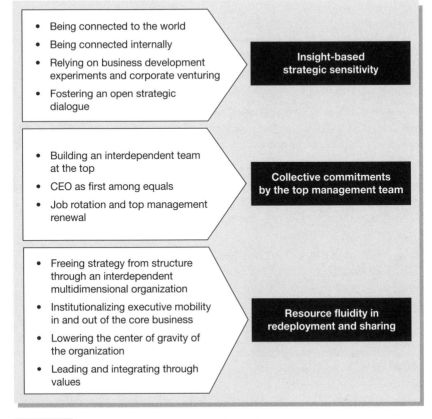

figure 3.1 **IBM's approach to strategic agility**

An interdependent multidimensional organization, decentralized entrepreneurship, rules for mobilizing resources and the emphasis on managing by values all contributed to greater and faster resource fluidity within IBM.

Conclusion

Over the past dozen years IBM has put in place a lot of efforts to learn to dance: the most important are listed in summary form in Figure 3.1 above. IBM today is fundamentally different from the failing company of the early 1990s. Among the large companies we studied it provides the most striking example of a business fostering strategic agility. Is it perfect? Of course not! There is perhaps no truly exemplary company; but it has gone further in the journey to strategic agility than most, and definitely started furthest behind in that long and arduous trip.

References

[1] The client-server architecture had decentralized the IT operations of most companies to department level, leading to fast cost escalation and compatibility problems in companies.

[2] Gerstner, Lou, *Who Says the Elephants Can't Dance?*, HarperBusiness, 2002.

[3] Hamm, Steve and Ante, Spencer E., "Beyond blue; never mind computers and tech services. IBM's radical new focus is on revamping customers' operations – and even running them", *Business Week*, 18 April 2005.

[4] This process was first implemented internally by Sam Palmisano in 2002, to gather feedback from all employees around the company values and aspirations. It provided useful information for debate in "Value Jams".

[5] Schlender, Brent, "How Big Blue is Turning Geeks into Gold", *Fortune*, 9 June 2003, Vol. 147 Issue 11.

[6] Authors' interview, Rod Adkins, Senior Vice President, Development and Manufacturing, IBM Systems Technology Group, 4 April 2005.

[7] Bruce Harreld, presentation at Strategic Management Society Conference, Orlando, October 2005.

[8] Authors' interview, Rod Adkins, 4 April 2005.

[9] Also Lou Gerstner changed IBM's Corporate Executive Committee working habits when he took over in 1993. He changed the name and charter of the group – but not its composition.

[10] In addition to the team meetings, Sam Palmisano has a monthly staff meeting for covering the ongoing, mainly administrative, issues of CEO's direct reports.

[11] Authors' interview, Sam Palmisano, Chief Executive Officer, IBM, 7 October 2005.

[12] Authors' interview, Sandesh Bhat, Director, Internal Operating Environment W3, 4 April 2005.

[13] Authors' interview, Hans Ulrich Maerki, Chairman, IBM EMEA, 14 March 2006.

[14] Authors' interview, Liz Smith, General Manager, IBM Global Technology Services, 13 January 2006.

[15] Hemp, Paul and Stewart, Thomas, interview with Sam Palmisano, "Leading Change When Business Is Good", *Harvard Business Review*, December 2004, Vol. 82 Issue 12.

[16] Authors' interview, Linda Sanford, Senior Vice President, Enterprise On Demand Transformation and Information Technology, IBM, 13 January 2006.

2

Fostering strategic agility

The first part of this book justified the need for strategic agility and defined its main dimensions. The key message was: companies need new approaches for strategizing and organizing which require new leadership styles. These new methods allow companies to thrive on change and disruption and leave strategically slower competitors behind.

The following three chapters explore, beyond the IBM example, the capabilities and managerial practices that companies need to put in place to foster and maintain strategic agility.

4

Sharpening strategic sensitivity

Insight is not gained in a vacuum, from armchair reflection only: insight results from connection, from a rich network of creative interactions. In fact, most significant ideas and innovations have originated from the confrontation and the combination of disparate sources of knowledge. Strategic insight is no different: it results from an intense interchange with the outside world as well as deep reflection. So, maximizing the channels and integrity of knowledge exchange with the outside world is a precondition for strategic sensitivity: there can't be sensitivity without exposure to stimulation!

Involving more, rather than fewer, people in the process pays off not least because many successful innovations resulted, in part, from positive surprises. To leave enough room for serendipity, companies need more external connections than they require operationally. Networking with the outside needs to extend beyond immediately felt needs.

❝ not all learning can be vicarious, not everything can be borrowed from others ❞

Exposure and knowledge exchange is not enough. Not all learning can be vicarious, not everything can be borrowed from others. A more experiential – and experimental – attitude toward strategy development needs to prevail.

Connectedness is hard to achieve unless you stand outside, away from your own position, your own context, at some distance, and mentally play with your own organization as if holding a model of it in your outstretched arm.

Connectedness, experiments, and modeling do not pay off unless you are really smart about learning from external stimuli. Results come from experiments, and from playfulness with one's own position. Some amount of creative tension, and of contradictory objectives, helps being attentive, intellectually stretched, and intensely preoccupied. For example, role-playing as a difficult customer or a competitor viewing your company's products or services helps some, while others like to envision viewing their company's operations from the top of a tall building or even from 30,000 feet up. Maintaining an active dialogue, involving many in the organization, around choices and commitments that are difficult, is a further way to help exploit external connectedness, learning from experiments and playful modeling. This chapter develops these themes and shows how strategic sensitivity can be heightened and made to contribute to strategic agility.

Maximize the knowledge exchange with the outside world

Co-strategizing (sharing of key scenarios, ideas, and assumptions about future markets, technologies, and competition) with multiple stakeholders helps companies increase their sensitivity to new opportunities as several parties share and test their insights regarding the environment of their future bets. An active and purposeful dialogue with key stakeholders allows companies to borrow the foresights and insights of others as "building blocks" for new business innovations. The more parties involved in co-strategizing, the more opportunities for breakthrough ideas.

Leading customers

Both IBM, as in the previous chapter, and HP, as well as Cisco and many of the other companies we studied, have created comprehensive processes and multiskilled teams led by senior general managers to interact continuously with their key global customers. In the case of these companies, the criteria for intense customer interaction are strategic learning and future business potential. This interaction includes both clearly structured formal management bodies and a lot of informal peer-to-peer communication across all levels and functions in both organizations. The purpose of this multidimensional interaction is not only, or even not so much, to find immediate new business and collaboration opportunities but rather to increase understanding of the future challenges for both organizations.

Non-customers

Incumbent companies should also try actively to build relationships with companies representing new types of customer needs and requirements. New disruptive technologies and business models often come from new types of customers seeking a novel solution to their needs. Without an active dialogue with these non-customers (who might be potential customers, or should already be customers), the risk of becoming hostage to traditional customer relationships and perspectives looms large. This risk is compounded by the sales organizations' natural bias towards and interest in existing customers – and difficulty in dealing with new, uncertain, and challenging business opportunities growing from the periphery. Sales people simply don't have an interest and incentive to actively drive business with potential customers whose needs may strongly contradict the needs and interests of existing customers.

This is why companies need systematically to use other functions such as internal consultants or R&D experts to learn actively from non-customers.

End-users

Companies also need to stay connected with the end-users of their product. Intel, for instance, as we saw, invests heavily in understanding end-user behavior and usage models driving the demand for its products and services. It does that with a strong anticipation focus, given the long lead-times of products and process development, and capacity planning in semiconductors. This deep understanding then helps Intel to direct its own market-making efforts in such a way that new "pull" for Intel products can be created – while decreasing the related technology risks. Consequently, the main purpose of being intimately connected to end users is to further understand and influence market evolution beyond one's own horizon – beyond the immediate customer concerns.

Partners and complementors

Various kinds of partners and complementors (particularly in the ICT industry) comprise another important stakeholder group for co-strategizing. Sharing strategies and roadmaps with these stakeholders is crucially important for building successful end-to-end solutions and for achieving positive network effects. Intel has for years invested a lot in sharing its future product and technology roadmaps with all major value chain members in order to secure alignment of the R&D efforts of all major contributors of an end-to-end solution.

Further, Apple's most recent success with i-Pod illustrates the strength of borrowing an insight from potential partners and applying it to another context. The company has been well known for its excellent devices and design for a long time, but these strengths alone would not have taken it to where it is today. It required Steve Jobs' active dialogue with the CEOs and senior executives of potential partners, Time Warner and HP in particular, to change the company's strategic direction. In a meeting, the head of Time Warner suggested to Jobs that i-Pod could be a solution to Napster's challenges and peer-to-peer exchanges. This dialogue quickly opened a completely new growth avenue for Apple.

Substance experts and think tanks

Active and broad-based co-strategizing with customers and partners and involvement with non-customers and end-users help companies to understand the interests and needs of their immediate business environment better, but this is not enough. Companies also need to understand the key trends and challenges of the broader society which ultimately drive the demand for their own ecosystem. This requires, for instance, active collaboration with multiple stakeholders beyond "pure" business as discussed in the previous chapter in connection to IBM Global Innovation Outlooks (GIO). These efforts help companies not only to learn more broadly but also to create new demand by aligning the interests and mobilizing various stakeholders to innovate and work on the same themes.

Don't shy away from experiments

Deep intellectual connectedness to various stakeholders allows profound learning but it seldom suffices for changing the way people behave. Reaching this target requires experimentation that allows people to deeply internalize highly embedded, systemic and contextual knowledge.[1]

Personal experimentation

The least risky way of experimenting takes place on an individual level. Thinking and acting in sequence enhances both individuals' and organizations' ability to generate new insights and gradually alter their mental models.[2] Nokia, for instance, actively encouraged its employees to experiment personally with the internet in the late 1990s to make people actively more familiar with this new disruptive technology and to help them come up with new insights regarding mobile internet. In the case of Nokia this practice had worked successfully before, as discussed in chapter 1. Nokia President from 1999 to 2005, Pekka Ala-Pietilä's passionate experimentation with the Apple Mac in the early 1990s made him understand that, like personal computers, given proper design, user interface and branding, mobile phones could quickly turn into consumer goods, and even fashion items, reaching market penetration levels well beyond the 5 to 10 percent of the population then anticipated. Such experiential insight, which would not have been possible through just outside observation, led Nokia's management to frame the emerging mobile phones business in a fundamentally different way to its competitors, as described in chapter 1.

Simulation, visualization, and play may also substitute for actual experimentation, with less risk and more drama! Philips, for instance, as it was struggling with new competitors and with the convergence of markets and technologies, organized workshops on specific issues and technologies for its management board – such as several days examining flat screen displays, exploring their potential and technology. It also set up a "war room", ostensibly on competitive threats, but also using the most advanced "converged" technologies available then, the medium becoming the message. What would have left key executives indifferent, if merely printed in a long report, hit them in the face as an interactive multimedia "war game" simulation. Today, Samsung's corporate university uses the same focus and drama approach to help the company internationalize and move beyond products to networks, systems, and solutions.

Corporate venturing

Corporate venturing with real businesses and people takes experiential learning to the next level – in potential gains, but also in risks. At best, corporate venturing helps to map changes in the core business trajectory and gradually transforms the mental models of the core business managers. For instance, Intel's Worldwide Interoperability for Microwave Access (WIMAX) venture helped its Communications division to "stay on the changing track" by first challenging its core development trajectory and later by becoming a core element of the division's strategy and value offer.[3]

❝ is there any scenario which would make the market bigger? ❞

In Intel, the WIMAX effort started as any venture in Intel's New Business Initiatives (NBI) unit in the early 2000s. After six months of hard work the WIMAX venture team was challenged with a question: "Is there any scenario which would make the market bigger?" The venture team thereafter continued to work on a new scenario based on creating direct end-user demand, rather than relying on Intel's core customers and distribution partners. It also proposed that Intel Communications Group (ICG) take over the venture to provide it with stronger visibility and boost. This proposal was first turned down by the ICG, which saw their main focus as WiFi (wireless technology – for the Centrino chip, a new micro-processor Intel was then developing), and this new effort as a deviation from their core development path. The venture team thus continued to work alone, and it decided to make a small acquisition to access more capa-bilities to accelerate Intel's WIMAX development.

The team also promoted the establishment of an industry-wide WIMAX Forum under non-Intel leadership. As a result of the WIMAX Forum's interest, and Intel's Solutions Marketing Group's (ISMG) market making efforts, as well as NBI's WIMAX own development efforts, the venture started to look more attractive from Intel's core business point of view. Finally, a year after first turning down WIMAX, ICG wanted to "take over" WIMAX development as one of Intel's core initiatives.

Experimentation with strategic partners

Creating new businesses and/or moving to markets together with strategic partners are the most difficult and risky ways of experiential learning. According to Steve Steinhilber, Vice President of Strategic Alliances in Cisco, the main challenge related to creating and/or moving to new markets together with selected partners relates to the fact that none of the partners really knows the market, each other's position, or the market potential.

Nobody knows the market and each other's final position in the initial phases of strategic market making and collaboration. These will all evolve over time and at best – if a new market can be created – everybody gets more than they had before.[4]

As a result, the participant companies must have the courage to live with a moving target and great ambiguity all the time. No clear roadmaps and milestones can be defined, but they have to be continuously adjusted as the joint understanding of the emerging business opportunity increases.

This requires a great deal of trust and acceptance of changes in companies' power positions. A market and competition "dominance mindset" would hamper companies' progress in these cases. Instead, companies need a mindset where creating a new market position is seen to bring new potential to everybody, regardless of the position. The fight for value capture starts only later. The means that Cisco uses change gradually to partial ownerships and acquisitions, reflecting greater confidence and commitment, depending on the case.[5]

Risk of creeping commitments

The main risk related to joint experimentation, though, is "creeping commitments" – where a company gets locked into a traditional supplier or way of doing things although new opportunities have developed. Successful co-strategizing evolves naturally to joint experimentation, requiring increasing investments from all parties. Over time companies' commitments to a given strategic direction or standard, as well as to various stakeholders (including customers), grows to a level from which there is no turning back. Perhaps the most dramatic, and certainly most costly, example of this was the way the whole telecom industry convinced itself over time that 3G was the only way to go, through a succession of reinforcing commitments to standards, applications, and licenses, leading to an auction "bubble" for traffic right and frequencies.

One way to manage creeping commitments is systematically to reduce the number of partners throughout the experimentation process. According to Chris Thomas, Chief Strategy Officer of Intel's Solutions Marketing Group:

You have to first pick up the most likely winners from the 360 degrees opportunity space and start supporting these intellectually and financially. Then you gradually increase investments in the most likely winner. By organizing a "social movement" around the likely winner you increase its chance of becoming the dominant standard. In any case, you limit fragmentation in the ecosystem and grow the market for the given solution.[6]

Be holistic and involve everyone

The ultimate value of co-strategizing and experimentation depends on the number and quality of people involved on your side. It is therefore very important that companies interact with different external stakeholders in multiple dimensions at all levels in the organization.

Senior executives

Peer-to-peer connections among CEOs and other top executives provide important insights and foresights to key trends and challenges at society and industry level. In-depth substance discussions among top executives may also provide important new business-level insights, as the Apple and IBM examples demonstrated earlier. In addition to this, peer-to-peer connections among top executives help build trust and commitment between companies on a personal level. This helps open doors to deeper collaboration and learning opportunities for other stakeholders in the company. The key role of top executive dialogue is thus to provide guidance and a framework for lower level co-strategizing.

Strategists

Corporate and business level strategists constitute another important stakeholder group in open strategizing. Their role is twofold. They drive and facilitate co-strategizing between different stakeholders at multiple levels in the organization in line with the top management guidance and framework, and they help integrate and synthesize key outcomes into cohesive strategies and action items.

For instance Cisco, Nokia and SAP have all assigned dedicated strategy people to drive and facilitate corporate-wide strategic collaboration with key partners. This is considered a necessary factor in order to maximize the organization's deep learning in a very dynamic environment.

Substance experts

Substance matter expert networks enable deep learning at an individual and team level. Many companies have assigned dedicated functional experts to key stakeholder relationships, but IBM has institutionalized this practice even further. As seen earlier, it has established an "independent" Engineering and Technology Services (ETS) unit for directly interfacing with R&D people in different companies across industries. This profit/loss responsible services organization does not report to any of the IBM global business units or sales and marketing organization but to IBM's global R&D organization. According to Kevin Reardon and Paul Ledak, heads of IBM's ETS activity: "R&D people want to deal with R&D people, not with sales and business people".

The ETS unit helps IBM establish deep relationships with different R&D organizations well beyond IBM's core business segments, which, in turn, open up avenues for new innovations and revenue streams beyond IBM's current business. At the same time, this approach enables IBM to influence standards and architectures in an indirect way. The other reason for keeping this activity separate from mainstream sales and marketing as well as service is that it empowers and trains the R&D organization to stay open and avoid the "not invented here" syndrome that so many R&D centers suffer from.[7]

Line managers

Line managers at various levels in the organization should also be actively interacting with their peers. This activity helps companies expand their learning base not only strategically but also operationally, as people in different functions and processes learn how other companies think and run their operations. Active interfacing with external parties also helps to keep the whole organization externally focussed. The more people in the organization understand the real customer needs, the better they can focus on truly value-adding activities. Cisco, for instance, has established a principle according to which all its senior managers, regardless of function and process, must interact with external stakeholders, preferably with customers, on a regular basis.

Creating a comprehensive architecture for staying connected

Cisco has created a comprehensive architecture for staying connected with the external world. At the top of the organization the CEO and his top team have an active peer-to-peer dialogue with various industry leaders, influencing and searching for new foresights and insights. In addition, Cisco has created a complete framework and process for guiding a wide range of co-strategizing activities, from intellectual co-strategizing and experimentation with multiple parties (for value creation) to minority and majority investments (for value capture).

In 1999 Cisco established a separate consultancy organization called Internet Business Solutions Group (IBSG) with three main targets:

1 to acquire a deeper understanding of leading customers' (existing and potential customers') business model drivers and future needs;

2 to accelerate customer adoption of internet technologies;

3 to educate and help Cisco as an organization to become a more customer and solutions driven company.

By sharing its value offering and product roadmaps with different external stakeholders the Cisco IBSG team gains valuable information about the key concerns of top management and a deeper understanding of the suitability of Cisco's products for the higher-level needs of potential customers. The direct reporting of IBSG to the CEO allows Cisco to learn from "any customers", and not just provide sales leads in the interests of the sales and marketing organization.

In addition to IBSG, Cisco has established segment councils to broaden its view on customer needs. The main role of these cross-functional councils is to drive segment-specific solution development across the company towards genuine customer-business improvement and higher added value. By gaining a better understanding of customers' needs, together with IBSG, Cisco R&D can develop smarter system architectures, allowing a better configuration of Cisco's and partners' resources and products into a full solution.

Cisco also encourages all of its personnel to associate closely with external stakeholders, particularly with customers and key partners, to understand customer concerns and needs, as well as to learn new best practices. It expects all senior executives to have regular meetings with their counterparts in Cisco's customer, potential customer, and partner organizations. According to Kate D'Camp, Cisco's former SVP of HR, this practice is also important for keeping the whole organization focussed on real and not internal customers.[8]

Cisco has also developed an open web-based tool for sharing its internal "user experiences" of Cisco products with the global community. This allows the company to establish and maintain an ongoing dialogue about its products and solutions with the outside world, including both existing and potential customers. The experiences to be shared with the external world are gained first by Cisco's internal IT via the "Cisco on Cisco" activity. This activity was started in the early 2000s as an attempt to understand better the question: "What are the integration challenges and issues with those Cisco products that Cisco uses itself?" This initiative quickly grew into an important strategic influencer and "test bed" role in the company, particularly in its enterprise business segment.

These experiences and business benefits of the "Cisco on Cisco" activity are shared on a corporate-wide basis, as well as with external customers in close collaboration with Cisco's Customer Advocacy function. The "Cisco on Cisco" web pages have today over 100,000 hits a month, providing valuable information to Cisco R&D and marketing and sales, drawing not only from Cisco's experience but also from those of external customers. "Cisco on Cisco" has also become a major internal influencer in

❝ the R&D units listen to the "customer voice" and are continuously making adjustments ❞

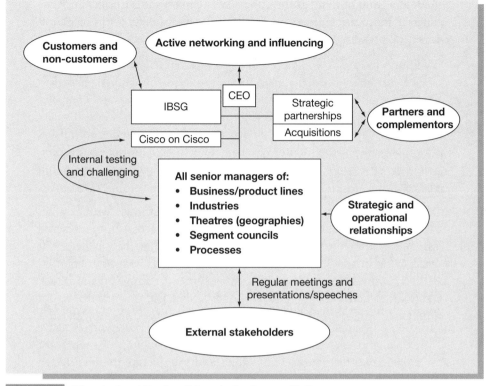

figure 4.1   Cisco's "architecture" for strategic sensitivity

prioritizing Cisco's product portfolio. The various R&D units listen to the "customer voice" and are continuously making adjustments/changes to their product roadmaps, including stopping and/or merging products already in the pipeline.

Cisco's architecture for staying connected is described in Figure 4.1.

Know where you stand

It is hard to make use of holistic co-strategizing and experimentation if the company doesn't know what it is and where it stands. New insightful interpretations call for an ability to see one's own organization as if standing outside, seeing it as an object, a shape, a structure, a set of processes that can be observed from a distance. Nokia's early insight to position mobile telephones as consumer goods resulted from the combination of experimentation and the "outside-in" modeling capability of the whole top team. It resulted in asking: "Why can't what is learned from the personal computer business be brought into the mobile telephony business?" Companies that do not have the ability to model themselves in relation to their environment cannot interpret strategic issues in a fresh way. The next sections look at the various ways in which companies can stay open to new interpretations.

Using the right language

Language conditions what management sees or doesn't see, and how it interprets what it sees, and whether or not what it sees provides a useful relationship to reality. Languages develop in context, for and from a particular practice, or business areas, as a way to express, codify, share, and teach knowledge pertinent to that practice or area. Hence, language may become constraining in its own right, adapted to a particular context, but not suited to a broader one. Having been at the forefront of GSM development, the language of which it had done much to create, Nokia was able to take leadership of the mobile phone industry. But that same language was not an advantage in multimedia applications, where software, video games, music, entertainment, sports, and the like became relevant. Such a highly contextual and specialized language as GSM technology may prevent companies from registering weak signals and interpreting them correctly. Indeed, movie and entertainment professionals have their own languages. With the understanding of key "shorthand" phrases comes the implicit expectation of a fully realized understanding of their meaning and usage in that industry context. To someone from a different business environment, such as telecom, just understanding the words does not provide an in-depth grasp of their meaning. For successful convergence and crossover learning to take place, a deep appreciation of each others' context is needed. Companies with a very specific industry jargon may be trapped in their own language!

A way to counterbalance that risk is to use a language that allows abstraction and analysis, i.e. not just a context-sensitive language, but also a concept-rich one.

Anticipation based on foresight is difficult in the absence of a concept-rich language, a language that allows systemic representation and modeling of trends and the ways they unfold, and of potential discontinuities and their consequences. Such a language is necessarily more abstract, conceptual, and universal, closer to the jargon typically used by strategy consultants. Such general and abstract languages are needed for executives in a company to make sense of what does not belong to their domain of experience, what they have to learn intellectually and conceptually, not simply by reflecting on their experience. Yet conceptual richness may not seem relevant, understandable, and useful to operational executives caught in their own cave. A stylized description and an abstract analysis of the world outside may not carry all that much meaning! On the other hand, situational learning based on insight is difficult and potentially hazardous in the absence of conceptual richness. In fact, both contextual detail and conceptual richness of language are needed for high strategic alertness.

Finding the right language is a challenging task for many companies. They find it most natural to rely on external consultants and/or academics for bringing new conceptual frameworks to the organization while keeping the internal language as contextual, or concrete, as possible. This approach secures the rootedness of the new conceptual tools in reality. The risk with this approach, however, is that the new frameworks are only seen "as applicable" when they confirm the old thinking patterns. A stronger vehicle for raising the conceptual capabilities of the company is to use internal consultants as facilitators of the strategic dialogue, or to hire people with an academic or consultancy background in the top team. This approach allows the top team gradually to learn a higher abstraction level language without compromising in contextuality.

Defining the core business in a broad manner

In the same way as the language used in strategy making needs both to combine a concrete "rooted" fit with the operational context of the company and also to be able to expand beyond it, so does the definition of their business the executives use. It needs to be concrete enough to represent accurately current activities and domains, and yet be able to transcend them – not an easy paradox to solve.

Defining the existing business in a slightly broader and more open way than just describing what the company does today lessens its mental dependency on current activity. Of course, the "What business are we in?" question is a timeless one that has haunted the strategy field for ever. All that is suggested here is a broader definition in terms of potential areas of application, and a tighter definition of how activities fit together.

Let's take an example, easyGroup. Although ultimately less than a brilliant success, it illustrates the point.[9] Although it started as an airline, from the beginning its core value creation logic was quite different from that of conventional airlines. The easy "X" concept builds on "easy anything" instead of on the process of running an airline. easyGroup is interested in any business domain or market with real-time elastic price services where it can leverage its strengths in dynamic pricing models, internet transaction capabilities and redeployable assets – such as planes that can be moved from serving one route to another as a function of dynamic learning from end-users. To easyGroup's way of thinking, the airline business is "just" one of many applications for implementing its core business idea. easyGroup's business definition is not tied to any given industry or market. Its internal capabilities are not tied either to any particular competences as they evolve continuously with the businesses easyGroup is involved in. From easyJet, easyGroup moved to car rental, movie theaters, hotels, cruise ships, internet cafés and even financial services. Success varied across businesses, but the fact that it defined its core business as a combination of capabilities applied to service businesses of a certain type, minimized its dependency on any specific business (which it saw only as an application area) and facilitated quick entry and, as needed, exit.

Recognizing opportunities on their own merits

New business opportunities should also be allowed to develop on their own conditions and merits. This does not mean that they should be left alone and evaluated only as stand-alone opportunities. On the contrary, new opportunities may sometimes contribute to the core business or the core may contribute to the new opportunity. The Apple i-Pod case described earlier is an example of the latter: Apple's core device business could contribute to the new opportunity by providing a good growth platform for the new business.

Marks & Spencer's entry into the food business is an example of recognizing opportunities on their own merit. When it first started selling "ready-made" food 30 or so years ago, Marks & Spencer's original idea was to use expensive basement space more efficiently and to generate lunchtime traffic in their clothing stores. Much more recently, management recognized that with the fitness trends, providing healthy food in Marks & Spencer's stores supported their image in the clothing business very well. However, they soon realized that health food could become much more than just a support activity for clothing. This led the company to enter the food market with a new "food only" store concept in which they could leverage their competences in retailing while building an autonomous new business. Although still small, this is a promising new opportunity.

Safeguarding new insights and opportunities

ff overambitious target setting and the wrong type of metrics can kill new insights JJ

Overambitious target setting and the wrong type of metrics can kill new insights and opportunities too early. As with IBM's use of different time "horizons", the type of dialogue and management process needed for managing new emerging businesses or issues differs from those used to running an ongoing business. Hence, a differentiated process for managing emerging strategic issues and opportunities is needed to prevent management from jumping to conclusions – positive or negative – too quickly, especially in new, unknown matters. Not only is IBM managing emerging business opportunities differently over time, according to their maturity, but it is also using the management process of EBOs in a way that emphasizes learning, with the objective early in the process being principally to gain clarity on the value proposition and strategy of the proposed business, then to gain a first, or a few, customers and co-learn with them, and later increasingly to emphasize, over time, the more usual business building objectives. Throughout, the emphasis is on creating and deepening new insights, and gaining precious understanding of how to make that business successful, not to impose approaches that might hamper the required learning. In other words, it's a simple but powerful "learn and reflect first, perform later" approach, managed with care and discipline in the relationship between the EBO team and its corporate sponsors and business group overseers.

Nokia has built a somewhat similar process to address emerging issues, not just emerging business opportunities, on an ongoing and flexible basis. To prevent too fast a judgment, Nokia has developed a strategic agenda and issue management process for generating and following up new emerging strategic issues in a systematic manner. Nokia's corporate strategy development team facilitates a corporate-wide process, generating a corporate agenda consisting of around 10 major strategic issues that are continuously followed up. These issues are typically emerging technologies, business models, or other important trends relevant for more than one of the Nokia business groups. The strategic issue management process attempts to increase understanding of an emerging issue and proactively manage actions related to it. As a result, this process aims at keeping top management on top of new developments by involving them in a continuous action learning process. At the same time, it prevents top management from jumping to conclusions too quickly.

Using tension to provoke people's thinking

Finding the right balance between complacency, which dulls the senses, and fear, which paralyzes people, requires great sensitivity from the leadership of an organization. Top management must be able to make the present look fragile enough to be watchful but not too fragile to be paralyzed. Paranoia[10] can hence be positive for an organization to the extent that it raises people's awareness to the non-permanence of success. There are various ways in which top management can raise the strategic alertness of their organization.

Stretched goals

Stretched goals, such as compelling, company-wide vision statements that let all employees understand the company's big picture aims and objectives, are an effective way to raise people's strategic awareness. They direct people's attention, providing for longer-term ambition and aspiration in the same direction, and encourage them to look for new solutions beyond current reality. Nokia's "Voice goes Wireless" vision statement in the early 1990s created a great deal of enthusiasm in the organization and in doing so raised people's awareness toward new opportunities.[11] This shared vision was simple and clear, and strongly challenged the prevailing telephony paradigm at the time when mobile penetration was still well below 20 percent in most developed markets. This challenging vision inspired people across Nokia to look for new technological and commercial innovations that would not only complement but replace fixed telephony. Many innovations in miniaturization, design, lifestyle branding, and so on were made during those days to make this vision come true. Very few of these innovations had their origins in the existing customer dialogue, important though it was in the emergent phase of the market. It was the vision that inspired people to look for new solutions beyond the obvious.

High-profile lead projects can also be used as catalysts for heightened strategic awareness. For instance, Nokia's Calypso program launched in 2001 was consciously profiled as a catalyst for new thinking, not just for new products. Anssi Vanjoki, then head of the Digital Convergence Unit in Nokia Mobile Phones business group, made the challenge visible to all by pointing out the screen of a mobile phone in a big internal Nokia meeting and showing how Nokia as a company had to make sure that all the new "non-voice related applications" such as cameras (at the core of the Calypso program) had to be brought as a service to consumers on the screen in an intuitive manner. This required development of not just a new product concept combining digital photography and mobile phones, but also the creation of many new partnerships to make the new value offering compelling for consumers.

Contradictory goals and paradoxes

People must think when confronted with choice and contradictory priorities. Some companies, such as Honda in Japan, have by design given contradictory goals to their product development leaders to force them to think about how to innovate.[12] Renault in France developed its highly successful and innovative Twingo car, at the low end of the market, by requiring engineers to break through the usually accepted trade-off between low cost, quality design, and good performance.[13] Overall, at the strategic level, the Japanese auto industry in general, and Toyota in particular, succeeded in the US by rejecting the commonly accepted trade-off between differentiation and low cost. Assigning managers contradictory goals at the strategic or product development level keeps them on their toes intellectually and forces innovations that shatter conventional wisdom.

Burning your bridges

In addition to contradictory goals, a CEO's public promises are a commonly used and very powerful means to increase strategic awareness. As goals designated at the top of the organization are typically taken seriously, and since there is no "route to return" from public announcements, the organization has to start behaving differently. Hasso Plattner, founder and ex-CEO of SAP, used this vehicle very successfully in the early 1990s to force the organization to quickly find a new technical architecture for what was to become the future SAP R/3 (enterprise resource planning) system. The public announcement made by CEO Plattner was considered as impossible and contradictory to the strategic trajectory that was familiar to most of the organization.[14] The only way to resolve the problem was to put the new application on UNIX computers instead of mainframe computers, a move which ultimately turned out to be hugely successful.

Establishing a multidimensional organization

All the companies we researched had adopted a multidimensional organization with intersecting responsibilities for customers, products, core competencies, and technologies. The reason was always the same: a desire to maximize business potential along multiple dimensions. At the same time, these companies intentionally introduced positive tension in the organization, as perceiving the same phenomenon from multiple perspectives always creates different interpretations and a basis for richer dialogue and higher strategic alertness.

Deeply integrated companies such as IBM, Cisco and SAP had all ordered themselves into several equally strong organizational dimensions. For instance in Cisco, the head of R&D runs all the product lines and technologies, the head of Sales and Marketing all geographies and industries, the head of Customer Advocacy runs the care and services businesses, and the head of Operations all the cross-functional operational processes such operations, logistics and sourcing. This enables Cisco to perceive and evaluate business environments from multiple perspectives and, as a result, make optimal trade-offs from the whole company point of view.

Nurturing high-quality internal dialogue

Maintaining a high-quality internal dialogue is difficult for most companies whose resources are tied up in operational tasks. Nobody has the time to prepare complex strategic issues – and to facilitate discussions on a neutral, objective, and consistent basis. Yet we know that comprehensiveness in strategic decision making and extensiveness of strategic planning have a positive impact on performance.[15]

❝cognitive diversity is a key precondition to high-quality internal dialogue❞

Cognitive diversity is a key precondition to high-quality internal dialogue. People with different ways of thinking register different things and interpret the same information in different ways. These differences provide a rich basis for internal dialogue and help companies prevent group thinking and avoiding difficult issues, behaviors so typical of many top teams.[16] How can companies then make sure that their top team cognitive diversity stays high?

Internal consultants as facilitators of strategic dialogue

Many companies are using internal consultants to bring factual and conceptual richness in their top management meetings and strategy process. SAP, for instance, has created a 30-person-strong internal consultancy team, consisting of individuals brought in from the best external consultancy companies and high-potential employees of the organization itself. The main purpose of this team is to improve the quality of strategic dialogue with the help of solid facts and common frameworks and concepts that allow rich interpretations of strategic questions. At the same time, it indirectly educates top management to adopt a more conceptual language for capturing reality outside its familiar business domain. According to Henning Kagermann, SAP's CEO, the team provides the necessary neutrality and rigor that enables "the quality of decisions that the Executive Board makes to get better and better".[17] Neutrality, according to Kagermann, can only be achieved by having the internal consultancy team report directly to the CEO. Earning the trust of the key line managers can best be achieved by transparency and job rotation. In the case of SAP, the Corporate Strategy Group (CSG) was set up with the explicit objective that after a period of three years colleagues move within the broader SAP organization. According to Henning Kagermann, "this turnover is a positive thing" and the concept is currently gaining traction within the wider SAP organization.

Cisco also uses its Internet Business Solutions Group (IBSG) discussed earlier to provide factual and conceptual richness to Cisco's strategy dialogue. In addition to their main role as external consultants, the IBSG people are facilitating many of the Cisco strategy discussions with facts and conceptual frameworks generated and used in dialogues with external stakeholders.

Selective inclusiveness in top team composition

Factual and conceptual richness can also be enhanced without dedicated internal consultants and strategy experts. Many companies enhance cognitive diversity by inviting selected substance experts and/or high potential leaders to participate in their top team meetings on a topic basis. In the case of IBM, as seen in chapter 3, this practice has been made more permanent by inviting high-potential leaders to be "semi-permanent" members of its three management teams.

Fundamentally, IBM's team-based top management meeting practice is a way to engage a number of the best brains *vis-à-vis* specific issues in strategizing and technology management for a limited but long enough duration (one year) in an intense way, on an ongoing basis, rather than rely on specialized permanent staffs or on members of the top team exclusively. In addition to increasing cognitive diversity, this practice constantly exposes and invites the highest executives, including CEOs, into an open dialogue with the most demanding managers and experts. According to Sam Palmisano, IBM Chairman and CEO, this change has played an important role in improving IBM's top management dialogue and organization-wide commitment to key strategic questions.[18]

table 4.1 Different approaches for increasing factual and conceptual richness

	SAP	Cisco	IBM
Main approach	▥ Dedicated internal consultant team (35) focussing on key internal: – Strategic challenges – Operational challenges – Organizational challenges (= internal orientation)	▥ Dedicated internal consultant unit (~ 150) focussing on external business consulting (= external orientation)	▥ Three top teams focussing on: – Strategy – Operations – Technology ▥ Consisting of top line managers and selected other "permanent" contributors (= informal and external orientation)
Main targets	▥ Improve the quality of top team decision-making through: – Neutrality – Objectivity – Transparency – Consistency	▥ Identify new business needs and improve customer business understanding ▥ Challenge and educate line organization in strategy and best practices	▥ Extend, deepen, and challenge top team's thinking through "best brains" and focussed agenda
Ownership	CEO	CEO	CEO
Other principles	▥ Resource acquisition from prime management consultancy companies and internally ▥ Rotation to line organization after max three years	▥ Resource acquisition from prime management consultancy companies, companies from other industries, and internally ▥ Rotation to line organization after max three years	▥ Additional resources selected to top teams by CEO for a year at time

Table 4.1 summarizes the three different approaches used by SAP, Cisco and IBM for enhancing factual and conceptual richness in the organization.

Using "shadow management teams"

Companies may also use "shadow management teams" to challenge their official top team perspectives on key strategic issues. Accenture started this practice in 2005 by appointing a diverse global team consisting of young (in their early thirties) high-potential leaders to create the company "vision for 2012". The purpose of this assignment was actively to use the "next generation" thought leaders to create the company vision – and to educate and challenge the views of the older generation's official top team. The synthesis of these perspectives not only created a more thorough vision but also a stronger commitment to execution.

The positive experiences from the "Vision 2012" exercise encouraged several Accenture regional leaders to apply the same principles in their regional management. For example, Accenture's Nordic region has used a "shadow management team" to develop their regional strategy and related operational model as, according to Markku Silen, head of Accenture Nordic, "anyway, the younger generation knows better how they want and need to work".[19]

Extending the strategy dialogue across the organization

A participative strategic planning process helps companies extend high-quality internal dialogue across the organization on critical strategic issues. Nokia has been running a highly participative strategy process for years. This process starts from a common vision phase analyzing the key megatrends affecting the company's business environment. Each of the key vision themes are owned by Nokia top team members, who "hand-pick" about 10 of the most capable individuals from any part of the organization to work on their vision theme.

After working together on these themes for a couple of months, the teams report their findings to the hundred most senior managers in the company. The purpose of this reporting is to provide direction to the strategy work conducted partly by existing business units and partly by cross-company task forces. The strategy work in Nokia involves practically all the key managers and substance experts across the company. During this phase, people are invited to a global web-based dialogue on some of the critical assumptions and questions related to the strategy. This interactive phase allows people to connect and align their views for a subsequent strategy formulation.

How does it fit together?

This chapter focussed on describing and analysing the key managerial practices behind strategic sensitivity. These practices can be further grouped into the following three main capabilities contributing to strategic sensitivity.

- **An open strategy process** that improves companies' sensitivity to different standpoints and orientations. This requires that companies actively co-strategize and experiment with multiple stakeholders in line with a comprehensive architecture for staying connected with the world.

- **Heightened strategic alertness** that improves companies' ability to frame strategic issues in a fresh and insightful way. This requires that companies improve their "open mindedness" through better abstracting capabilities (language and business definitions) and intentional tensions that provoke people's thinking.

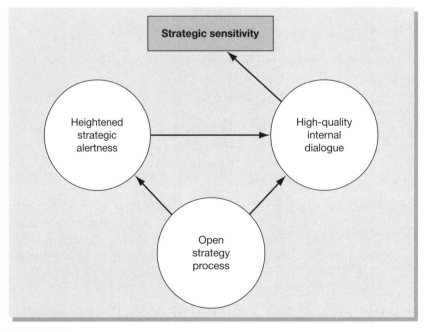

figure 4.2   Interdependencies between strategic sensitivity capabilities

■ **High-quality internal dialogue** that improves companies' ability to turn individual insights and foresights into shared strategic direction. This requires that companies systematically bring factual and conceptual richness and cognitive diversity into their top team as well as the whole organization.

As Figure 4.2 illustrates, an open strategy process provides the foundation for strategic sensitivity as it connects the company with its external world on a broad and continuous basis. Heightened strategic alertness and high-quality internal dialogue are valuable only if they are deeply and broadly rooted in the surrounding reality. Heightened strategic alertness, again, improves strategic sensitivity only via a high-quality internal dialogue, which turns individual insights into common strategic direction via a collective sense-making process.

Consequently, none of these capabilities alone suffices to achieve and maintain strategic sensitivity. An open strategy process does not add value without open-minded people capable of insightful framing. Neither of these, again, is valuable unless companies can sustain high-quality internal dialogue, which helps them turn individual insights into shared strategic direction.

References

[1]   Doz, Yves, Santos, José, and Williamson, Peter, *From Global to Metanational*, Harvard Business School Press, 2001.

[2]   Schön Donald, *The Reflective Practitioner: How Professionals Think in Action*, Basic Books, 1983.

[3]   Authors' interview, Chris Thomas, Chief Strategist, Solutions Market Development Group, Intel, 19 January 2006.

[4]   Authors' interview, Steve Steinhilber, Vice President, Strategic Alliances, Cisco, 22 July 2005.

[5]   Ibid.

[6]   Authors' interview, Chris Thomas, 7 April 2005.

[7]   Authors' interview, Paul Ledak, Vice President, Engineering and Technology Services, IBM, and Kevin Reardon, Vice President and General Manager, Global Electronics Industry Sales and Distribution Group, IBM, 25 January 2006.

[8]   Authors' interview, Kate D'Camp, former Senior Vice President, Human Resources, Cisco, 21 July 2005.

[9] Doz, Yves and Balchandrani, Anita, "Extending the 'easy' Business Model: What Should easyGroup Do Next?" INSEAD case study, 2003.

[10] Paranoia as a term was brought to the attention of the business community by Andy Grove's well-known book: Grove, Andrew, *Only the Paranoids Survive*, Currency, 1996.

[11] Nokia's original Vision 2000 introduced in 1992 (Global, Focus, Telecom-oriented, High Value-Added) provided clear direction for the company at the time it was still only a European conglomerate.

[12] Nonaka, Ikujiro and Takeuchi, Hirotaka, *The Knowledge-creating Company: How Japanese Companies Create the Dynamics of Innovation*, Oxford University Press, 1995.

[13] Midler, Christophe, *L'Auto Qui N'existait Pas : Management des Projets et Transformation de L'Entreprise*, Dunod, 2004.

[14] Transcript of a video history interview with Hasso Plattner, 9 April 1997.

[15] Comprehensiveness here refers to the extent to which the top team utilizes a thorough decision process when dealing with immediate opportunities and threats. Extensiveness, again, refers to the number of longer term alternative solutions that are seriously considered and the extent to which qualitative analyses are conducted. See more in Chet-Miller, C., Burke, L. and Glick, W., *Cognitive Diversity Among Upper Echelon Executives: Implications for Strategic Decision Processes*, John Wiley & Sons Inc., 1998.

[16] Interestingly enough, as demographic diversity doesn't explain cognitive diversity well, a top management team from one country, one gender, and one educational background may have more cognitive diversity than a demographically very heterogeneous team (see more in Kotter, J. P. and Heskett, J. L., *Corporate Culture and Performance*, Free Press, 1992).

[17] Authors' interview, Henning Kagermann, Chief Executive Officer, SAP, 6 June 2005.

[18] Authors' interview, Sam Palmisano, Chief Executive Officer, IBM, 7 October 2005.

[19] Authors' interview, Markku Silén, Chairman of the Nordic Geographic Council, Accenture, 30 November 2006.

5

Building collective commitment

Strategic sensitivity is of little use unless top management can agree on critical strategic redirections and commitments. However, this is easier said than done. Most top teams are, for natural reasons, collections of independent individuals with strong opinions rather than inspiring and innovative teams.[1] In fact, in many companies this is implicitly why the top team members are there. The selection process of corporate leaders simply favors independent types with strong power and autonomy needs.

This behavior is amplified by the complex operations high-powered executives need to run well on a day-to-day basis. They simply don't have the time for in-depth dialogue since they have the interests of their own units to cater to and the loyalty of their staff to keep building. The bandwidth of discussable items among top team colleagues gradually shrinks and collective decisions affecting the power balance between top team members are harder and harder to make, leading at worst to decision stalemates. Instead, top team meetings turn into a contest among influential individuals for resource allocation, a series of border incidents about organizational turf, and perhaps tournaments for recognition and power.

As natural as this leadership approach may be in top teams it is becoming increasingly insufficient in today's global business environment where opportunities come and go at an increasing speed. Top teams simply need to be able to function as a team in order to cope with shifting industry structures, frequent technology disruptions, and changing business models in the middle of relentless performance demands.

Stronger business focus and greater concern with corporate value-added issues have also driven companies towards searching for a higher level of strategic integration between their businesses and subunits. Traditional diversified companies with decentralized organizations did not require their top management to function as a team, but today's globally integrated companies do. Taking care of the numerous strategic and operational integration needs across the company while boosting business level differentiation calls for a different – more united – way of working among the members of the top team. Delivering on an integrated strategy is very difficult if not impossible when business units are run as fiefdoms.

❝in an integrated company, each unit head feels responsible for the performance of other units as well as for their own❞

In a conventional top team, building on delegated leadership, unit heads perceive themselves as a sort of baseball team, in which every player has a distinct role. If one player consistently fails to perform to expectations, the manager will draft in a replacement. If the business, not the manager, falters, it will be sold off. In an integrated company, however, each unit head feels responsible for the performance of other units as well as for their own, and actively looks for ways to help them deliver. If a division is struggling, its problems are not necessarily attributed to the division head – nor is solving them considered purely his or her duty. The team as a whole brainstorms to arrive at a solution. Of course, the head of the struggling division will implement the agreed-upon strategy – collective responsibility for strategy does not mean collective responsibility for implementing every decision.

Beyond intellectual understanding of the requirements of an integrated strategy, making it happen is very challenging and calls for a major shift in the company's culture and norms of interaction. Multidimensional organizational structures not only enhance strategic sensitivity (as discussed in chapter 4) but they also force top management to work together on a continuous basis. When capital and people are allocated along multiple dimensions in the organization all top team members become deeply dependent on each other in practically all matters. They become interdependent contributors to an integrated corporate strategy instead of independent subunit "barons" pursuing separate business strategies and agendas. The following approaches are not the only ways to promote mutual dependence, though they are the most common.

Organizing for mutual dependency

Organizing along value chain or functions

Companies with relatively focussed business portfolios can foster engagement among senior executives by simply abandoning the stand-alone unit as the organizing principle of the top team. They can give the executives formal responsibility not for a business unit but for different stages or links in the company's value chain. SAP did that as part of its 2005 reintegration into a more unified organization. Each senior executive took responsibility for just one step in the value chain and now the entire top team has to collaborate closely in developing and implementing the company's overall strategy.

Cisco has gone in the same direction by organizing its top team along purely functional lines. All key dimensions in Cisco's organization have an internal profit/loss objective to help optimize their business. And yet at the same time, none of the top team members can function alone, as a big part of their resources reside in their colleagues' organization. Decisions have to be taken together, and commitment must be joint. Collaboration is a must to overcome the intentional tensions.

Common functions as integrators

Companies whose business portfolios are less focussed than Cisco's or SAP's can't always go as far as those organizations. They take a lighter approach to integration and collaboration. Such companies may find that organizing on a matrix, with crisscrossing business and functional units (all represented on the top team), makes more sense. Nokia took this approach in its 2004 reorganization. The company was divided into four business groups: mobile phones, multimedia, enterprise solutions, and networks, each with global P/L responsibility. These vertical groups were served by two horizontal groups – customer and market operations and technology platforms – and a number of other common corporate support functions and processes. The horizontal groups and functions, with their company-wide knowledge of asset needs, were mandated to probe and challenge as well as to support the vertical units.

In June 2007 Nokia announced a new, more integrated, organizational structure starting from 1 January 2008. The new Nokia organization consists of three units: two "What to Sell" organizations, Mobile Devices and Software and Services, and one "Go to Market" organization, packaging and

selling complete mobile experiences to both consumers and trade customers. Together these three units form one highly interdependent entity
with one P/L statement. No major business decisions in the new organization can be made without full alignment between all three units. The
networks business of Nokia was already (earlier in 2007) merged with
Siemens to form a new Nokia-Siemens Networks enterprise.

Common value creation logic as an integrator

Companies that are seemingly widely diverse are likely to emphasize the
shared learning opportunities provided by a common value creation logic
across different businesses. As seen, easyGroup, for instance, may appear at
first to be a travel and leisure conglomerate, with an airline, cruise ships,
budget hotels, car rentals, and so forth. To its founder, Stelios Haji-
Ioannou, it is anything but a conglomerate. It is a single business model –
involving low-priced services of a scheduled, and thus perishable, nature:
low cost, particularly effective dynamic-pricing and yield-management
practices; distribution on the internet; and mobile redeployable assets –
leveraged across a whole range of opportunities. Common learning about
these elements, particularly dynamic pricing, yield management, and innovative approaches to cost reduction, provides the basis for a corporate
business model. In a physical reflection of this model, the company office
is a huge round room (actually a former train depot) called the Rotunda, in
northern London, where key executives and their respective business teams
sit together, with Stelios and his staff in the middle. At the end of every
work day the group carries out a joint review of all businesses in a meeting
room next door. Despite its logic and shared management processes,
easyGroup has faced difficulties. By overemphasizing what was common
across all its businesses it may have overlooked the specifics of each, and
ignored the deeper business understanding needed to run each of them
successfully.

Distributed leadership roles

Companies can also enhance mutual dependency by designing and
assigning separate corporate roles for key top team members. This helps
companies to shift the criteria for team participation away from the size of
the units represented to the quality of individual contribution.

The key principle in designing these roles is a clear distinction between a
person's unit responsibility and corporate-wide responsibility. Adoption of
a true corporate perspective is not possible if the corporate role is sub-

❝companies can balance power-distances between people with corporate-level roles❞

ordinated to the "primary" line unit management role. After all, the whole purpose of assigning additional corporate roles to key business line executives is to shift their attention to corporate issues in the top team meetings.

Companies can also balance power-distances between people with corporate-level roles. Assigning the biggest corporate-level role to the head of the smallest unit not only makes him or her take it seriously and learn new perspectives but also changes the power balance in the top team. Assigning an important corporate responsibility to the head of the smallest business unit may help neutralize the power advantages that accrue naturally to the heads of larger units.

These additional corporate roles typically relate to one of the key leadership dimensions of the company. Many global companies assign additional regional responsibilities and/or global business process responsibilities to their line managers. Nokia also assigns to individual unit heads corporate-wide responsibility for such assets as the brand, major global customers, and relationships with strategic partners. The quality of dialogue at the top has been noticeably affected, because key line managers now play a corporate role in all executive board meetings. (Their specific unit agendas are discussed primarily in business group boards.)

Working together

Organizing for mutual dependency in the top team is only part of achieving collective commitment. You can create organizational interdependencies, but unless you put the right processes and practices in place, interactions at the top will quickly prove dysfunctional. As many experts[2] have demonstrated, it is all too easy for top teams to fritter away the time they spend together. IBM in the 1980s gave up on exploiting its interdependencies partly because it had lost the ability to manage them.

Learning to work together as a team is not easy for executives used to running their own "fiefdoms". Many CEOs and top team members feel most comfortable in managing their company or business through delegation and outcome controls. Hence the high emphasis on various kinds of scorecards as well as over-scheduled and sometimes overly choreographed, formal top team meetings. As important as timely and accurate reporting is (as a factual foundation for dialogue), it should not become an end in itself. Managing an integrated company requires that most of the time in top team meetings is allocated to open, constructive, and substantive dialogue on difficult corporate-wide matters.

Focus on corporate issues

The charter of top team meetings largely defines the way in which members interact with each other. If this charter emphasizes business-specific matters and reporting, then meetings tend to center around one-to-one reporting with little dialogue and interaction across businesses. The CEOs in the companies studied were very particular about what went on the agenda for executive team meetings.

For instance, IBM's Corporate Executive Committee (CEC), put in place by Lou Gerstner in 1993, did not accept delegation of problem-solving from the business units, nor did it sit through presentations and make decisions for the business units. It focussed solely on policy issues that cut across multiple businesses.[3] All top team members already possessed a wide general management competence with a great deal of overlapping expertise. This created the basis for an active dialogue, encouraged and expected by the CEO.

Similarly, Nokia's strategy development staff is assigned to collectively create and maintain a list of the 10 or so most important corporate strategic issues to be put before the monthly strategy panel meeting. That helps senior executives to learn about emerging strategic issues and to respond to them in a proactive and, more important, collective manner. Jarkko Sairanen, Nokia's head of corporate strategy, explains:

Having a corporate-wide agenda makes top team members focus on common challenges instead of specific subunit agendas.

Shared incentives

Shared incentives support collective commitment. Most of the companies studied have recently increased the weight put on shared corporate incentives over business-specific results. The rule of thumb seems to be a direct relation between the interdependence of the organization and the weight of common corporate incentives. At one extreme, SAP's executive board members have 100 percent common incentives whereas most of companies seem to float around 50 percent. According to Claus E. Heinrich, executive board member of SAP, this practice has greatly helped SAP's top team collaboration.

If I see Léo [Apotheker, Deputy CEO, a fellow board member and the President of Customer Solution Operations] doing a great job, I say, "Wow, great!" I am quite willing to subordinate some of my own priorities to help him achieve the common goal.[4]

Transparent goals and fair process

Collective commitment also requires fairness between the different units' goals and targets. Fairness in this context should not, however, mean only fairness in outcome but also fairness in process. Many companies pay a lot of attention to making sure that everybody in the top team feels equal pain regarding the ambition level of their targets. The outcome of this exercise may be productive in the short term, as people feel fairly treated, but it may be very counterproductive in the long term, as equality is anti-strategic. Strategy is about choices, which means non-equality in outcome. The process for reaching non-equal outcomes can, however, be fair.[5] When people understand the strategic reasoning behind the non-equal level of pain it is easier for them to accept it.

Nokia's top team has adopted a practice in which all top team members' personal goals ("What do I need to achieve in the next two years?") are discussed and shared openly by the top team as a whole. In this process each member can comment and add perspectives to his or her colleagues' targets to make sure that there is full alignment and "equal stretch" for everybody in the group. Also the key interdependencies between the key top team members are openly shared and discussed. In connection to the goal-setting each member also articulates clearly what they need and expect from their colleagues to achieve their targets. The outcome of this process leads to more realistic and shared target-setting for the whole top team.

Building on overlapping areas of expertise

Dealing with emerging strategic issues and conflicting organizational interests on a constructive basis requires understanding of colleagues' points of view. Making sure that the top team members have sufficiently overlapping areas of expertise is hence very important. Having an experience-based view on colleagues' responsibility areas makes constructive dialogue much easier. It helps members to relate to and build on their colleagues' points of view rather than creating a "right or wrong" debate between people.

Institutionalized job rotation – where individuals are often moved from one activity in the company to a completely different one to give them a more rounded view of all aspects of the business – combined with a principle that members are expected to experience multiple different roles before reaching the top team, is hence good practice for building a top team with overlapping areas of expertise. In many companies – as in armies – this rotation is expected to cover both line and staff responsibilities. This is particularly important for organizations with an integrated strategy, as understanding the corporate perspective is key to all top team members.

Embracing conflicts

Constructive dialogue also requires embracing rather than avoiding conflicts. However, this is not natural for many well-established top teams. On the contrary, many of them develop a very smooth way of communicating as they become more familiar with each other over time. This easily leads to group thinking and declining intensity of dialogue. As the CEO of one large US chemical company describes it:

ff constructive dialogue requires embracing rather than avoiding conflicts JJ

In the executive committee we have these polite exchanges, everyone agrees publicly, and we leave with a warm feeling of consensus. Nothing happens, and then I hear that as soon as they were back in their offices, some group VPs started complaining about misguided corporate decisions and essentially discouraged their own subordinates from any wholehearted implementation. It's a case of public consent but private dissent.

The key means to avoid the negative consequences of familiarity is to embrace conflicts and related substantial dialogue in top team work. By calling for participants to reveal systematically their underlying assumptions, and ensuring others understand them, dialogue builds on common ground and fosters the development of a common language. Claus E. Heinrich, member of the executive board at SAP and responsible for global human resources (HR), summarized the essence of constructive dialogue as follows:

When I joined the board, I was impressed by how open the discussions were there. To create openness and collaboration, it's not the props, tools, lunches, etc. The real recipe is to discuss first as a team at the top. We like each other, but we are really tough with each other in discussions. We work as a team on all matters – not with the attitude, for instance, of "I am HR, so I should stay out of product development". If I disagree, I have something to say, no matter where I come from or what I am in charge of.[6]

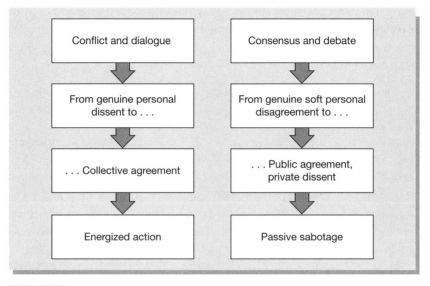

figure 5.1 **Quality of collective decisions**

Conflicts and disagreements on how to work should not be avoided in the process of reaching shared understanding and collective commitment as there is no evidence that these would lower the team performance[7]. As Figure 5.1 demonstrates, conflict and dialogue surface and resolve genuine personal disagreement, which leads to collective agreement and finally to energized action. The alternative – and too often seen as the route – to collective decisions is based on consensus and debate. This approach enables only soft, polite disagreement, which leads to public agreement but private dissent, and finally, at worst, to passive sabotage.

Keeping the dialogue informal

Senior executives at successful, integrated companies are comfortable with direct, informal dialogue. HP and IBM put their top team members on one floor in a largely open layout to ensure casual and frequent contact. At Canon, CEO Fujio Mitarai holds a meeting from 8:00 to 9:00 every morning. These meetings have no set agenda, but a lot of information is shared, and a number of decisions are at least implicitly made. "It's not a meeting that executives will choose to miss," says Kunio Watanabe, the head of corporate planning development at Canon. Even formal meetings at these companies have a deliberately informal tone. Lou Gerstner, for example, refused to let executives use overhead transparencies and banned executive assistants from IBM's meetings, both of which can be used by executives as props to distance themselves from others.

Making time for reflection

Beyond substance, top team members' personal motives and styles have a big impact on the quality of dialogue. One of the main reasons for misunderstandings and personal mistrust among members relates to not understanding fully each other's deeper motives, personal values and drivers in life. This may be the case even between top team colleagues who have worked for years side by side. Getting a deep enough understanding and appreciation of these differences takes time, and this is typically difficult to achieve in the course of normal management team work. Taking extra time as a group to share deeply each others' personal values and drivers strengthens the basis of dialogue. Henning Kagermann, the CEO of SAP, makes a point of holding quarterly off-site meetings with the executive board. At Nokia's off-site meetings senior executives talk about their corporate goals, which helps ensure mutual understanding and respect for the efforts, contributions, motives, and ambitions of everybody in the group. Informal, spontaneous interactions over time are felt to be essential.

Another less exposing way to learn to know each other more personally is systematically to spend more time with each colleague. These more informal exchanges can most naturally take place for instance by traveling together. Spending time socializing together doesn't hurt either, although this practice doesn't necessarily expose people to deeper sharing of their drivers and motives.

Developing adaptive leadership skills

Like team behavior, adaptive leadership[8] skills are rare among typical top team members. Senior executives are used to "knowing better" and thus when approached for advice they are used to deciding, using their wide experience and best expert judgment. This is often a good decision-making style when operating within a known and stable market place, but it is certainly not effective when the company faces increasing ambiguity and needs to choose a new course, or perhaps even construct a new business landscape. Leaders in this situation should not try to provide answers, as nobody is likely to know them for sure, but rather set a context and guide the search for a feasible answer to the challenge at hand. The role of the leader in this situation is to provide a foundation for collective work. In the process of searching, individual members transcend their initial position, reframe their understanding and gain personal commitment to the collectively developed solution. This applies to all work across the organization from top to bottom when in search of strategic agility.

A supportive and humble attitude in asking questions and providing context for people often leads to better results than giving fast answers. The energy and joy stemming from finding a solution and from being forgiven after a failed attempt to try something new cannot be underestimated. After all, the main target of an adaptive leader is to make other people "shine" and excel in the company by reducing obstacles and fear in the organization. Acknowledging the importance of luck and the value of other people's work, including competitors', is also important when trying to sustain objectivity in the middle of success.

Changes in the top team

❝ doing the same job for too long leads to declining dialogue and personal motivation ❞

Top team changes are the third key managerial mechanism to improve and sustain collective commitment. Mutual dependency and collaborative work relationships enrich top executives' interaction patterns and work content, but doing the same job for too long automatically leads to declining dialogue and personal motivation.

Changing roles

Changing roles by rotating top team members' core responsibilities is an effective mechanism not only to increase cognitive diversity (as discussed in chapter 4) but also to improve collective commitment without disturbing the social coherence within the group. New responsibilities force experienced leaders to learn new skills and face their colleagues in a new way. At the same time, the often hidden internal pecking order created around the key leaders in their respective organizations is being destroyed. Many successful companies have been able to initiate timely strategic redirections or reorientations by changing their top team members' roles and responsibilities in anticipation of future changes.[9]

Nokia rotated the jobs of its key top team members in the beginning of 1998 when it was just reaching the number one position in mobile telephony markets. The President of Mobile Phones made room for the President of Networks. A new man was put in place to lead mobile phones business in a new business situation. At the same time, the President of Mobile Phones was appointed President of Nokia, with the special task to create new growth for the company. The CFO was assigned an additional corporate-wide responsibility for overseeing Nokia's business in the Americas. The number two person in the Networks business was promoted as President of Networks business while also overseeing business in Asia. As a result, the four key line managers and top team members of Nokia completely changed their jobs in anticipation of a new phase in business. The outcome of this move was new energy and drive, which further strengthened Nokia's market position.

Renewing the top team composition

Bringing new people to the top team is another powerful way of renewing top team dynamics and hence improves collective commitment. The caveat to this approach is that renewing one person at a time is seldom enough for a real change. A new person is easily absorbed into the old thinking pattern and ways of working. A more useful approach is to analyze the top team as a whole and make changes to more than one person at a time. In a similar manner, CEO succession should not be regarded as a separate phenomenon from the top team.[10] Mere CEO succession may not introduce sufficiently new and diverse experience or knowledge to alter established understanding and entrenched activity patterns in the company. Moreover, even a radically different new CEO may not be able to implement changes.[11] Without extensive team changes, incumbent team members with vested interests in the status quo and with stronger ties to the existing organization may undermine a new CEO's attempts at change.

The combination of CEO succession and substantial turnover in the executive team is likely to provide a sufficient critical mass of new skills and experiences to promote organizational change.[12] This approach does have its risks, though. While externally promoted CEOs may be most likely to initiate substantial organizational changes, they do so at the cost of decreasing ties to the old system. A wholly new executive team, especially if led by an externally recruited CEO, will lack well-developed political networks inside the organization and knowledge of its multiple strategic, organizational, and cultural linkages. Such new executive compositions may have difficulties in implementing changes. As Lou Gerstner, ex-CEO of IBM said:

It would have been absolutely naïve – as well as dangerous – if I had come into a company as complex as IBM with a plan to import a band of outsiders somehow magically to run the place better than the people who were there in the first place.[13]

First, Gerstner changed the key support-function personnel, such as those in finance, HR and strategy. This provided him with sufficient support to implement both operational and strategic integration across the company while keeping the business running.

The most effective executive succession events may therefore be those where an internally promoted CEO initiates substantial changes in the executive team. In this case, the new CEO takes advantage of existing organizational knowledge and relationships even as they equip the organization with more heterogeneous expertise and understanding through a new team.[14]

Nokia's recent top team change reflects these principles in practice. In anticipation of a new phase in business Nokia's board appointed Olli-Pekka Kallasvuo as the COO in October 2005 and the CEO of the company in June 2006. The gradual top team change had already started in early 2004 and continued until spring 2006. During this two-year time-frame six out of the nine executive board members left the company and eight new members were appointed. Three members, including the new CEO, stayed with the company. Only one of the new executive board members was recruited from outside, while the rest were promoted from within the company.

Letting the "old heroes" move on gracefully

The way in which high-powered executives move out from the core team in connection to top team renewal matters greatly. A graceful exit or transfer of those core team members who have naturally outgrown the new organization is very important. These executives have typically served the company successfully for many years and people across the organization have great respect for them and want to see them treated well. Yet they can seldom continue in the new top team, particularly if the new CEO comes from inside the company. It is difficult to change well-established interaction patterns with an ex-peer and, secondly, these executives have typically outgrown those roles that are available in the new organization. They would simply not start from an equal basis with the rest of the new team, which, again, would harm the team-building efforts described earlier. Furthermore, accepting a smaller and less meaningful role is not motivating and would not look respectful and credible in the eyes of the organization.

It is therefore very important to link the retirement or transfer of senior executives to changes in the market place and the subsequent top team renewal. This way there is a natural business reason for the change and it happens to several key people at the same time. People in the organization understand these reasons and hence transferring loyalty from old leadership to a new top team is easier.

Leadership style and capabilities of the CEO

❝successful top team collaboration requires a CEO who is comfortable with a strategic dialogue in the top team❞

For the reasons already discussed, many CEOs feel most comfortable in one-to-one relationships[15] with their direct subordinates and shy away from personal exposure in top team meetings. For most top executives, adopting a dialogue mode by becoming an equal, being "just" a member of the team, is difficult. However, successful top team collaboration requires a CEO who is comfortable with a strategic dialogue in the top team and with treating individuals as intellectual contributors rather than just business result deliverers. CEOs of integrated companies also need to be able to elicit emotional loyalty and provide intrinsic rewards rather than rely only on incentives and extrinsic rewards.

CEO first among peers – building a team of equals

CEOs ultimately make the difference in balance between a real team and non-team performance at the top. They set the tone, provide the leadership philosophy, and pick the leadership team with which they want to work in different roles. It is very hard for the rest of the top team to adopt new kinds of interaction patterns and roles if they can't see their CEO appreciating these behaviors. If the CEO, for instance, sees efficiency and predictability as the key drivers for the company, then they are likely to emphasize coordination and control in the top team interaction. Learning and trying new business experimentations are hard under these circumstances, since they may appear to go against the grain of the CEO's preferences.[16] Members' relative status in the context of the team also influences team dynamics. Large differences in power and status between the CEO and the rest of the team, as well as between the members, influences team members' willingness to participate in critical inquiry.[17]

In spite of the challenges, the benefits of building a team of equals are overwhelming. The capacity of the team increases substantially compared with a single leader model. When a team and its members learn to play multiple roles and shift team leadership dynamically from one person to another, it can draw on the full capacity of the diverse group instead of being subordinated to a single leader's point of view. As other senior executives become accustomed to assuming more leadership of the top team, the CEO can step back from day-to-day issues to think about where the company's long-term future lies.

IBM's top team meeting behavior and CEO Sam Palmisano's conduct in these teams address this point in practice. Palmisano himself doesn't chair any of his three meetings (strategy, operations and technology) but participates as a team member on a "first among equals" principle, intervening and summarizing in his CEO role only when needed. According to Palmisano, such a transition has not been easy or natural for him or his team. Shifting roles dynamically within a single meeting requires practice and adaptation from the whole team. It is also intellectually, socially, and emotionally very demanding because personal strengths and weaknesses become much more visible in this approach.[18]

How does it fit together?

This chapter described and analysed the key managerial mechanisms behind collective commitment. After all, strategic sensitivity is of little value without the top team's ability to make collective decisions and commitments regarding the strategic direction of the company. No unified action will follow without collective commitment!

The four groups of managerial practices discussed in this chapter can be summarized as follows:

- ■ **Mutual dependency.** Enhances top team members' willingness and incentive to make collective commitments, and fight against creeping "management divergence".

- ■ **Working together.** Enhances top team members' ability to work as a team by building on constructive dialogue.

- ■ **Top team changes (rotations and renewals).** Helps companies to improve and sustain high-quality collaboration over time.

- ■ **Leadership style and capabilities of the CEO.** Enables companies to maximize the output of their diverse but integrated top team.

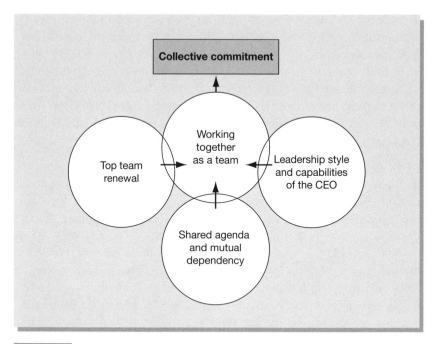

figure 5.2 Interdependencies between capabilities contributing to collective commitment

As Figure 5.2 illustrates, mutual dependency is the foundation of collective commitment as it provides the reason for the top people to function as a team. Figure 5.2 also shows how top team renewal and the team-oriented leadership style of the CEO are "vehicles" to improve top team collaboration.

References

[1] Katzenbach, John R., *Teams at the Top: Unleashing the Potential of Both Teams and Individual Leaders*, Harvard Business School Press, October 1997.

[2] Mankins, Michael, "Stop Wasting Valuable Time", *Harvard Business Review*, September 2004, Vol. 82 Issue 9.

[3] Gerstner, Lou, *Who Says Elephants Can't Dance?* HarperBusiness, 2002.

[4] Authors' interview, Claus E. Heinrich, member of the executive board, SAP, 6 June 2005.

[5] Mauborgne, Renée and Kim, Chan, "Fair Process: Managing in the

Knowledge Economy", *Harvard Business Review*, July/August 1997, Vol. 75 Issue 4.

[6] 100 percent of SAP's top team's incentives are based on corporate goals.

[7] Kotter, John P. and Heskett, James L., *Corporate Culture and Performance*, Free Press, 1992.

[8] Heifetz, Ronald A. and Laurie, Donald L., "The Work of Leadership", *Harvard Business Review*, January/February 1997, May/June 1997.

[9] Virany, Beverly, Tushman, Michael L., and Romanelli, Elaine, "Executive Succession and Organization Outcomes in Turbulent Environments: An Organization Learning Approach", *Organization Science*, February 1992, Vol. 3 Issue 1.

[10] Ibid.

[11] CEO legitimacy may also be dependent on the culture of the company. Companies with high respect for positional power accept a new CEO and the new order more easily than companies with low respect for positional power.

[12] Several case studies on organizational turnarounds indicate that both a new CEO and a completely revised executive team were necessary to implement system-wide changes (*see* Virany, Tushman and Romanelli, 1992).

[13] Gerstner, 2002.

[14] Virany, Tushman and Romanelli, 1992.

[15] One-to-one relationships between executives and the CEO are counterproductive from a collective commitment point of view as they create an atmosphere of competition and distrust among the top team members (*see* Nadler, David, *Champions of Change*, Jossey-Bass, 1997).

[16] Schwandt, David R. and Gorman, Margaret, "Foresight or Foreseeing? A Social Action Explanation of Complex Collective Knowing" in *Managing the Future*, Tsoukas, H. and Shepherd, J. (eds), Blackwell Publishing, 2004.

[17] Ibid.

[18] Authors' interview, Sam Palmisano, Chief Executive Officer, IBM, 7 October 2005.

6

Enabling resource fluidity

Without resource fluidity, strategic sensitivity and collective commitments toward new strategic opportunities remain useless. As you will recall from chapter 2, resource fluidity is the ability to redeploy resources quickly toward strategic opportunities as they develop. Only the ability to mobilize and reallocate resources toward new strategic opportunities with maximum fluidity makes strategic agility real. Intelligence and commitment without swift action in fast-developing strategic situations bring no advantage.

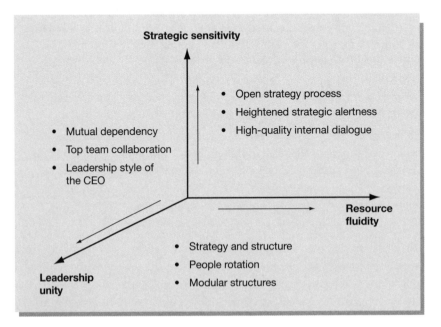

figure 6.1 Key capabilities enabling strategic agility

The managerial capabilities described in chapters 4 and 5 and in this chapter are the essential drivers of strategic agility. They allow companies to thrive on change and avoid strategic paralysis, which often results from singleminded attention to operational excellence. As illustrated in Figure 6.1, an open strategy process, and heightened and high-quality internal dialogue, are the key drivers for strategic sensitivity. Again, mutual dependency, top team collaboration and the leadership style of the CEO are the main drivers of leadership unity, enabling collective commitments. This chapter concentrates on the managerial practices that enhance resource fluidity.

The resource fluidity challenge

As discussed in chapter 2, both capital and people are often locked in support of existing activity systems in incumbent companies, leaving little leeway for redeployment. A conventional hierarchical organization often compounds this problem. Hidden reallocation of resources can occur since top executives do not always see how resources are actually being deployed. A CEO may not know precisely who, someone several direct reports away, is utilizing resources. Transparency down into the organization is not always possible, and when it is, many budgetary "games" can be played all too easily.

Consider a real example. Visiting a foreign manufacturing site of a very successful multinational, and seeing a lot of R&D and engineering work being performed, we asked the local manager whether he also had an R&D "center of excellence" mandate of some sort. Very sincerely, the man answered:

Of course not. But you see, we have become really productive. More than we really need to report. The core business division has been categorized a "cash generator" in a corporate strategy and, as a mature business, it is starved of resources for product development. So the division manager and I agreed to do more and more R&D work here, and report the expenses as part of manufacturing cost, and process improvement expenses.

Needless to say, this "informal" resource allocation "arrangement" went totally unnoticed by top management. Although few executives will talk about such agreements so openly, they do not seem that unusual, and many are probably at least partly justified. The division manager to whom we also spoke, said in essence this was the only way to guarantee the future of his business, and he secured the collaboration of the local country manager by transferring more and more production work there, which reduced costs. From his standpoint he was doing the best for the company, and he may well have been right.

❝ resource fluidity is a complex interpersonal and political issue within companies ❞

So, between proclaiming dynamic resource allocation and achieving true resource fluidity in a strategic way, there may be a wide gulf! That is the point: resource fluidity is a complex interpersonal and political issue within companies, not just a matter of management structures and systems.

Management systems in hierarchical organizations, however, often compound the problem since they are typically designed to support resource allocation discipline within divisions, not strategic resource reallocation across them. This is partly a matter of how costs are allocated. Cross-unit efforts – such as when marketing coordinates some special work with manufacturing – are often not very clearly measured nor rewarded. Account teams in IBM's new organization – with its principle of lowered center of gravity – need to negotiate commitments with a large number of product and service divisions to offer an "integrated" solution to their customers. We are no longer in the age where IBM cross-unit sales were loaded with a "per unit" transaction cost – making small ticket items such as PCs hard to sell and very unprofitable. But, between such blatant and absurd margin distortions (which did contribute a lot to the lack of success of IBM in some businesses in the 1980s) and full, fair exchanges and transparency of cost and benefits, some progress is still needed. So, without even knowing it, many companies discourage collaboration and resource allocation to cross-unit projects. Units that have very different margins, cost structures and, more generally, business models will find it difficult to collaborate. Their managers will have very different assumptions on pricing, on volumes, and on costs.

Rather than foster creativity and collaboration, this will lead many unit managers to guard resources jealously, limit "see through" transparency from the top, and cut side deals (such as the one described above) between the core business division and the most efficient manufacturing location. This makes the evaluation of resource utilization efficiency across the company difficult. Many companies find all too late that they keep over-investing in mature core businesses and starving new business development initiatives.

Riding the storm of fast growth also encourages companies to develop "fit for purpose", highly specialized, and tightly integrated activity systems with proprietary architectures. Business-specific differentiation, speed, and cost efficiency call for this. The performance of these systems separates success from collapse. In the mobile phones industry, volume manufacturing and global logistics have been a key competitive differentiator for all companies for years. Many otherwise successful companies, such as Motorola or Nokia, suffered near supply chain "meltdown" in periods of fast growth. The risk is frighteningly real. Once systems are in place, the fear of changing elements of these partly tacit and complex activity systems, with sometimes less than fully known causalities, often accelerates this "convergence to fit" process.[1] Like software systems cobbled and patched over time to answer specific needs individually, many activity systems are poorly understood, poorly documented, and no one may have an operating functional overview of how they actually fit together. Hence, change, adaptation, and redirection become perceived as unduly risky. "If it works don't fiddle with it" becomes the implicit principle. Perhaps good for efficiency, but certainly not for agility!

Designing modular activity systems capable of changes and reconfiguration, and fostering collaboration is difficult. The rush to shortcut rigorous business systems designed to meet exploding demand growth is tempting. Problems typically arise only when a business matures and changes have to be implemented. Then the need for more flexible business systems is felt. Highly efficient business systems, well honed to one particular product and business model, for one purpose, do not support other purposes well. Instead, they turn into major rigidity factors. Proprietary activity systems, at the level of individual business groups or divisions, do not allow efficient resource sharing and people rotation. Different standards, processes, practices, and tools make it difficult for people to move from one role to another.

This chapter explores three key challenges related to resource fluidity. First, managerial practices that help corporate leaders to mobilize capital. Second, how to foster people mobility. Third, those managerial practices that help companies to de-risk business entry or exit by deploying modular shared resources and dynamic capabilities.

Mobilizing capital resources

Providing multiple channels to access resources

Hierarchical organizations are often terrible at resource fluidity because they allocate and organize resources into subunits in a very stable pattern that cannot be changed without major reorganization or intensive cross-unit collaboration. A multidimensional organization that functions like a living organism can allocate resources along multiple axes: products, geographic units, core technologies, customer groups, etc ... so it is not only more sensitive and collaborative (as discussed in the previous chapters) but it can also respond faster than a hierarchy. A new opportunity or threat perceived by any of the dimensions in the organization receives resources from senior executives preoccupied with that dimension.

As an example, imagine yourself as a project manager at Nokia, developing a new mobile phone. You are, *de facto*, at the intersection of vertical product units and of horizontal shared technology units. Although in the end you may need everyone's agreement on the funding of your project, and you may see this as multiple hurdles, how you negotiate each hurdle and in which order you negotiate them to build support may well be your choice.

More generally, having access to multiple channels to obtain resources usually offers commitment advantages. Managers are much more committed if they know they can knock on multiple doors, get feedback on how to develop and improve their proposals from multiple places, and expose themselves to the need for dialoguing with more potential sponsors and earn their support, but are not locked in a bilateral hierarchical dependency relationship. They keep the choice and the initiative, but are not at the whim of the idiosyncrasies of a single boss of a hierarchical organization.

The existence of multiple resource allocation channels also means that multiple forces remain strong: senior executives representing various perspectives, and perhaps more sensitive to some stakeholders than others, all keep a voice. They have the power to play on the high-stake resource allocation table. When rules of open dialogue, adaptive leadership, and norms of leadership unity are operating, the true beauty of a multidimensional organization is revealed: it contributes to agility.

To use an analogy: today's fighter planes are highly maneuverable, in fact, contrary to large airliners, they are designed to be unstable and kept flying only by the constant micro-balancing exercised by powerful computers on their controls. Fluid, agile organizations are no different. Strong but contradictory forces are embedded into their organizational design, reflecting different priorities: industries, customer groups, product lines, processes, functions, and technology, to mention a few. This allows these companies to flexibly adjust their efforts to reflect the changing strategic priorities.

In practice, though, most senior executives and CEOs hate such multidimensional organizations. Why? First, because they are an acid test of the underlying quality of management processes and systems. You can fall on your face all too easily if you don't do things right. As will be developed more fully in chapter 10, a multidimensional organization introduced without the underlying management system and process infrastructure – and without a culture of collaboration and reciprocity built and earned over time – may be hell. Managers become mired in endless negotiation and the leadership group bogged down in difficult divisive arbitration. The fabric of the organization is further torn apart, rather than woven back together.

> **a true multidimensional organization, puts an end to the comfort of bilateral relationships at the top**

Second, as seen in chapter 5, a true multidimensional organization, including multiple channels of resource allocation, necessarily puts an end to the comfort of bilateral relationships at the top, where resources are allocated "privately" on a "one-to-one" basis between CEOs and major business groups or regional barons. So, it is not that multidimensional organizations are bad, more that they are more demanding, more exposing, for senior executives. The coziness of bilateral deals disappears, or at the very least, is made visible.

One of the key constraints for flexible resource allocation relates to the way external profit/loss is reported. If a company with an integrated strategy reports its P/L externally by business units or any other main dimension, it easily "locks" its resources to current business trajectory. External visibility to subunit performance leaves little room for anything but meeting the stock market expectations by optimizing short-term performance for each business separately. This may prevent companies from investing sufficiently in future opportunities in line with the corporate growth strategy. Resource reallocations between businesses, as circumstances change, become more visible and unplanned shifts may disappoint short-term driven investors and undermine management credibility. It is sometimes difficult for outside investors to distinguish strategic agility from reactive confusion. In doubt, they will fear the latter. This is why so many companies go private.

This does not mean, however, that a company with an integrated strategy cannot have a clear internal financial target setting for its main business dimensions. On the contrary, it is very important to have clear accountability and internal key performance indicators (KPIs) for all key organizational dimensions in order to see how efficiently resources are being utilized at any given time. Discipline and transparency are key to fluid resource allocation.

As discussed in the previous chapters, Cisco's organization reflects multidimensionality in practice. Each key dimension of the organization is aligned with one of the top team members, making each of them completely dependent on all others. Revenues and contribution in Cisco are internally calculated for all key dimensions to provide a factual basis for internal resource allocation. As a result, the contribution of all organizational dimensions is needed to create and make the Cisco corporate strategy come true. A change in the assumptions or operations of any of the dimensions forces the other dimensions to adapt.

Having only one set of performance data

For adaptation to take place with as little friction as possible, multidimensional organizations must be able to provide one single set of performance data for all key dimensions of the organization. Each key activity in the organization must be able to see the same common performance data from its own perspective. Profitability, for instance, must be seen from product, geography, and customer channel points of view. In a similar manner, a product line manager responsible for a particular set of products globally must be able to follow up their delivery and sales data throughout the supply chain and all the channels, even though the primary management responsibility for that activity rests with company-wide head or heads of supply chains and channels. The same applies naturally to the managers of various development programs of the company. One set of performance data allows each dimension in the organization to optimize their work without sub-optimizing the whole. It also provides a factual basis for a constructive dialogue where people can compare the same data from different points of views.

Dissociating business results from resource ownership

Multidimensional organizations also allow companies to dissociate business results from resource ownership. In practice, this means that no single dimension or unit in the organization, no matter its charter, "owns" all the resources needed to conduct its business. Deeply integrated companies such as IBM, Cisco and SAP do not even have their organizational dimensions aligned on "businesses" as less integrated companies such as HP do. Still, in their case, business results are clearly dissociated from resource ownership.

Global business units in these companies "own" only the most distinctive resources, and access the other needed resources from internal and external resource providers. Such an organizing principle requires a major attitude change in the minds of executives. Instead of valuing the mere ownership of the resource, executives need to put more emphasis on the cost and flexibility of the resource in question, no matter who develops and runs it. They are accountable for results which depend on resources they have to negotiate and access with others in the organization.

HP had, for instance, developed five common supply chain and three common go-to-market models for dealing with the thousands of products and customers of its various business units. Each HP business used these common models and processes ("owned" by HP's Global Operations organization or one of the business units) based on their business needs. Most HP businesses need several supply chain and go-to-market models at any given time, but the needs for these capabilities vary over time. A product and/or a customer can move from a "high touch supply chain" and "direct sales model" to a "low touch" and "indirect sales" model over time. Businesses can use the same business processes and share their cost, and can also develop new business configurations quickly by using existing supply chain and go-to-market capabilities.

Ann Livermore, EVP of HP's Technology Solutions Group, emphasized the importance of being able to run simultaneously many different business models:

We have an advantage of having multiple business models and can hence migrate products between the different business models as products and businesses mature or markets change. When we, for instance, take a high-volume supply chain management (SCM) process and apply it to servers, too, the cost and time savings are huge. Developing new business models and related capabilities takes on average six years and when we can migrate to new business models in months you can understand the difference.[2]

Establishing dynamic governance mechanisms for balancing business unit differentiation and corporate integration

The balance between business unit differentiation and corporate integration needs to be managed on a continuous basis. Business situations change fast, and the organization needs to be able to reallocate resources and reassign responsibilities across the different dimensions in a fast and flexible manner. It may, for instance, make sense to move back a shared activity to business divisions in a situation where divergence between the businesses increases.

In order to institutionalize continuous balancing between corporate integration and business-specific differentiation, HP has established corporate-wide councils for each of the key "horizontal activities". One of the key purposes of these councils is continuously to evaluate and adjust the division of labor between the different "horizontal" corporate-wide activities and "vertical" business-specific activities.

Working through programs and projects

❝ this program-driven operational model helped Nokia achieve an unmatched product renewal rate ❞

Programs and projects are another vehicle for dissociating resource ownership from business results. By planning, creating, and delivering work under purpose-specific cross-company programs and projects, a company releases resources for company-wide use. By organizing its R&D work in the early 1990s into cross-functional product programs, Nokia dramatically improved its competitiveness through better time-to-market accuracy, speed, and cost efficiency. Together with the smart product architecture splitting the product into "basic engines" and actual products, this program-driven operational model helped Nokia achieve an unmatched product renewal rate which enabled the company to pace market development for years.[3] In the Nokia model, cross-functional product programs have the responsibility for planning, creation, and implementation of all the key activities for making the new product successful in the market place. This process includes not only actual product development but also, together with the respective functions, the planning and positioning of the product, implementation of the needed mass manufacturing, and marketing capabilities to make the product successful. All product programs in Nokia follow the same product creation process, handing over the product to the delivery process only after successful mass-production capability has been achieved.

Since the mid-1990s, all key cross-functional development work at Nokia has been carried out by using a similar program-based operational model. For instance, all new business process and related IT solutions are developed as company-wide "business infrastructure" programs.

Full visibility of the overall program portfolio through, for instance, a corporate program office is a key prerequisite for fluid resource reallocation across programs. In addition, the role of a program office is to provide the methodology, facilitation, and tools for anyone in the organization to propose and plan a program – and if approved by the line organization, to run and follow up the program progress. In the Nokia case, all new programs are systematically prepared and presented for decision-making in connection to the company's regular planning cycle. A program planning team prepares a business case for the program, including business benefits, time schedule and resource requirements (such as capital, human resources, and other assets). This proposal also often includes a clear specification regarding the amount and type of resources, sometimes even the names in connection to scarce ones, needed to complete the task in a given time. These resources are then released, either full or part time, to the key programs from the line organization, to which people return after the completion of the project. The primary role of the line organization is long-term human development and administration. The program organization takes care of the task management and short-term competence development.

Adopting an adjustable planning process

Companies' conventional planning processes may also hinder rather than enhance resource fluidity. First, they seldom question the primacy of the core businesses, and second, they are based on calendar rather than real market events. To overcome these shortcomings Nokia, for instance, has replaced annual planning and budgeting with a more adjustable, assumption-based planning process. At the most strategic level, Nokia is maintaining the validity of its strategic agenda through an issue-based planning process to make sense of the most important emerging topics and to trigger actions when needed. In addition, Nokia is reviewing its three-year corporate and business unit strategies (drafted on an annual or need-be basis) at least twice a year to discover if any changes in the core assumptions have taken place. If so, the company is prepared to initiate the needed actions regardless of the official financial planning and incentive cycles.

To increase the flexibility of its capital resources allocation, Nokia does not practice conventional annual budgeting but continuous planning, with six-month, short-term plans supported by monthly latest estimate process. The incentives of most people are tied to the six-month plans but they can also be tied to longer-term projects. Together, the strategic planning, short-term planning, and individual incentive planning make what is called "integrated planning process" in Nokia. The main benefit of this process is improved timeliness of actions but the process also helps the company to allocate capital resources in a more flexible way across the company.

Restricting over-investment in core business

Another way to prevent over-investment in legacy activities is to allocate resources through a transparent corporate-wide "channel" (for example, a program office discussed earlier) that manages a portfolio of development opportunities rather than letting separate business units have "fixed" budgets of their own.

SAP, for instance, prevents core business from absorbing too many resources by carefully managing investments in its core application functionality versus investments in new areas required to support its new middleware/platform strategy. SAP has consolidated all its vertical (industry) and horizontal (different product layers) development areas under the leadership of the CEO. Aided by a rigorous portfolio planning and management process, he is able to make the required trade-offs that maximize SAP's return on development resources.

Setting resource allocation rules

Companies can also put safeguards in place to guide resources toward areas of greatest returns and avoid resource misallocation. For instance, resource allocation rules can make resources move to where they contribute the greatest margin. With this approach strategy becomes subject to an automatic efficiency constraint for the allocation of scarce resources. As a result, market mechanisms are brought inside the company. For example, part of the resource fluidity of Intel over time can be attributed to its "profitability per wafer start" resource allocation rule.[4] In essence, this auctioned its wafer (the silicon crystals from which chips are cut) manufacturing capacity to the most profitable opportunities. Product and business unit strategies were subject to this profitability safeguard: insufficiently profitable products simply did not get production capacity. It became a "Show me the money" case for products.

Reallocating work and responsibilities

Not only resources but also responsibilities may be allocated. In other words, a way to reallocate resources is to broaden or narrow the responsibilities of specific units, for instance through allocating new products and new businesses to one or another. Such reallocation can be a top-down corporate allocation, or a process through which subunits "compete" internally for the allocation of new responsibilities.[5] Such reallocation can help the most efficient and presumably best managed units grow faster, by "absorbing" new product and gaining new responsibilities over time. In HP, for instance, Singapore gained a growing role in printing cartridges, as HP Singapore became more efficient and more innovative. In other words, work and responsibilities migrate to where they are best performed and exercised. Better than resources being reallocated, work is allocated to the highest performing resources.

The specific array of tools and approaches used will obviously vary across companies: the capital allocation challenge of HP, with a wide and diverse product range, bears little resemblance to Intel's, with a strong core business. Complex, expensive capital assets, such as Intel's wafer fabs, are another obvious constraint on fast resource reallocation, except to an extent within the confines of core business. Service-based organizations, such as Accenture or IBM, can redeploy themselves faster (for example, by hiring thousands upon thousands of people in India) than capital-intensive companies, but they also feel more knowledge development and cost reduction pressures from new competitors.

So, beyond the specifics of any individual company, the key point is for management to be constantly attentive to unnecessary self-made constraints on resource fluidity. Most of these find their origins, as outlined above, in features of the organization and in characteristics of the planning, budgeting, and measurement process that can easily be changed.

Fostering the mobility of people

❝ hard-pressed managers of operating units will always find it difficult to release their best people ❞

Managers of businesses may hoard people in the same way as other resources. Despite the obvious and politically correct lip service to people's development and mobility, hard-pressed managers of operating units will always find it difficult to release their best people to other units. Whether it is to pursue new strategic opportunities or to allow career development, or both, actually matters little. Left to their own volition, senior executives may not encourage people's mobility. People who feel good in their current role may sometimes not really want to move either. Right after its fast growth, Cisco, for instance, found it difficult to move people from one unit to another.

With growth slowing down, tougher performance targets made managers hold on desperately to their best resources to meet their goals. People also preferred to stay where they were, as their expertise was appreciated most in their home domain, and moving into new domains would be risky.[6]

Establishing measurable targets for job rotation

In order to overcome this hurdle, Cisco's top management established clear and visible measures for rotation. It aimed to have 10 percent of its workforce shift to new positions every year in order to keep people "on the move" for personal development, growth, and to overcome imprisoned resources.

Using systematic leadership reviews

Companies also need to establish processes such as leadership reviews to institutionalize a process through which all key individuals are reviewed openly on a regular basis. This process makes it difficult for managers to hide high performers and keep them out of rotation for too long. At the same time, this practice provides every manager an opportunity to justify why a specific high performer, otherwise ready for rotation, should not move on to new challenges until later. All of the companies we researched have put in place systematic leadership review practices over recent years. Reporting of subunit performance was made to include a measure of mobility.

In addition to enhancing job rotation within the company, companies may also want to extend their rotation principles beyond the core organization. Letting people go and work for a partner may sometimes develop a person more than any available internal rotation alternative.

Providing an open job market where "jobs can find you" to identify talents

Companies also need to make sure that their job rotation principles and practices support everybody and not only the most vocal and active individuals. Many companies have developed open job markets in which all new job openings are made public by posting them on the company intranet and/or public internet. This practice widens the development opportunities of individuals whilst providing equal opportunities for everybody. This practice does not, however, maximally utilize the rotation potential of the organization as it leaves the less active people untapped – and at the mercy of their manager who may or may not develop them in the best possible way. This practice also leaves room for opportunistic mal-practice by letting the most active people exploit the system.

Cisco has tried to overcome these challenges by introducing a "jobs can find you" rotation principle. According to this principle, Cisco is changing work, not people, and individuals are expected continuously to look for job openings that are close to their aspirations. The key difference between this and the more traditional open job market principle is who plans what. According to the "jobs will find you" principle, the company first plans, based on its strategy, what kind of competences and jobs/roles it needs in the medium and long terms. It then makes this strategy and the related job openings visible to all people to help them achieve their individual career and competence development plans. People then apply for those new openings that reflect their aspirations most closely.

Providing visibility for individual career development potential and opportunities

Providing full visibility for career development and opportunities is another important enabler for enhanced people mobility. People need to be able to see and feel that their competence and personal contribution is valued by the organization, now and in the future. The earlier and more honestly people learn about company needs, and the potential and limits of their own contributions, the better they can prepare for the future. Hence the importance of practices and principles such as Cisco's "jobs can find you" which help people to explore, find, and align their own interests with the company strategy and competence requirements. These practices also emphasize the role of managers, who need to be able to coach and support individual contributors to find a suitable career path for them.

Considering moving teams, not just individuals

In addition to career paths, people often anchor their self-esteem to a pro-fessional community or a team. Companies should therefore pay special attention to the social ties people have to their professional communities and team members. The performance of a team is often more strongly linked to the team dynamics than the work content itself. In these cases, moving a whole team and making it perform a new task is more productive than breaking it up and assigning people to different tasks in different parts of the organization. Armies have for years been applying this principle when addressing difficult tasks. Teams with strong social cohesion and common work disciplines are moved from one place to another, not individuals.

Paying attention to fairness and track record in personnel evaluation

The more mobile people are expected to be, the more important "personal anchors" become for them. People are not willing to take personal risks if they cannot trust that their performance is fairly evaluated in a transparent environment. And they are certainly not willing to take risks unless they feel that the organization cares for them. Care gives rise to trust, empathy, help, courage, and lenient judgment – all needed for resource fluidity.[7]

The importance of fairness and track record in personnel evaluation increases as the traditional "anchors" such as organizational structures become more fluid, and people have to change their "home base" more and more often. In such an environment, people have to be able to trust fully the evaluation system around them. According to Gill Rider, former Chief Leadership Officer of Accenture, a fair and transparent performance management process is paramount for a professional service company like Accenture to ensure that people stay motivated and that the strategy is delivered consistently. To reach this, Accenture has defined common global performance criteria for all roles at all levels in the organization. Each leader has similar expectations in their role as a "business operator, value creator, and people developer".[8]

An evaluation system based only on the measurable performance during the most recent period does not, however, capture everything. Companies also need to pay attention to how people achieve their performance targets. Many companies, such as IBM, Nokia and Cisco, have developed a list of behavior and value-driven attributes describing the way performance has been achieved. In the case of IBM, managers' "values-based behavior" is being regularly measured. The company has also established special improvement programs, such as "help my manager to become a better manager", to address systematically the behavioral elements of performance management.

People evaluation must also include an element of history. Everybody has ups and downs in their life and performance does not always follow a stable pattern. An evaluation system must therefore include a clear track record of past performances. When judging a person's eligibility for a promotion, both value-based behavior and historical track record, in terms both of what has been achieved and how, need to be taken into account. One more factor needs to be considered: fairness. This is very difficult to quantify and therefore contains some risks. The feeling of fairness is largely a result of the previously mentioned elements, but there is sometimes more to it. The belief that one has been given a fair chance to succeed by the boss is often very important. These matters must also be brought up in discussion to provide people with a true feeling of fairness in evaluation.

Having a pool of senior managers as corporate resources

Finally, people mobility can also be improved by creating a pool of senior managers which is managed directly as a corporate, or CEO, resource. Rapid redeployment of high-quality management talent calls for corporate management, in fact the CEO, to follow and lead the cadre of promising high-potential executives. At the same time, developing key talents as one corporate pool increases the cohesiveness and collaboration capabilities of this group. At an individual level, a strong corporate identity as opposed to a subunit identity helps in motivating these individuals to take new challenges across the company. At an entity and management level, the fact that these key people have a direct relationship with the CEO lowers the hurdle of managers, letting these people take new challenges.

Most of the companies studied have established a corporate pool of key resources for enhancing people mobility and improving collaboration and learning among their key personnel. SAP, for instance, has established a corporate function for taking care of top talents, and especially senior managers ranked amongst the top two percent of performers globally. The purpose of this function – reporting directly to CEO Henning Kagermann – is to facilitate the company-wide identification, accelerated learning, and promotion of its top performers. This includes special training and learning opportunities, encompassing additional roles such as "fellowships" in other lines of business or functions. SAP also monitors the success in leveraging this talent pool in staffing management positions across the company, to ensure the relevance of this program.[9]

This is not a book about managing people or designing people management systems. However, in the same spirit as that for barriers to capital reallocation, a more systematic attention to the array of practices, tools, processes, and mechanisms that promote people mobility can go a long way toward fostering strategic agility.

Reducing business risk and market entry/exit risk

££ allocating resources strategically and facilitating people's mobility helps companies to overcome resource imprisonment 🡆🡆

Allocating resources strategically and facilitating people's mobility, as discussed earlier, not only helps companies to overcome resource imprisonment but also to reduce the risk of business entry and/or exit by redeploying resources and people with little conflict or trauma.

Common modular business processes and interchangeable subunit models can also contribute to resource fluidity. At best, the majority of processes and IT systems needed to run a new business can be put in place by copying and combining existing process and system modules. Cloning and replicating small units with standard operating procedures – such as a customer account team in IBM – also allows rapid build-up and deployment. Individual mobility can also be supported by systems that provide relatively "complete" work environments. Taken together, these three approaches allow faster ramp-up toward – and if needed, less traumatic exit from – new businesses and markets.

Increasing speed and efficiency through modularity

Well-integrated modular organizational structures based on interchangeable business processes and IT systems allow companies to make fast organizational changes.[10] For instance, in the case of Nokia, the modular logistics process and related IT systems first developed for the mobile phones business (after the 1995/1996 logistics crisis) could be later leveraged across the company to all logistics and administrative processes. In addition to the increased global business transparency and related fast decision-making, these processes and systems architecture made it possible for Nokia to make fast and cost-efficient organizational changes.

The adaptability of Nokia's organizational structure was seriously tested in two major reorganizations in 2002 and in early 2004. Both of these changes, where thousands of employees changed jobs, were implemented in a matter of few weeks, without business disruptions – and at negligible extra cost – by reconfiguring the cost centers using the common processes and systems. In Nokia's case the core asset providing this capability is one single-instance Enterprise Resource Planning (ERP) system running all

Nokia's finance, people management systems, and logistics transaction processing for all units worldwide.

Replicating subunit models

Modular organizational structures can also be used for creating and replicating multiple small units of a large multidimensional organization without losing the benefits of global transparency and economies of scale. This helps global companies like IBM (as discussed in chapter 3) to lower their "center of gravity" in decision-making closer to markets and customers.

Dissociating individuals from roles and tasks

The principles of modularity can be brought down to individuals as well. Company intranets are currently being transformed to comprehensive work-flow and people management environments in many companies, as discussed in the case of IBM in chapter 3. When designed correctly, these new work environments enable dissociation of individuals from roles and tasks. This, again, enables individuals to contribute effectively in various roles and tasks independent of time and place, and allows companies to plan and follow up work progress from anywhere. This kind of a working environment means companies can dispense with many of the local hierarchies and controls previously needed for managing individuals linked to roles and tasks. Instead, companies can now use the "freed" managerial resources in more value-adding work.

Accessing and growing resources

Lastly, we suggest that the availability and use of resources should not only be seen as a static problem of resource allocation and people mobility, but also as a means of developing processes that allow smooth growth of the resource pools and human talents available to a company. Resource fluidity is not just a matter of best using existing capital and talent, but also, and perhaps even more importantly for strategic agility, of developing approaches and mechanisms that allow the company quickly to access, integrate, and leverage new competencies and skills. We call these generative mechanisms and processes.

Learning to learn

Cisco's expansion to new market areas demonstrates the use of a generative process in practice. Cisco has been developing its acquisition process in connection to over 100 acquisitions, and today the main process consists of a lot of well-defined, explicit subprocesses and experience-based rules. Tim Merrifield from Cisco's acquisition integration team emphasized the generative nature of Cisco's acquisition process:

Acquisitions are a fundamental building block of our business strategy. Not an event, but a key process we continuously refine and measure. We dedicate a set of resources to it, a rapidly evolving process we refine as a function of what has been successful, what works well. Business development function leads the effort. IT, finance and other functions each bring specialist skills. Integration of IT, governance and business processes and applications come first. It's all treated as a repeatable systematic process. We pay very close attention to the dynamics of individuals, evaluation, technical details, as they need to evolve all the time.[11]

At a business level, Cisco's "domain translation" strategy follows the same generative process principles. According to Guido Jouret, Vice President at Cisco/IBSG:

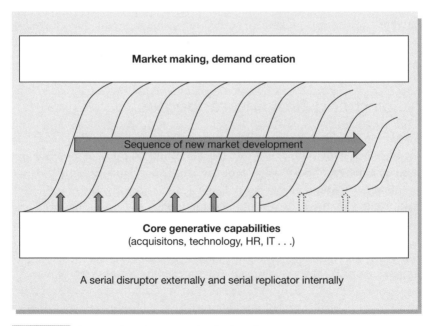

figure 6.2   Leveraging the "growth platform" strategy

We take skills learned in one domain and redeploy them to bring disruption or development for another domain. For instance, from switching we did virtual area networks and introduce a whole series of new features. It's a configuration of similar competencies applied to new domains.[12]

Cisco's "domain translation" strategy is illustrated in Figure 6.2.

The high-level generative processes of Cisco comprise a set of well-defined and continuously evolving processes, such as alliance management, minority investments, and acquisition integration skills. The more the company uses these processes, the better it becomes at using them. Active systematic alliance management helps the company to invest in minority positions at the right time to follow up market development – and to disrupt with the right timing – when needed. The acquisition integration processes, together with efficient support practices in IT and HR, help the company quickly to change the "rules of the game" in the newly absorbed business area. This organizational platform, together with its IP networking product platform, help Cisco to move quickly to new business areas without internal disruptions.

Creating new businesses

Generative processes' capabilities can also be leveraged for building completely new businesses. Intel has, over the years, built a special competence in ecosystem building and fostering. This has been necessary as the company's core business is at the end of the "food chain" and it needs to find ways to manage the risk related to its huge core business investments.

❝ Intel uses ecosystem strategies both to create and develop markets faster, and to contain its innovation risks ❞

Market development in Intel's case may take many routes (fragmenting the overall demand) and risks are highest in the discovery and early adoption phase. Once the major software houses and system integrators get on board, the risk level drops. This is why Intel needs to be actively influencing the market development already in the early phase. Intel uses ecosystem strategies both to create and develop markets faster, and to contain its innovation risks.[13]

In the case of WIMAX (Worldwide Interoperability for Microwave Access), for example, Intel's main motivation was to "eliminate a barrier to purchase" and to market growth (of laptops with Intel processors). As it had in the past seen the risk of fragmentation of peripheral interface standards as a threat, and introduced the USB port interface to prevent such fragmentation, Intel now saw break-up of the broadband wireless market as a major threat to its core business. Market growth would stall unless a reliable and efficient way was found for laptops to stay connected to the internet. Intel thus wanted to promote the creation of "one single, cost-efficient and quick-to-deploy solution" for broadband wireless in metropolitan areas.

Intel did not really care what this "one solution" would be, as long as it was the one (and the only) standard.[14]

According to Chris Thomas, Chief Strategy Officer of Intel's Solutions Marketing Group:

Our basic logic in WIMAX was the same as in all the other ecosystem cases. You first pick up the most likely winners from the 360 degrees opportunity space and start supporting these intellectually and financially. Then you gradually increase investments in the most likely winner. By creating a "social movement" around the likely winner, you increase its chance of becoming the dominant standard. In any case, you limit fragmentation and grow the market for the main solution.[15]

In substance, in its "outbound" ecosystem building process, Intel supports "likely to win" solutions and picks up the probable winner for E2E (end to end) solution demonstration, giving the impression of an "aligned" industry and creating a "social movement" around the wanted solution. This can be achieved in months.

To complement its ecosystem activities, Intel also consciously increases the "barriers to entry" to the industry. It uses its large R&D muscle and software design capability to raise the abstraction level of a chip from a product platform to a solution platform. Instead of providing a single functionality, Intel aims at developing chips that can fulfill complete end-user experiences which enables it to differentiate with wider functionality and move to new end-user application areas in a less risky manner. When successful, all of this naturally creates more volume to Intel's core manufacturing machinery.

Developing a full analysis of acquisition selection and integration processes, or of building alliances and collaborative ecosystems, would take us well beyond the scope of this book, and away from its main purpose. The section above merely highlights, using briefly the examples of Cisco and Intel, how important it is to think of resource generation access and leverage. Resource fluidity is as much about this as it is about the allocation of scarce resources. Developing process competencies around key areas such as acquisition integration or alliance and ecosystem development is part and parcel of resource fluidity, and contributes greatly to strategic agility.

How does it fit together?

This chapter described and analyzed the key managerial practices that help corporate leaders to enhance resource fluidity. These practices can be grouped into three main "clusters":

■ **Mechanisms enhancing reallocation of scarce resources such as capital and people.** Help companies address new business opportunities quickly by avoiding the "natural" imprisonment of resources into organizational "silos".

■ **Mechanisms enhancing resource redeployment through modularity.** Help companies de-risk business entry/exit by avoiding the "natural" ossification of activity systems and structures.

■ **Mechanisms enhancing resource access.** Help companies learn, adapt and influence to changing market circumstances quickly.

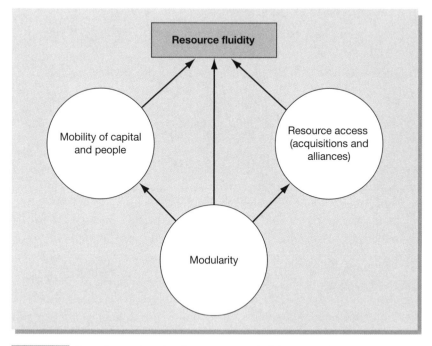

figure 6.3   **Interdependencies between capabilities contributing to resource fluidity**

Each of these clusters impacts positively and directly on resource fluidity and there is no specific sequence in which these clusters should be developed (contrary to strategic sensitivity and collective commitment), as shown in Figure 6.3. Modularity does, however, reinforce mechanisms behind dynamic capabilities and capital resource allocation. Within resource reallocation clusters we can also conclude that capital and people mobility reinforce each other.

References

[1] Siggelkow, Nicolaj, "Evolution Toward Fit", *Administrative Science Quarterly*, March 2002, Vol. 47 Issue 1; Lippman, Steven and Rumelt, Richard, "Uncertain Imitability: An Analysis of Interfirm Differences in Efficiency Under Competition", *Bell Journal of Economics*, Autumn 1982, Vol. 13 Issue 2; and Porter, Michael, "What is Strategy?", *Harvard Business Review*, November/December 1996, Vol. 74 Issue 6. In a high efficiency activity system, resources interplay in tight lockstep, with little slack or leeway, in a highly fit but not flexible way.

[2] Authors' interview, Ann Livermore, Executive Vice President, Technology Solutions Group, HP, 27 April 2005.

[3] Brown, Shona and Eisenhardt, Kathleen, *Competing on the Edge: Strategy as Structured Chaos*, Harvard Business School Press, 1998.

[4] Burgelman, Robert A., *Strategy is Destiny: How Strategy-making Shapes a Company's Future*, Free Press, 2002.

[5] Galunic, Charles and Eisenhardt, Kathleen, "Architectural Innovation and Modular Corporate Forms", *Academy of Management Journal*, December 2001, Vol. 44 Issue 6.

[6] Authors' interview, Kate D'Camp, former Senior Vice President, Human Resources, Cisco, 12 April 2005.

[7] von Krogh, Georg, "Care in Knowledge Creation", *California Management Review*, Spring 1998, Vol. 40 Issue 3.

[8] Author's interview, Gill Rider, former Chief Leadership Officer, Accenture, 6 February 2006.

[9] Author's interview, Ted Sapountzis, Vice President, Corporate Strategy Group, SAP, 16 January 2006.

[10] Galunic and Eisenhardt, 2001.

[11] Authors' interview, Tim Merrifield, Director of IT Acquisition Integration, Cisco, 18 January 2006.

[12] Authors' interview, Guido Jouret, 6 April 2005, former ISBG Director, Global

Innovations Team Lead, Cisco. For details on Cisco's acquisition processes *see* Wheelwright, Steven, C., Holloway, Charles A., Kasper, Christian G., and Tempest, Nicole, "Cisco Systems, Inc.: Acquisition Integration for Manufacturing", Harvard Business School case study, 2000.

[13] Authors' interview, Chris Thomas, Chief Strategist, Solutions Market Development Group, Intel, 7 April 2005.

[14] Ibid.

[15] Authors' interviews, Chris Thomas, 7 April 2005 and 19 January 2006.

3

Rebuilding strategic agility

Sustained strategic agility is far from a given for most companies. Most successful businesses have it – in fact they would not have made it in the first place without it – but they lose it after a while. As they grow, become successful, and mature, most companies are not able to maintain strategic agility. The toxic "side-effects" of continued growth and success are simply too strong, and the management too focussed on operational success to anticipate the need for strategic agility. Corporate history is full of examples of organizations that have died of strategic paralysis. There are fewer examples of companies that survived and even fewer of those that have been able to build permanent strategic agility to thrive on change. The real challenge, after all, is not just how to survive and redirect your core business once, but how to weave strategic agility into your organizational fabric.

7

Strategic agility – lost and found

Most leaders of successful growth companies would readily agree high performance often, and largely, results from:

Clear direction

- a clear vision for the future of our core business
- a sustained effort at leveraging our core business to the maximum extent
- a tight focus on continuous improvement
- a leadership position in everything we do
- a strong action orientation.

High efficiency

- strong business units with sufficient autonomy as they grow
- highly efficient business systems and processes
- deep collaborative relationships with our key customers and partners
- the ability to learn from own experience.

Strong leadership

- clear charters and missions for all organizational units
- strong leaders with proven track records
- strong expertise brought into decisions
- long-tenured leadership teams.

The curse of success

The sources of growth and high performance listed above allow companies to excel on their current growth trajectory, i.e., to do more of the same better and better over time. Yet, the longer a company manages to extend the life of its core business, the more difficult it is to change the fundamentals of the business model. The mental hurdles to consider other models grow, and the capabilities to change and transform the existing one decline.[1] At worst, instead of true renewal, these strategies only perpetuate the *status quo* and, at best, they postpone the day of reckoning! The very same sources of high performance that help companies expand and endure successfully for years, gradually become major obstacles for change and renewal. The very focus that drives success also erodes strategic agility.

A big part of the challenge relates to the invisible and slow nature of the deterioration process. As with a heart condition for an individual, it is difficult to notice before it is too late. It is also difficult to prevent purposefully, since decline is a systemic and slow process; and preventing strategic sclerosis requires actions in many dimensions, as does changing

table 7.1   **The erosion of strategic sensitivity**

Driver	Consequence	Toxic side-effect
■ Clear vision for the future of the core business ➡	■ Considering everything outside the core as non-relevant ➡	■ Tunnel vision
■ Sustained effort at maximally leveraging the core business ➡	■ Framing everything in the light of the core business ➡	■ Tyranny of the core business
■ Tight focus on continuous improvement ➡	■ Short-term internal orientation ➡	■ Strategic myopia
■ Leadership position in everything we do ➡	■ Reluctance to open collaboration and experimentation ➡	■ Dominance mindset
■ High action orientation and self-confidence ➡	■ Action hero syndrome, no time and interest for alternatives ➡	■ Snap judgment and intellectual laziness

your life habits to prevent heart disease. Even smart corporate leaders, acting in good faith with a long-term perspective and ambition, fail to detect the loss of strategic agility.

Single-minded attention to clear direction has various harmful consequences if you are not careful. The very same strengths that help companies endure as growth performers turn, over time, to tunnel vision, tyranny of the core business, strategic myopia, dominance mindset, and a tendency toward snap judgments and intellectual laziness, all eroding strategic sensitivity, and making strategic redirection difficult. Table 7.1 summarizes the deterioration process, which is explained in more depth in Appendix 1.

In a similar manner, strong leadership gradually erodes your collective commitment, as illustrated in Table 7.2. The same factors – clear missions and charters and self-confident leaders – that help companies become strong gradually turn into inhibitors of collective decision-making and strategic change. Management divergence grows when over-self-confidence – or hubris – gets in the way. Too much self-confidence leads individual executives to fully take charge of decisions in their area and to no longer seek dialogue or collective decisions. Finally, high-powered executives, having won many battles, may start suffering from emotional apathy; the future

table 7.2   **The erosion of collective commitment**

Driver	Consequence	Toxic side-effect
▓ Clear charters for all organizational units ➡	▓ Declining intensity of dialogue and decreasing need for collective commitments ➡	▓ Management divergence
▓ Strong leaders with proven track-record ➡	▓ Inflated egos, overly bold commitments, implicit pecking order ➡	▓ Heady charm of fame and power
▓ Strong specialized expertise ➡	▓ Decisions elevating to the top team; decisions made by the "same" experts ➡	▓ Expert management
▓ Experienced long-tenured leaders ➡	▓ Tired hero syndrome; future opportunities looking less thrilling than past experiences ➡	▓ Emotional apathy

can't quite be as exciting as the past, and their passivity starts undermining energy throughout the organization.

"the very same strengths on which success was built gradually turn into toxic side-effects"

Finally, let us turn our attention to the consequences of a single-minded pursuit of high efficiency. Why does the drive for efficiency easily result in increasingly stable resource allocation and tend to perpetuate the *status quo*? Here too, Table 7.3 shows how the very same strengths on which success was built gradually turn into toxic side-effects hindering renewal. Companies start suffering from resource imprisonment due to overly strong divisions hoarding resources and playing it safe. Their business systems become ever more optimized for only one purpose. In addition, valuable customer and partner relationships and architectural "lock ins" – the tendency to use the same suppliers and services instead of keeping an eye open for alternatives – grow into ties that bind. And companies find out that their general management skills are no longer sufficient to rebuild strategic agility.

table 7.3   **The erosion of resource fluidity**

Driver	Consequence	Toxic side-effect
Strong business units with sufficient autonomy as they grow	Core business managers "sitting on their resources"	Resource imprisonment
Highly efficient business systems and processes	Increasingly differentiated and specialized ("fit for purpose") activity systems	Activity system ossification
Deep collaborative relationships with key customers and partners	Customer and partner "lock in" and decreased strategic freedom	Ties that bind
Learning by doing and building on experience	Forgiven and hidden shortcomings	Management mediocrity and competence gaps

Why is it so difficult to regain strategic agility?

Once lost, strategic agility is extremely hard to regain, as a piecemeal approach to assembling the capabilities described in chapters 4 to 6 is unlikely to succeed. The interdependent and complementary nature of these capabilities makes building them one by one unlikely to work: each is fostered and exercised by the interaction with the others. Building each one at a time would not only be a self-defeating, slow process, it would also be unfeasible. Yet you need all of the capabilities at the same time. Take one out, and the whole edifice will collapse, as when removing a beam from a roof. The capabilities behind each of the strategic agility dimensions are interdependent and need to be built in a certain sequence. For instance, heightened strategic alertness and high-quality dialogue build on open strategy process, and top team collaboration builds on mutual dependency. Modular structures help companies mobilize capital resources and people as well as share resources and knowledge in a more efficient and flexible manner. In other words, having some of the capabilities for strategic sensitivity, resource fluidity, and leadership unity, but missing others, does not help.

The risk of dead ends

Further, building and sustaining strategic agility is also not easy because its three key dimensions (strategic sensitivity, collective commitment, and resource fluidity) are not naturally mutually reinforcing. Being strong on one dimension does not help strengthen the others. In practice, this means that putting a high priority on one of the dimensions typically makes the development of the others more difficult since some unbalanced configurations between the three dimensions are naturally stable, but also dysfunctional. In other words, as explained below, putting first a strong emphasis on one dimension, to the detriment of others, and then trying to build the missing ones subsequently may simply not work. The interdependencies between dimensions of agility are important to understand, in order to build a truly strategically agile company.

Lopsided emphasis to a selected dimension may actually stall, rather than help, the process of achieving strategic agility, by creating a stable – but inadequate – configuration of capabilities. Let's start with resource fluidity, an area emphasized by many companies as a cornerstone of strategic agility, but perhaps to the point where it affects the building of other capabilities.

The perils of resource fluidity

Organizational design researchers as well as consultants and IT solution providers have recently emphasized the importance of flexible, modular organizations, built around key processes, as does this book. Ravenously following their good advice, many companies are today investing in the capabilities underlying resource fluidity. Our observations suggest that this is all fine as long as companies don't concentrate on resource fluidity only. There are two reasons for this. First, resource fluidity is a necessary but not a sufficient condition for strategic agility, and secondly, too high an emphasis on resource fluidity may hurt strategic sensitivity and collective commitment.

Single-minded emphasis on resource fluidity leads to declining strategic sensitivity as it fosters an internal orientation. The complicated organizational design and process development efforts needed for high resource fluidity absorb a lot of management attention and energy, and may make the whole company focus on itself, often at the cost of external orientation. Further, a high reliance on resource fluidity may lead to overlooking the need for foresight and insight, and overall strategic alertness. Companies may start believing that they can afford to wait until others make the first move, and then react speedily based on the fluid and fast deployment of their resources. In other words, resource fluidity does enhance agility, but perhaps to the point where the false comfort of fluidity exonerates top management from the need for strategic sensitivity.

High resource fluidity may also harm leadership unity since management conflicts over resource allocation are likely to emerge as resource fluidity increases, particularly in the absence of common corporate-wide value creation logic. HP, for instance, was not fully able to realize the benefits of its integrated and dynamic organizational design for years. It knew that it had the capability to move in various directions, but in the absence of common strategic value creation logic across all of its distinct businesses, to which all these businesses would fully commit, it could not utilize its common capabilities at their best. At the same time, the highly interdependent structure required a lot of corporate-wide coordination. This partly diluted accountability and attention from the distinct core businesses. Everybody accepted common services providing economies of scale, but the more strategic integration efforts in the customer interface were considered counterproductive by some managers.[2] A common value creation logic in new "transverse" areas, such as mobility, intelligent homes, or rich digital media, could only emerge and be sharpened over much time. This takes years, and only recently has HP begun to reap the fruits of the integration strategy first proposed by Carly Fiorina early in her tenure.

Consequently, we recommend that companies be careful not to overemphasize their corporate-wide resource fluidity development unless they have a clear common value creation logic emphasizing strategic integration across their businesses, or build well-functioning internal markets. Too high an emphasis on resource fluidity may lead to conflicts that deteriorate leadership unity and to an excessive internal orientation that weakens strategic sensitivity.

The risk of being too smart

❝ companies confident in their strategic foresight are likely to overlook investments in resource fluidity ❞

Let us next look at companies that are putting a priority on strategic sensitivity. Not surprisingly, our observations suggest that this may decrease attention on resource fluidity. Companies confident in their strategic foresight are likely to overlook investments in resource fluidity since they believe they can either shape the markets according to their plans, or have plenty of time to adapt, due to their superior foresight. Recognizing the importance of emerging strategic insight, on the other hand, naturally leads to a desire for resource fluidity. High strategic sensitivity does not, however, naturally decrease collective commitment. On the contrary, investments in strategic sensitivity, and particularly in strategic alertness and high-quality internal dialogue, are likely to increase collective commitment. High-quality internal dialogue and high strategic alertness pull people together into a closely knit team, as seen with Nokia in the early 1990s.

The risk of being too fast

Finally, let us look at the natural consequences of putting a high priority on collective commitment. Interestingly enough, high emphasis on collective commitment is likely to improve resource fluidity since it promotes natural collaboration across boundaries. Cabinet responsibility and high collaboration capabilities make sharing and re-use of resources easier across the organization.

But emphasizing collective commitment does not necessarily improve strategic sensitivity in the same way as giving priority to strategic sensitivity increases collective commitment. On the contrary, placing high emphasis on collective commitment alone may decrease strategic sensitivity if it leads to group thinking. In this case top team members simply become too familiar and comfortable with each other to challenge each other's views.

The natural outcome of putting high emphasis on collective commitment is, thus, an "agile organization" with high collective commitment and resource fluidity but low strategic sensitivity. The strategy of such a company emphasizes responsiveness because it has confidence that it can adapt to any changes in the surrounding reality better than the competition.

Accenture, for instance, succeeded very well for years without a great need for strategic foresight. Its swift transition from an internet consultant to outsourcing company is a good example of agility in practice. In three years approximately 25,000 people left Accenture (mainly from consulting) whilst another 50,000 were recruited. As Tim Breene, Chief Strategy Officer of Accenture, described it:

As a services company, completely client-centric, Accenture has always been very good at ongoing adaptation to needs as they surface. Although the true potential of the outsourcing/off-shoring opportunity was not clear in our Horizon 2010 work in 1999, once we saw the markets moving this way we responded much faster than our competitors. In less than two years we developed and implemented a completely new business model with new economics.[3]

But this change also brought Accenture to a new business model that could not be run in a mere "sense and respond" mode. Managing long-term off-shore commitments led the company to create a new strategy function and a lot of new practices related to open strategizing. According to Steve Rohleder, COO of Accenture:

In the old operating model we tended be a "sense and respond" organization driven by clients. But today, we need to be agile and be ahead of the curve rather than in step with it or slightly behind it.[4]

In sum, one has to be careful not to rebuild and nurture only one set of forces enabling strategic agility, to the detriment of others. Such lopsided emphasis would not only fail to contribute much to strategic agility, it would also make further steps to rebuild strategic agility by then emphasizing other dimensions even more difficult.

The risk of misfits: strategic agility cannot be the same for all businesses

The nature of a business has an impact on the balance between strategic sensitivity, resource fluidity, and collective commitments of a company. Accenture needs more strategic sensitivity now than a few years back, but may lose some of its resource fluidity. Among the other companies researched, Intel, for instance, has to be strategically very sensitive, develop foresight, and think long term because its strategic advantage requires huge long-term investments which carry significant risks. Good foresight and active ecosystem building efforts are thus required from companies like Intel to manage the risks of large investments.

On the other hand, professional services companies, such as Accenture, can in principle change, train, replace, and promote consultants, and recruit software developers in India. The individual contributor is the unit of investment. Of course, at Accenture, the intensity of training and professional development, the use of detailed common methodologies, the inculcation of common values, and the development of norms of interactions and social networks among its employees take considerable time and constrain resource fluidity. But still, achieving and sustaining high levels of resource fluidity is easier for Accenture than it is for Intel. At Accenture, the unit of change is the individual whereas at Intel it is the next fab, a multibillion-dollar investment, which takes years to conceive and build, at the leading edge of not only Intel's innovation, but also of some of its key suppliers, such as Applied Materials, and up to a year to ramp up to efficient yields.

So, it is particularly difficult and it requires special efforts for companies like Intel to build resource fluidity. But this is increasingly important even for such capital-intensive companies: converging markets and technologies change the competitive landscape quickly and companies need to be able to turn faster. In a similar manner, companies like Accenture have to invest in strategic sensitivity in order to anticipate and proactively influence the market development. Mere reactive agility is not sufficient anymore.

Rebuilding strategic agility in a balanced manner is difficult

Developing strategic agility in a balanced manner is not easy. Let's revisit IBM. In 1993, the need for developing each of the strategic agility dimensions was urgent and profound. As a multi-business company it also had to develop differentiated capabilities as some of its businesses required long-term foresight and active market development whereas other businesses, for instance services, required fast client responsiveness.

In spite of the high requirements for balance between the key drivers of strategic agility, IBM first paid more attention to collective commitment and resource fluidity, to break the paralysis of decentralized product lines and geographic organizations, and only later towards the end of 1990s, after the initial recovery, did it put higher priority on systematic strategic sensitivity development. Apart from becoming well connected with existing and potential customers, all the management practices helping the company to become more externally oriented, including active new business development, took place after 1999.

Systematic development of resource fluidity started in parallel with development of collective commitment in IBM immediately after Gerstner took over in 1993. The integrated company envisioned by Gerstner needed high resource fluidity and high collective commitment at the same time. Otherwise efficient resource utilization across businesses and geographies would not have been possible. As a result, Gerstner's first development actions focussed on establishing a new top team charter supporting an integrated company. This new management practice emphasizing collective commitments would not have made sense without change in cognition regarding what IBM was (a globally integrated company) and a change in resource allocation principles. The change in resource allocation was achieved by a change in organization towards a multidimensional matrix consisting of global businesses supported by geographies and common business processes. The required change in cognition was achieved by opening up the strategy process. So, enhancing leadership unity required simultaneous development of resource fluidity (fluid reallocation of capital resources) and strategic sensitivity (open strategy process).

Towards the end of the 1990s IBM had made tremendous improvements in its resource fluidity and leadership unity. As a result, it had become an agile but not yet strategically agile company. The systematic development of strategic agility in IBM started only in the early 2000s. In search of new growth IBM decided to start investing in various practices enhancing an open strategy process as described earlier. But this required the development of new resource fluidity and leadership unity principles and practices. Getting the Emerging Business Opportunities (EBOs) up and running required new job rotation principles that allowed moving high-powered people in and out from the core business to new business opportunities without "losing face". This change was achieved by consciously prioritizing process over people. In practice this meant that changing a person from one job to another had only a minimal impact on their personal salary or job grade. Changing from one job to another was part of the company career development process, not a personal loss or win.

❝ changing from one job to another was not a personal loss or win.❞

Beyond EBOs, getting the whole of IBM to innovate and look for new business opportunities required more effort. Achieving the true benefits from Global Innovation Outlooks and Jams required a fundamental change in the company culture and leadership behavior of the top management. Knowledge sharing and people mobility had to become even more fluid than before. This required putting high priority on values-based behavior as part of the management system throughout the company. Also, the leadership behavior of the top team had to change. Top team members, including the CEO, had to develop into active coaches and facilitators of strategic dialogue in addition to taking their conventional decision-making role. Capability to play multiple roles and to act as "first among equals" had to become the new leadership norm. Enhancing strategic sensitivity therefore required resource fluidity and leadership unity as well.

In sum, strategic agility is a systemic capability for IBM that requires a very holistic development approach. It matters in what sequence the various capabilities inside each strategic agility driver are developed. And for developing true strategic agility it matters that all the drivers and their capabilities are developed as an interactive system of complementary forces, as can be seen in the IBM case.

Strategic agility is everybody's and nobody's business

The second main challenge in building and sustaining strategic agility, beyond the need for a balanced approach to all three dimensions and each dimension's components, relates to "ownership". It is hard to find a natural owner – other than the CEO – for strategic agility. Most companies find it much easier to delegate power than to reintegrate responsibilities. The division of labor in large incumbent companies simply calls for delegation of all matters to one of the corporate functions or business units. How do you delegate strategic agility? Functional and business unit executives may address some of the perspectives of strategic agility but none of them has an interest and incentive for holistic long-term development of strategic agility. Most companies do not have a systematic long-term development approach for organizational capabilities, the "hows" behind the "whats". Organizational and managerial capability and innovation development all too often receives too little attention. All companies have roadmaps for developing various products and markets but very few have roadmaps and assigned responsibilities for developing organizational capabilities needed for strategic agility.

New requirements for the corporate management process

Many companies are still today run as conglomerates, in spite of the increasing integration activities across their businesses. In these companies, the only management process most people see and know is the annual planning cycle followed up by monthly operational business, financial, and HR reports. Unfortunately, these do not contribute much to strategic agility.

Yet we know – based on the findings of this research – that the role of top management is dramatically changing as a result of increasing integration needs in global companies. The management process of an integrated company has to accommodate management of various tensions at the same time. In addition to excellent collaboration skills discussed earlier, top teams need new types of processes and tools for managing their business portfolio (consisting of businesses in different time horizons) in a dynamic manner.

Top teams also need new processes and tools for managing capital and human resource allocation across the different businesses and dimensions in the organization in a more agile manner. This calls for deeply substantial and specific targets for each organizational dimension in the company. This requires new types of governance mechanisms. As discussed in chapter 6, HP, for instance, has set up separate steering groups to manage resource allocation between each "horizontal" unit and business units.

These few examples demonstrate the kind of activities the management process of an integrated company has to accommodate. Embedding strategic agility as an integral part of your company's management process ensures that it will become a permanent capability of your organization. This may, however, be easier said than done if your company lacks a coherent corporate-wide management process, as so many incumbent companies do. You may have excellent processes within various corporate functions such as finance, IT, and HR, but have they been integrated into a company-wide management process in a similar manner to the way you have integrated your business functions (such as sales, marketing, R&D, operations, etc.) into logistics and product creation processes? Maybe not quite!

New roles for corporate functions

The holistic development of strategic agility poses a major challenge for conventional corporate functions. At the same time, it is a major opportunity for adding new value. A CEO is much more likely to listen to a HR manager if she can promise improved leadership unity rather than talking about teamwork on a general level. In a similar manner, a CEO is likely to be more interested in finance people improving resource fluidity instead of just reporting. However, the challenge is that none of this can be promised by any of these functions alone. They all need to collaborate to design and deliver these capabilities. Good collaboration, within a shared strategic agility development framework, would prevent the various corporate functions from addressing one or other aspect of strategic agility in a non-direct and non-coordinated fragmented manner. At the same time, analysing how well the company handles the various components of each dimension of strategic agility is likely to reveal "white spots" in the contributions of corporate functions.

❝ making a multidimensional organization work requires collaboration between all corporate functions ❞

For example, making a multidimensional organization work requires collaboration between all corporate functions. The finance organization's contribution is needed for designing the right decision-making rules (in line with the agreed division of labor between the key dimensions) and building up the right reporting principles and structures. The IT organization is needed to design and implement the right information architectures and "plug and play" processes and IT systems. The HR community is needed to develop behavioral norms and policies that support generalized reciprocity and foster trust. Otherwise a multidimensional organization, so important for all the key dimensions of strategic agility, cannot be made to work.

The same need for collaboration between corporate functions applies to developing and running an assumption-based, continuous planning process, as illustrated by Nokia in chapter 6. This cannot simply be developed without close collaboration between strategy, finance, and HR. The strategy people should play a lead role in designing and running an increasingly open strategy process for the company. However, the finance people should be closely collaborating with the strategy people in order to provide financial expertise for evaluation of the different strategic alternatives. Finance people should also be deeply involved in the strategy process in order to be able to take it over seamlessly when the planning process moves to their special expertise area, such as annual or semi-annual financial and action planning. HR people should be involved throughout the process because of their people and competence development perspective. The other reason for taking HR people onboard is the fact that they are responsible for individual level performance management process. Consequently, HR people need to be deeply involved in short-term planning to secure smooth transition from short-term plans to individual performance plans.

How to get going depends on where you start

The loss of strategic agility may result from two very different situations, which provide different starting points for its rebuilding, depending on the underlying vitality of the core business. The first situation, characterized by a vibrant core business that still gains momentum, makes a change in strategic direction difficult. The company has a lot of energy, and momentum, but its development trajectory is locked toward a particular direction that may no longer be appropriate. The simpler the company and the more dominant its core business – both in dwarfing other growth opportunities internally and in maintaining market leadership externally – the greater the risk of being firmly set on a strong, hard to bend, development trajectory. Leaders of some companies thus feel the need for regaining strategic agility not because they have reached a crisis point, but because they anticipate, or fear, reaching one in the future and finding themselves unprepared to face it. As Dan Scheinman, SVP, Corporate Development of Cisco, put it:

What keeps me awake at night is that we may reach an inflection point without being aware of it, and not be able to react and change in time.[5]

The second situation is characterized by a very different starting point: rather than running full steam ahead, the company has run out of steam. Typically, it has suffered a growth stall, seen its stock market valuation collapse, and shareholders, employees, and even customers lose faith in its leadership's ability to rekindle growth. Top management itself may well feel relatively powerless to handle the situation. In 1995, for instance, Lew Platt, then CEO of Hewlett Packard, commissioned a study which showed that most high-growth companies would end up hitting a growth stall, seeing their market capitalization cut by half and employment by a quarter, and would never fully recover. By 1996–7, HP did indeed hit a stall, and its yearly growth rates halved to 10 percent despite the phenomenal success of printers. In 1997, sales fell in absolute terms by nearly 10 percent, the first decline in HP's history. New growth initiatives, such as capitalizing on the internet, did not have much substance and failed to gain traction. By 1998, Lew Platt shared his frustration openly:

Frankly, we are tired of delivering excuses. We want to deliver results . . . Some of you probably remember Peter Finch's famous line in the movie Network. *He said, and I quote, "I am mad as hell and I am not going to take it anymore". That pretty well describes my mood.*[6]

Critical levers

Moving forward from either starting point – momentum or stagnation – requires a deep understanding of the critical levers of leadership.

What are these levers and how do you use them?

Ask most CEOs, or change management "gurus", how they lead change and they will answer in terms of changing the organization, "unfreezing" and "refreezing" authority and power relationships, rejigging measurement and reward systems to redirect priorities, and changing people. In other words, their view of change is one of organizational and social engineering: change the organizational structure, the management systems, and the constellation of key executives, and strategic redirection will follow. Of course, this well-accepted view is not inaccurate; it has been tried and tested.

However, our observation of companies struggling with the strategic agility challenge suggests this is only a partial view, and one that needs to be complemented when considering how to rebuild strategic agility. While organizational and top management changes no doubt do play a key role in regaining strategic agility, they are simply not enough.

Cognition and emotions

One critical challenge in regaining strategic agility is not to define too narrowly where to go – risking a blind charge into the unknown, and potentially off the cliff should a new strategy not be successful – but to provide a wider perspective rooted in a broader and deeper concept of what the firm's business system and value creation logic are all about. In some cases this may involve weaning the company's managers from a narrow but energizing vision –third generation mobile communications in Nokia's case – without dampening their energy. For Nokia's managers, to be committed to the more tenuous "life goes mobile" concept was intellectually and emotionally appealing but operationally difficult to pin down, and to become "access agnostic" (i.e., to embrace a plurality of diverse technologies) was difficult too for people who gave birth to the lead mobile communication technology, carefully nurtured its growth, and built its success on its adoption by major mobile telecom operators. They now needed to adjust to a wider perception, and a deeper understanding of a more complex environment comprised of many more interacting players. So, initiating positive change in strategic sensitivity calls for change in cognition.

In other cases, regaining strategic agility may require re-energizing dejected and discouraged managers, as when Lou Gerstner struck the integration chord with old-time IBMers and sang with them the "IBM is back" mantra. Like access agnosticism and the broad "life goes mobile" vision for Nokia, IBM's commitment to services, progressively leading to the "On Demand" concept and customer "big problem"-solving priority, provided a broad direction-setting and identity-defining framework within which many initiatives could then recognize themselves. The change in this case was largely driven by emotions.

In other words, we can conceive of leadership action as affecting four different forces. Most of the time hardly visible, but constantly present, are the cognitive and emotional ones. What members of the organization perceive, pay attention to, and how they frame what they perceive, and think about it, makes the cognitive force: the provision of attention, and the provision of meaning. Strategic sensitivity is obviously conditioned by the quality of attention, and the relevance of meanings assigned to perceptions.

What members of the organization feel individually, let others perceive and respond to, and perhaps openly share with each other, and how their feelings take them toward or away from constructive action and intense energy, defines an emotional force.[7] Cognition and emotion are ongoing at all times among human beings. They are the strong forces in organizations. Intense emotions drive strong actions beyond the call of duty, but may also lead to the passive resistance behavior so detrimental to strategic agility.

In most organizations, though, despite their powerful influence, the cognitive and emotional forces remain primarily private, and strangely unknown to top management. Top management may not know what middle managers think, or what they feel. This is not just ignorance, shyness, or oversight. In high momentum organizations in particular, what members of the organization perceive and think is not really important, they are engulfed in action. Action dominates thought. Emotions remain private. Beyond the simplistic rule that emotions should not be allowed to become part of organizational life, momentum is like steering a fast sailboat through high winds: it requires so much ongoing attention, and provides so much elation, so much "flow", that it leaves little need and little room for other emotions.

Although not always visible, and sometimes seen as outside the realm of "proper" management or leadership, both the cognitive and the emotional spaces are very much part of organizational reality, and both can provide opportunities for leadership action.

Organization and power

More conventionally, you find the usual realm of managerial action: the organizational and political forces. They provide the opportunity for a context the leadership of the company can set, both for action and for redirecting the emotional and cognitive forces. For instance, a political context that makes visible a well-functioning closely united top management team elicits positive emotions and heightened commitments. An organizational context that supports actions and initiatives, and allows people to thrive at work and feel trusted and autonomous, also elicits powerful positive emotional commitment. In turn, a highly committed workforce may have a strong positive impact on the working of the top team. Conversely, a divided, corrupted, or simply acrimonious top team elicits negative emotions.

In a conceptually similar fashion, how an organization is defined and self-perceived helps direct and focus cognition, if only by providing job boundaries and contents and by defining interdependencies. Measurement and reward systems also obviously help focus attention. And the definition of the organization has an impact on the political context too, if only by defining the differentiation and integration needs among members of the top team. New cognition, in turn, may justify organizational changes and legitimize relational ones.

In considering how to lead the process of rebuilding strategic agility it useful to organize our observations around four forces – cognitive, organizational, political, and emotional – thus adding to the usual repertoire of organizational and political change levers another two levers, acting on the cognitive and the emotional forces, to the range of levers of leadership available to a CEO to regain strategic agility.

The four levers of leadership

Put differently, if you consider how to unlock the energy of an organization, applying levers of leadership to all four forces is essential. New

❝ new cognition is a precondition to challenging myopia and tunnel vision ❞

cognition does not necessarily by itself enable heightened strategic sensitivity, but it is a precondition to challenging myopia and tunnel vision, and showing the cost of ties that bind. New cognitive evidence may also both create the awareness of the need for a different organization, and also justify the change to such a new organization. Reciprocally, shifting organization structures and management systems may guide and redistribute the attention and priorities of managers. In other words, strategy and structure both influence each other. Unlocking power configurations and patterns of integration among key executives leads to new relationships and to restoring collective commitment. Finally, concrete fast implementation actions stem from emotional energy supported by flexible organizational architectures, discussed in chapter 6.

In sum, regaining strategic agility requires action on four fronts (*see* Figure 7.1). Although all levers of leadership affect all key dimensions of strategic agility, one of the levers plays a "leading role" in initiating change in each of the dimensions. A declining strategic sensitivity cannot be "turned around" without active use of the cognitive lever. Regaining collective com-

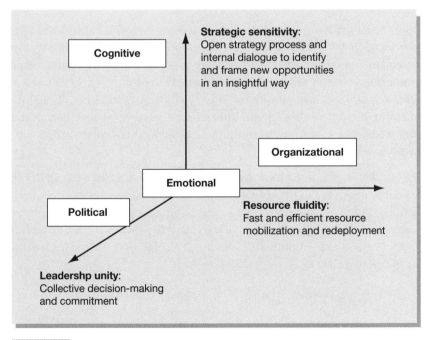

figure 7.1   Regaining strategic agility

mitment and leadership unity always requires use of the political lever, and rebuilding resource fluidity calls for organizational changes. Finally, re-energizing an organization suffering from the toxic side-effects of continued growth and success calls for active use of the emotional lever of leadership.

Summary

Most companies fall victim to the curse of success. As they grow and mature, strategic sensitivity is dulled by inward-looking operational priorities. Leadership unity is eroded by specialization and the all-absorbing preoccupation of senior executives with continued growth and operational performance. Resource fluidity is undermined by specialized activity systems, business models, and supplier and customer relationships.

And strategic agility is not easy to regain, once lost. It is a systemic capability – where many forces have to play in unison – so it can hardly be rebuilt one component at a time. It calls for more difficult top management skills and more demanding behaviors. It cannot be delegated by the CEO, but yet needs to involve all key corporate functions in well-coordinated action.

Further, as discussed below, there is not a simple, single recommendation for rebuilding strategic agility – which action sequence to consider, which path to take are contingent on where a company starts from: sustained momentum or stagnation and inertia.

References

[1] See Burgelman, Robert A., 'Strategy as a Vector and the Inertia of Co-evolutionary Lock-in". *Administrative Science Quarterly*, June 2002, Vol. 47 Issue 2.

[2] Authors' interview, Bob Wayman, former Executive Vice President and Chief Financial Officer, HP, 28 October 2005.

[3] Authors' interview, Tim Breene, Chief Strategy Officer, Accenture, 12 May 2005.

[4] Authors' interview, Steve Rohleder, Chief Operating Officer, Accenture, 12 May 2005.

[5] Comments made at the Cisco Trusted Advisors' presentation, 20 September 2006.

6 Lew Platt's presentation to security analysts, May 1998.

7 Weeks, John, *Unpopular Culture: The Ritual of Complaint in a British Bank*, University of Chicago Press, 2004.

8

Mobilizing minds

The more successful a strategy has been over time, and the more momentum it has gathered, the more constrained the resulting field of vision. Success, and its explication and interpretation in the organization, create a system of mutually reinforcing perceptions, which grow into routine ways of doing things based on taken-for-granted truths – and strong beliefs. Cognition turns into beliefs. Beliefs, in turn, and in a reinforcing circle, then condition what issues receive attention, how these issues are articulated, how they are framed and what language is used to describe and analyse them. Beliefs also determine how the environment is enacted, i.e., how market, competitive, and regulatory reactions to the company's actions are perceived, interpreted, and given a meaning. New information – or knowledge – is recognized or not, and validated, in its truth, accuracy, importance, and significance, through the existing cognitive lenses of the company and of its members.

Traditional camera companies challenged by digital photography fell into that trap. Most strikingly Polaroid, the most innovative camera maker, and the father of instant photography, saw the threat looming and had developed all the technologies required to shift to digital photography. But its very success in selling (at a high price) the "peel-off" film cartridges that allowed instant processing of pictures made it hostage to a "camera and film" business model.[1] In that model cameras were sold at a rather low price, and films at a high price (like printers and ink cartridges today). Polaroid's management, or Kodak's a few years later, found it impossible to abandon their belief in the "camera and film" model, despite mounting evidence that their business model and value creation logic were doomed.

Beliefs are hard to challenge, and even harder to change, particularly after they become translated into action rules and routines. It is easy to remember a rule, and follow it routinely, but to forget the underlying belief. Beliefs become resilient to contradictory evidence and, over time, they are invested with an emotional value. In other words, they are not only ways to assign meaning, they also become valued as part of the system of sense-making of key individuals and of the business model of the organization. Coherent systems of beliefs develop a "gestalt" – they become both all-encompassing and pleasing. Attempting to change them creates a sense of loss, before any new cognition can emerge.

Yet, provided we can change them purposefully, the very strength of cognitive schemes and of the beliefs that lie behind them, as providers of attention, meaning, decision rules, and action routines, makes them a powerful lever of leadership. They very much condition how and where the organization members are going to put their attention and their energy. If cognitive schemes can be made to evolve, or if new cognition can be adopted by the organization, they provide a powerful approach to rebuilding strategic agility.

Barriers to cognitive change

But strong beliefs cannot be tackled head-on; successful people and organizations first reject dissonant cognitive evidence. Changing cognition faces a series of difficult challenges. Beliefs can be made to evolve, over a period of time, through the accumulation and the mindful processing of disconfirming evidence, or can be reframed into a different context, placed in a different light, and there given a different meaning. Put differently, people act on perceptions, on beliefs, on what they assume to be true, and this can be purposefully shaped; sometimes surreptitiously. Let's take an unusual example. Lou Gerstner, quite early in his tenure, argued that "the last thing IBM needs is a vision", but also made momentous decisions at roughly the same time to focus on services and to keep the company together rather than float off a series of businesses; decisions that would shape how IBMers and customers perceived the company, and its relationship to customers and employees for many years. These were identity-defining choices.

❝Lou Gerstner, argued that "the last thing IBM needs is a vision"❞

Of course, few CEOs can enjoy Gerstner's initial advantage. Few bring a pre-existing cognitive frame to an organization desperate for change, and even fewer provide a frame which reminds employees of their best achievements and resonates with the deep identity of the organization. Most CEOs confronted with the strategic agility challenge need to articulate a new frame, to discover a new "gestalt", an untested and truly innovative one.

Articulating a new "gestalt" is difficult. Change is seldom an epiphany – a "Eureka!" moment – if only because most of us are not searching for a radical reconceptualization of our perceptions of the world. Continuity of habits, consistency of thought processes, certainty of future events are reassuring, and provide us with the basic anchors of a safe daily life. In fact, they are critical to the stability and efficiency of all organized activities. As they become widely adopted and shared in an organization, most cognitive schemes come to provide for more perceived stability over time and predictability of the future than is justified. As a result, they delay adaptation and action. And the need for change does not appear suddenly, either.

Wolfgang Krips, SVP Partner Care and Enablement Services, SAP very aptly put his perception of this risk:

When you move into adjacent areas and they take you progressively further away from your original course, it's difficult to perceive the need for a new vision. You still believe you are on the same course. As a result, you move operationally in an incremental and invisible manner away from where you were supposed to go. The perception and the reality differ and diverge.[2]

The observation above is typical of how a creeping departure from expectations leads to a progressive divergence from goals and direction, and results in a slow build-up of stress over time. In an organization, low levels of discrepancy, or divergence, between goals and achievements are likely to be interpreted first as a failure of "execution" and to result in renewed attention and energy down the existing strategic trajectory, not a questioning of the trajectory itself. Stress and momentum conflict. Increasing but low levels of stress first tend to reinforce momentum (reinforcing persistence in "trying harder" in the face of weak, disconfirming evidence) before the divergence between goals and actual direction becomes big enough for direction to be challenged.[3]

So, change is seldom radical, at least until an actual major crisis hits – reflected in massive losses, lay-offs, withdrawn credit lines, threats of bankruptcy, downscaling of retirement benefits, and the like – and painful awareness sinks in. Readiness for change may slowly build up in periods of prolonged stagnation, without a major crisis.

Ironically, the financial performance of a company is seldom as good as just before a crisis. Transitions in business models (e.g., from lease to sales at IBM or Xerox), the high performance of one single business unit (e.g., printers – and their cartridges – at HP), or overall underinvestment in business renewal may for a long while hide the deepening strategic crisis. This was described years ago as "satisfactory underperformance" (at least for a while) by Sumantra Ghoshal, exploring the causes of failure of major companies.[4]

Higher-order barriers

Cognitive change in an organization faces an additional three higher-order barriers: First, how we, human beings, make sense of something is largely tacit (nearly all our cognitive processing is unconscious) and thus hard to change purposefully. Second, such change is even more difficult because cognitive schemes – how something is collectively understood – are also part of a social regulation process. Cognitive schemes are neither just "given" nor neutral. There are winners and losers in how something is framed, and what sense and meaning are attached to it. Third, strategic agility calls not just for changing cognition once but for creating permanent cognitive awareness, a sort of third-order learning.

First, like all systems and processes used to create, apprehend, and assign meaning to new knowledge, beliefs are largely tacit. Knowledge in an organization – for instance an understanding of customers – cannot itself encompass and make explicit the rules that led to its creation and articulation. Since they become beliefs – confirmed truth – cognitive schemes are therefore deeply rooted and hard to change. In other words, the world, as we see it, is a constructed reality, where multiple perceptions are made to converge over time into a consistent representation.[5] Once set, that representation is remarkably resilient, because we forget why we have it and accept it as truth. The cognitive story we have built, which is just a way to organize and summarize our interpretation, is treated as if it was reality.

Second, cognitive representations may also reflect a social structure of accepted relative positions of influence, and a set pattern and network of relationships. This may lead to the perpetuation of power positions and social structures that are obviously rewarding to the "winners", and are made acceptable to the "losers" through the very mode of their representation.[6] In other words, cognition is a social control tool, not a neutral intellectual reality, it cannot be detached from power and politics. As stressed earlier in this chapter, this makes it a powerful lever of leadership but also, once set, a remarkably resilient and hard-to-reset one. In the same way as history is written by the victors, so is cognition structured by the winners in an organization. The interpretation becomes a tool of control and stability to relationships within the organization, hence its leaders, and even members of the organization who may not objectively benefit from such interpretation, will cling to it.

The combination of the tacit nature of cognitive rules and their role for social control makes them doubly hard to change. When existing cognitive rules are not seriously challenged by prolonged crisis, they can only evolve slowly. As suggested earlier, developing a richer language is a key to changing cognitive rules. A more concept-rich language allows one to take some distance from day-to-day reality and to do some modelling of one's situation. Repeatedly and experientially chipping away at rules of cognition and action routines, for instance through corporate ventures making forays into new territories, can also foster the emergence of new cognition rules. We know human beings normally coach themselves into thinking differently, so only new experiences, in new contexts, which cannot be accurately predicted by using old rules, lead to learning new rules. What new rules of cognition members of an organization will adopt cannot be fully predicted, and even less determined. Short of sect-like conditioning and brainwashing, something that is not and should not be part of the corporate context (or of any context where there is respect for the individual), rules will simply emerge.

❝ rules will simply emerge ❞

Third, there is a fundamental difference between changing cognition once, in the traditional unfreezing–changing–refreezing sequence, and providing for a permanent, stable, broader, and more strategically aware and alert cognition. The former leads to core business redirection, a one-time change (but usually not to greater strategic agility), a capability to constantly pursue wider growth options and keep changing. This creates an additional challenge to using the cognitive lever for developing a permanent strategic sensitivity. Sustained strategic sensitivity calls not only for specific reframing, or changing cognitive schema once, but for the capability of such frames to keep evolving over time. This has been seen as third-order change, or learning: learning to learn and adjust over time.[7]

Approaches to cognitive change

To avoid, and anticipate, a crisis, cognition needs to change early, yet the paradox, obviously, is that cognition only changes in response to a crisis! Many of the management practices of strategically agile companies described in chapter 4 (e.g., open strategy process and broader business definition, factual and conceptual richness, etc.) provide ways for broadening cognition before the crisis hits. Yet, except in very fortuitous circumstances when a readily acceptable new cognition suddenly appears to prepared minds (e.g., Lou Gerstner at IBM), changing cognition is mostly an incremental and experiential process. You need to start experiencing the "deviation" between the prediction made by existing cognitive schemes and reality – the discrepancy between expectations and outcomes – before cognition changes. The very loss of strategic sensitivity prevents this.

Crises – intellectual, operational, strategic – as triggers

To overcome inertia, only the very deliberate introduction of new ways to organize information, new ways to consider the familiar reality, to put it in a new light, and thus to reframe it from new vantage points and perspectives, and to give it emotional salience by making it more tangible, more immediate, and more challenging, can help trigger new awareness and understanding. For instance, a decade ago we took a group of very senior Nokia executives on a seminar to Japan. More than the insightful lectures and revealing company visits we organized, an afternoon we set up for them individually to visit Akihabara (Tokyo's consumer electronics' market, looking like a Japanese version of a Middle Eastern bazaar but selling only electronics), each accompanied by a junior Japanese Nokia employee, opened their eyes to the reality and nature of emerging Asian competition, distribution of telephones in Japan, and to the challenges Nokia faced in Japan. This prompted participants to rename that particular seminar "How we make Japan an insider in Nokia" rather than its official title "Making Nokia an insider in Japan".

Crises can sometimes also be created, not only intellectually but also operationally. Stretched and conflicting goals and/or the "unreasonable" public CEO promises described in chapter 4 help companies break out from existing cognitive schemes. Striving for seemingly impossible goals or struggling with apparently contradictory ones calls for new thinking and does focus the mind. They put people under tension, beyond their "comfort zone", and force both new thinking and a questioning of hidden assumptions. Forcing an explicit questioning of taken-for-granted assumptions is a key to changing cognitive schemes.

As an extreme case of forcing the questioning of assumptions and beliefs, actual deliberate investment mismatches can also be used as a vehicle to break conventional thinking and bring reality back in. Timken's acquisition of a plant in Poland provides a, perhaps extreme, but powerful example[8] of experiencing the deviation from existing cognitive schemes and reality. Timken, the leading US tapered roller bearings (a type of bearings used in aerospace, automotive and other industries) maker had internationalized early by establishing fully fledged subsidiaries in various countries, a sensible approach in an age of geographic market fragmentation. But, like Ericsson being faced with Nokia's irruption in the early 1990s, Timken had become a victim of its success: new Japanese competitors were taking global markets by storm from strategically located global factories, and SKF, Timken's traditional European competitor, had rationalized and integrated its global supply system.

In 1996, Timken's European management proposed, and got support for, the acquisition of a plant in Poland. The proposal was framed as an entry into the Eastern European markets, following logic fully consistent with Timken's multi-domestic approach. Some key managers in Timken Europe knew better, though: Eastern Europe was opening up, the plant in Poland was a Japanese-built, highly focussed global factory, which had produced relatively few bearing types, of modest quality, in very large volume, at a low cost, for the Soviet bloc markets. It was a total misfit with Timken's approach. However, it had huge merit: the "What the hell should we do with that plant and its products?" arguments that followed the acquisition made the debate of Timken's strategic redirection toward a global approach much more tangible. What had hitherto remained a largely academic discussion became a real strategy discussion. Through several stages this led to a complete shift in Timken's strategy. Timken today is a highly efficient integrated global competitor, with a strategically agile deployment of resources and manufacturing capacities in a global supply network. The key Poland brought to unlocking the situation, initiating change and bringing new strategic agility to the company, was a real problem that had to be solved, and a tangible "object" to be acted upon (the plant), not a mere intellectual discussion.

To gain momentum, receive support, and be seen as legitimate in the face of uncertainty and ambiguity, processes and experiences of cognitive change need to be cast to fit well in the current cognitive logic. Yet they also undermine that very logic, sometimes in unpredictable ways, given the strength of cognitive beliefs. Columbus started with the mission to find a more direct westerly route for the spice and silk trade with China, and to find a passage around whatever land might lie in between, not to strike gold in a new continent. Yet the value of gold and silver from America would quickly dwarf that of spices and silk from the Orient. Had he crazily proposed looking for gold and silver in a yet undiscovered, hypothetical continent, his expedition would never have been funded.

Bringing new cognition to an organization calls for concern with three requirements:

- **First, initiating.** Short of a "return to roots" epiphany brought by a new prophet (such as IBM's), it takes time to break away from strategic myopia, tunnel vision, ties that bind, and the cognitive perception of the core business through which all developments are seen, described at the beginning of chapter 7, in particular when the core business still retains a lot of momentum and when new understanding of a complex nature (e.g., multimedia service business models for a hardware device manufacturer such as Nokia today) needs to be gained. So, engaging early in change experiments in parallel to continued commitment to the core business is key. This obviously generates tensions.[9]

- **Second, broadening.** Strategic agility requires a wide angle of vision: strong peripheral vision, not tunnel vision. Yet a wider vision, over a vaster and broader landscape, provides less clearly signposted avenues for growth and renewal than a single clear way. It is easy, intellectually, to find a broad perspective (such as "Life goes mobile" for Nokia) compelling and energizing, but how to make it real, what actions to take, remains more elusive. It provides a mobilizing force, but does not give a clear and focussed sense of direction. So the old, the incremental, as the key to sustaining momentum, have to co-exist with the new. Regaining agility is difficult because members of the organization have to be weaned from the cognitive certainties and the emotional comfort provided by clear vision mantras, mission gospels, and strategy statements. Thinking of a broad, fertile territory to farm is higher-order thinking than just plowing a given path through such territory.

- **Third, challenging.** Such co-existence between the old and the new can only be difficult, as the new becomes a substitute for the old. How to imagine and morph into a new business system, conceive of a new

❝true dialogues should allow cognitive schemes to evolve, while not undermining leadership unity❞

value creation logic and build a new relational and organizational system are major challenges; challenges to the capability to change for most individuals, from machine operators to CEOs. Continuous cognitive broadening results from open and flexible ongoing strategic dialogues, provided the dialogues feed on sufficient cognitive differences, and rich inputs. They need to be true dialogues, that lead to common sense-making, and cognitive convergence. They should allow cognitive schemes to evolve, while not undermining leadership unity. By embedding multiple cognitive perspectives in the organization, the organizational lever may help provide such capability for sustained strategic agility.

Change without crisis

Essentially, change is more difficult the more the organization is at peace with itself, the less tensions are felt internally. Let's come back to Nokia as a company which addressed the challenge of changing without a crisis. By the later 1990s, having surmounted a logistics crisis in 1995, Nokia was growing extremely rapidly, more than doubling its sales of mobile phones every year, and in 1998, for the first time, wrestling industry leadership from Motorola.

Its development path was well marked, and the way ahead clearly sign-posted. Mobile phones would continue to grow fast, with high replacement rates and large developing markets in Asia and Latin America allowing sustained growth. Mobile operators were snapping up all that Nokia could produce, so the company could maintain price levels, in a sellers' market.

Operators were also building Nokia's brand, meaning the company could dispense with having to see, or seek, customers beyond the rapidly growing cellular operators. Absorbed with their own growth plans, these operators were ready to pay fortunes to governments to acquire third generation ("3G") licenses, for data communication, smart phones, and value-added services. These built on Nokia's technical strengths; Japan would adopt the same standard, and play a leading role in application (particularly entertainment) development. The future appeared glorious and profitable.

Nokia was emotionally exhilarating to its employees. The company was going through an extraordinary period of profitable growth, and was further increasing its leadership in the market place. Stock options offered promises of bounties. The potential tension between the main two business groups had been handled over time by letting Nokia Networks (NET) and Mobile Phones (NMP) deal more independently and separately with customers, and by avoiding "tie deals" (whereby telecom operators would commit to order infrastructure equipment only if their orders of new, recently introduced handsets got priority treatment). Complacency was creeping in, and the role of fortuitous circumstances was partly forgotten in the organization. So, although the organization had a lot of momentum, and even added energy, it was becoming self-satisfied, emotionally.

Nokia was also organizationally in a stable state, where the two business group heads of NET and NMP played a key role. Over time, each group had developed its own strategy and activity systems, although they did share common support services and business infrastructure (business processes and IT). Role definitions among members of the top team had also evolved into a relatively stable pattern in the mid-1990s, following the upheavals of the early part of the decade. Although the company was no longer really diversified, the conglomerate heritage to an extent endured; and business group and corporate leadership roles were well delineated.

As a result, Nokia's cognitive challenge was huge. Its core business was successful, and the transition from 2G, GSM phones to 3G multimedia phones seemed assured, with the operators' commitment to 3G technologies clear and well secured. This paved the way for Nokia's continued growth and development along its existing strategic trajectory. Its reliance on major operators and co-evolution with their strategies reinforced this orientation. Nokia did not just have momentum, it still enjoyed a lot of renewed energy.

Initiating change

Given such adverse initial conditions, how can change start? In Nokia, as in the other companies we observed, change did not start suddenly. Change had started to develop earlier, not very visibly, through a plurality of initiatives that converged and coalesced into triggering a widening of the strategic scope considered by the firm. In other words, seeds of change had been planted, neither very consciously nor deliberately, and they provided the origin of a change process. At Nokia, seeds of renewal were sown when Nokia New Ventures Organization (NVO) was created to search for a third business beyond networks and cellphones, while the core business was actively searching for internal renewal.

Seeding change: corporate ventures as change seeds

In Nokia, therefore, change would have to proceed incrementally, both fitting within the dominant logic of the core business, and slowly bending it, without departing too far or too suddenly from it. The precedent of Nokia Ventures demanded caution. Having started in 1998 as an attempt to discover and build a "third leg" (beyond handsets and network infrastructure), a remnant of the risk mitigation through diversification logic of the "old" (pre-telecom focussed) Nokia, Nokia Ventures did not quite meet expectations. As the quest for a third big "leg" was gradually abandoned, the role of Nokia Ventures evolved in the early 2000s toward acting as a "scout" for the core business.

According to Pekka Ala-Pietilä, who supervised Nokia Ventures at the time:

The success of NVO was not fully appreciated at the time, for at least two reasons. First, even mature people in mature businesses suffer from NIH [not invented here], so in NVO we consciously promoted people who would not compete but collaborate with the core business people. If there was a better home to develop a business, they were happy to pass on the idea.

Second, almost necessarily, the very function of ventures emphasizing longer-term business development means that we were pushing against conventional wisdom. So naturally, you have few allies in the organization, and your success may become visible only way down the road.[10]

Because of this difference in time horizons, the key managers in the core business, following their 3G trajectory, saw Nokia Ventures' efforts as too far from their immediate preoccupation.[11] Further, some of its projects called for new business models, not so codependent with operators, which Nokia found difficult to implement, given its reliance on operators.

Faced with that gap, Matti Alahuhta, who headed NMP, strengthened NMP's own new business development activities and entrusted them to Anssi Vanjoki by assigning him to lead a Digital Convergence Unit (DCU) in 2000. Initially, these activities were framed very much as a way to extend and further the growth of the core business, not to redirect it. Opposite to Nokia Ventures, NMP's new business development activities were more strategically focussed but benefited from strong core business support. It was becoming clear that the move from voice to data and multimedia services through 3G technologies was gathering considerable momentum, as testified by the astronomical amounts telecom operators were willing to pay governments to acquire 3G licenses. Alahuhta and his team knew they had to develop smartphones, and foster applications and market creation for these.

This would provide the impetus for their development, and allow their evolution from mere experiments along the assumed future trajectory of the core business to sources of energy that, together with selected ventures, helped widen the core business trajectory to new application areas, and later to alternative access technologies, co-evolving with further application areas.

Triggering change: acquisitions as change triggers

❝ widening the scope of strategic attention from a position of strong momentum requires great strength ❞

Widening the scope of strategic attention from a position of strong momentum and sustained energy along a narrow trajectory requires great strength. Acquisitions sometimes provide a triggering event. They create a cognitive break and bring in new people with different perspectives. Let's turn to SAP's experience here. Like all incumbent IT companies, SAP saw the emergence of the internet as a mixed blessing: a threat and an opportunity. It had to be able to enable its business applications for the internet. "mySAP.com", an integration of the business applications, portal and market place that resulted from a mix of internal corporate venturing and acquisitions (in particular, Top Tier, an entrepreneurial portal company based in Silicon Valley developing internet based e-commerce platforms and headed by Shai Agassi, an Israeli entrepreneur that SAP acquired) provided a prototype of sorts. Although "mySAP.com" had emerged as the cobbling together of disparate capabilities built or acquired in response to the internet, it did evolve into a platform, and the business applications suite was built on top of it.

SAP Portals and SAP Markets (Top Tier) were merged and reintegrated into SAP. Portals evolved into a set of integration technologies that were collectively given the trademark "SAP NetWeaver". In 2000–1, this was at the leading edge of SAP. Some top talents had been attracted to Markets, and Top Tier brought 200 to 300 people of high caliber. At that time Hasso Plattner (SAP's co-founder and Chairman) was the Chairman of SAP Portals and SAP Markets.

This experience with "mySAP.com", in turn, could be reframed in a wider strategic context because, conceptually, platform thinking was gaining currency, and because SAP was developing its own capacity for knowledge absorption and reframing. Independent of SAP, platform thinking and its strategic value were being articulated both in academic[12] and in business circles.[13] Internally, the creation of the Corporate Strategy Group (CSG), partly with veterans of SAP's internet ventures, and partly with strategy consultants, provided the receptacle and the voice to apply the platform concept to SAP's predicament.

SAP's top management could frame the platform integration effort in a way that was both backward-compatible and forward-looking. It fitted well with the problem-solving, "fix-it" tradition of SAP. SAP itself had an integration problem. It also fitted well with the culture of customer responsiveness. Emotionally, it solved the conflicts that plagued the business unit organization, whether focussed on industry groups, application domains, or both. It could contribute to restore leadership unity, which had been steadily eroded by the organizations adopted since 1998. A new organization, based on key contributions to the value creation process, around a single common platform to which applications could fit in a standardized way (what would become known as the "SAP NetWeaver platform") would allow reintegration and foster unity. The flexible – variable – combination of platform and applications would allow for built-in strategic agility.

Broadening cognition

In Nokia, cognitive change could not be triggered easily, given the very "comfortable" initial conditions discussed. So, cognitive broadening had to result from the accumulation, step by step, of new evidence and new experiments, growing seeds of change into a major transformation. This broadening had to precede actual change, and could not take place fast in one go. Let's review that process.

The strategic widening that took place at Nokia in the first half of the 2000s finds its origin in 1994–5. Somewhat fortuitously – following vision, values, and operational excellence being chosen in the early 1990s as yearly "campaign" themes to mobilize Nokia – Pekka Ala-Pietilä came across Gary Hamel's and C.K. Prahalad's just-published ideas[14] around intellectual leadership and picked them up as a development theme for 1995. As part and parcel of the intellectual leadership drive came the emphasis on new ventures as vehicles to explore and understand new areas for potential business development. This approach was strongly supported by CEO Jorma Ollila, who also wanted to invest in the future while the core business was still doing well.

Nurturing seeds of change

A small task force in a Nokia research lab in Tampere, a smaller town in central Finland, identified in 1996–7 the internet-based datacom development as a potential disruptive innovation for Nokia. The corporate market, however, was not yet seen as a potential mobility market, so the new cognition remained largely peripheral to Nokia's center of attention. At the end of 1997 Nokia acquired Ipsilon, a mid-size entrepreneurial company in Silicon Valley, specializing in firewall technologies.

In the meantime the Tampere lab, with limited and discreet support from top management, had developed a first generation "communicator" (a hybrid between a phone and a laptop with a "qwerty" keyboard, easy-to-use short messaging service (SMS) and calendar functionality, which made it attractive for corporate use). The project was initially "bootlegged" under the leadership of Reijo Paajanen, the local R&D head. A new mobile data unit started selling this product. Lack of applications limited sales to small volumes, so it was not a commercial success, but it was another step in Nokia's cognitive evolution. Similarly, partly in connection with the "communicator" development, Nokia had developed WLAN (wireless local area network) capabilities in the 1990s, only to conclude there was no real market for them yet, and disbanded the team.

Closer or further from the core?

All these efforts, via NVO or at NMP proper, grew seeds of change that introduced some cognitive variety. Even in periods of great success of the core business, seeds of change can be nurtured. Ideally, these should be sown at varying distances from the assumed core business trajectory, perhaps not directly in its path, but fanning out not too far from that trajectory. Such "distance" from the core trajectory is obviously hard to measure and assess, and can only be subjective. Complementary mechanisms could be used to discover opportunities closer and further from the core. Some, such as the Digital Convergence Unit (DCU) in Nokia, could be grown close to the core business, others, like the New Venture Organization, further afield.

Experiments or just "thought experiments"?

These seeds of change can be more or less experiential or intellectual. Experiential, action-driven probes are needed when an unknown new environment needs to be "enacted", i.e. when actual patterns of action and reaction are required to understand an implicit emergent system. Intellectual thought experiments suffice when the system is known and visible. To a large extent at SAP, the initial response to the internet was experiential. It involved a mix of acquisitions, such as Top Tier, and start-ups, such as e-business market places. Both were subsequently folded and integrated into SAP's core. More recent seeds at SAP have become more intellectual, with the development of the Corporate Strategy Group. In the late 1990s and early 2000s Nokia was really exploring new territory, new not just to the company, but to the world. Intellectual seeds thus might not have yielded much insight: they would have had to assume much what was already known when, in fact, the territory was unknown.

Backward fit, forward misfit?

❝ initial nurturing is facilitated if seeds of change are seen as relevant to the core business ❞

Nurturing seeds of change requires support. For intellectual seeds, the attentive ear of the CEO and the top team is perhaps enough. For experiential ones, management skills and other resources are required, beyond consulting-like projects. Initial nurturing is facilitated if these seeds of change are seen as relevant to the core business, i.e., if there is a "backward" fit with the core: they fit close enough to the expected core trajectory, and look initially close enough to the assumed future trajectory to deserve and receive support, formally or informally.

At the same time, to succeed, seeds of change need to be able to maintain some uncertainty or ambiguity in their future relation to the core business – hence the "forward" fit: where the seed is planted in relation to the future core position to muster support. And yet, how distant it will come to be from the core needs to be ambiguous – a potential forward misfit. Cognitive diversity in the top team and in the ventures or internal think tanks themselves needs to resist premature judgment of position *vis-à-vis* the core business. The Digital Convergence Unit (DCU) and some of the Nokia ventures could succeed in challenging the 3G dominance only because they were not too tightly mandated.

As it worked on these various projects, and since 3G was progressing more slowly than expected, the DCU team soon understood that Nokia had to put more emphasis on so-called alternative wireless access technologies, such as WLAN and Bluetooth (in a sense breaking the tunnel vision that had set in).

In practice, the wider cognition of the DCU unit did not impact much on NMP's core activities until the mobile device market stalled in spring 2001. Until then, the real renewal needs were not there, since markets for the new businesses did not yet exist, and applications were not ready. Further, the growth and health of the core business before mid-2001 called for full attention and left little room to worry about the more distant future.

Stronger action was triggered when, in mid-2001, for the very first time, market growth forecasts were not met, rather than routinely exceeded. Although Nokia managed to overcome this operational challenge successfully, it was now clear to all that mobile voice communication was maturing and commoditizing. 3G alone would not provide the second wind. New growth avenues now needed to be actively developed.

Moving from experiments to commitments

As a result, Matti Alahuhta, who headed NMP then, added momentum to new business development in spring 2002 by tasking Anssi Vanjoki, head of the DCU within NMP, with the development of new "value domains" (market-oriented domain definitions) beyond voice. For instance, Mobile Imaging – today the core of Nokia's Multimedia business group – and Nokia Enterprise Solutions, a separate Nokia-wide business group, emerged from pilot projects at the DCU. In addition to this, another major move was made in NMP. Pertti Korhonen, head of NMP's operations, logistics and sourcing, was appointed in the fall of 2001 to head the new Mobile Software Unit, aiming to create an alternative horizontal middleware platform for smart phones.

Opening spaces and providing fora for sense-making dialogues

Experiential learning takes place only through the interaction between action and reflection. Nokia's strategy and venture staff created opportunities for such interaction through a variety of fora – meetings and discussions large and small. These allowed dissenting or visionary voices to be heard in a way that could not be ignored, avoiding what Intel's top management calls the "creosote bush" syndrome of groupthink and no dissent. In addition to the Strategy Panel already established in late 1996 to oversee all Nokia's new business development efforts, a new Nokia Business Development Forum (NBDF) was established to accelerate cross-company strategy dialogue and prepare decision items for the Strategy Panel. New

Venture boards at Nokia and business group levels oversaw the development of new ventures in a systematic manner.

Pacing the exploration journey to gain credibility

ff products can be learning successes without being commercial ones ッ ッ

Timing is everything, so the saying goes. As we saw with Nokia's WLAN development, you can be too early and fail to build credibility and commitment, because there may be no market yet, only to find out critical resources have been disbanded and capabilities dispersed when they are really needed. Products (e.g., the communicator) can be learning successes without being commercial ones, so there perseverance pays, and the effort can be stretched or accelerated (as with communicators) when the opportunity calls for it. Network technologies and standards such as WLAN raise more complex issues: the ecosystem building effort is either "on" full steam, or not, but there is no in-between.

Reframing opportunities away from the limelight

Most companies value reliability of forecasts and credible plans. Reframing does not sit well with these, and their yearly rhythm. Unless understood in context, reframing is hard for managers, almost like a stigma attached to not knowing what to do and not having credible "numbers". Reframing is thus best done in relative isolation with periodic, but not excessively frequent, updates. These periodic updates require active top management involvement, but with a more exploratory process, where generating new knowledge, and making sense of what is learned, are the clear priorities, not budgetary control.

Formally, the Nokia Ventures Board and Strategy Panel, and informally the new Business Development Forum, played this role, allowing an open discussion – in a learning mode rather than in a review mode – of the evolution of Nokia's various ventures.

The processes of new venture development, and the requirement for evolving strategic frames, can be more or less structured and more or less tightly defined. IBM, in its Emerging Business Opportunities (EBO) venturing process had developed a more formal approach not only to tolerating but actively fostering frequent reframing. IBM's priority for EBO leaders, in the early phases of a venture, was to achieve "strategic clarity". According to John Thompson, the Vice Chairman of IBM who oversaw EBO ventures early on:

It would take a year, or a year and a half, to get a strategy we were happy with. It would change three or four times. You'd meet a few milestones, but fail or miss others. So you just kept interacting, iterating and iterating.[15]

Individual EBO management teams would meet on a monthly basis with the heads of strategy and ventures, and representatives from R&D, marketing, finance, and other senior executives the EBO team felt should be involved. These meetings were devoted to collective brainstorming, issue resolution, and strategy articulation, not the usual financial reviews. Each meeting contributed to reframing and kept all key players involved and abreast of the strategy creation for the new business opportunity.

Matching level of attention to level of learning

For reframing to be useful, though, it must be shared and diffused widely enough. Yet too much attention too early may be detrimental, because it may force and fix framing, i.e., create articulated perception and perspective that cannot be changed easily later, even when they should evolve. So, visibility and top management attention must be made to increase as the relevance of the new learning increases and its validity becomes more plausible.

Clustering and bending

As the exploration process takes place, and learning accrues, the seeds may develop more significantly in one area than in another, leading to a natural clustering process. These clusters may play a role of attractor, almost as in astrophysics, bending and widening the development trajectory of the core business toward a cluster of new but unforeseen opportunities, following different trajectories. The mobile TV experiments in Nokia's venturing organizations – later in 2004 brought in to Nokia Multimedia business group – helped the company to learn about new application areas for mobility. The process is emergent, and probably, like gravity, self-reinforcing, i.e., the closer the core business trajectory comes to a cluster of new opportunities the stronger the attraction by that cluster.

Although in a more compressed time-frame, in the period between the acquisition of Top Tier and the announcement of the Enterprise Services Architecture Strategy in 2006, SAP went through a process rather comparable to Nokia's. The acquisition of Top Tier and the venturing move into SAP Portals and Markets had planted seeds of change, and broken the unitary logic of SAP. Some of the best people, and best minds, went to the new ventures, (as the communicator project or the initial camera-phone project called Calypso had drawn some of Nokia's best engineers). This provided strong seeds of change. Vanjoki's support at Nokia, and Agassi's at SAP – two strong, colorful, and bright leaders – lent credibility to the effort. The Corporate Strategy Group (CSG) of SAP gave the spaces for well-informed and grounded dialogues, providing facts and analysis that would widen cognition. The growing presence of SAP in California, through Top Tier, additional recruitments, the expansion of SAP's development activities there, and Hasso Plattner himself (in an informal role of chief futurologist and development officer, spending at least a quarter of a year in Palo Alto) all contributed to bring new voices and new cognition into the top management dialogue at SAP.

SAP NetWeaver itself, as an architectural integration platform, evolved from a way to solve SAP's own integration problems into a concept of how to compete using an integrated platform and open application interfaces, allowing both SAP and independent third-party developers to provide a wide range of applications on the platform. The experience, for some at SAP, was very much a process of "acting yourself into believing", an experiment easier to do first on one's own organization.

Nokia's new perspective

By 2007, Nokia was still the strong leader of mobile communication, poised for continued success, but the road had included many more unexpected turns and challenges than anyone would have guessed 10 years earlier. Of course, by the mid-2000s, GPRS (generation "2½") and 3G were still attractive opportunities and Nokia's second and third generation offering was competitive – but the wireless technology road had forked into many paths, such as Bluetooth, WLAN and most recently WIMAX.

The convergence between personal computers and mobile phones was accelerating, and the enterprise mobility market developed rapidly, fuelled by the growing "office-less" population of nomad knowledge workers (which we observed, among many other places, at Cisco, Accenture, and IBM). Nokia had invested massively in middleware development in order to enable different applications to run on mobile devices, starting with the Symbian operating system and S60 user interface, the development of which had started in the late 1990s (based on an earlier operating system for PDAs, contributed by Psion to Symbian[16]). This was strategically important to stop Microsoft alone taking the lead in software development, and to stop others capturing the value from software development.

Although the effort had to be massive, consuming huge amounts of resources, and requiring Nokia to learn a completely new business (software and its development), it was starting to pay off. It had staved off a threat by Microsoft to massively enter the mobility market and to use enterprise mobility as a springboard toward consumer markets, and Nokia had also positioned itself to develop and lead the mobility market.

In the mobile multimedia space, by 2006, Nokia had become the largest supplier of digital cameras embedded in mobile devices. These multimedia terminals were the largest business of the new Multimedia business group Nokia set up in a major reorganization at the beginning of 2004. Nokia Multimedia business group already accounted for 17 percent of Nokia's sales in 2006. Other multimedia applications were a bevy of new venture-type efforts in audio, video, gaming, and other entertainment areas. Although none amounted to much yet, they clearly opened potential growth avenues to interesting new business areas with new business logics.

Finally, Nokia was starting to dare to wean itself from the strong dependency on cellular operators.[17] After being "pushed back" from digital

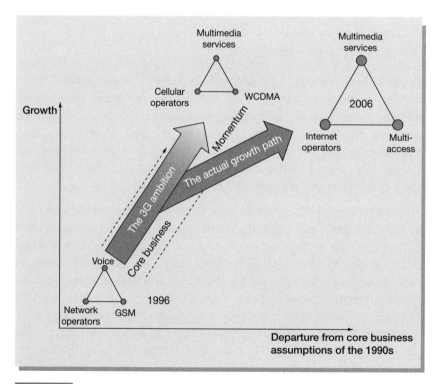

figure 8.1 Redirecting Nokia's core business

consumer services in the early 2000s, the organization was coming back to this new business area, now in collaboration with some cellular operators. New internet protocol (IP) based networks and related new service providers like Skype, Google, and others were emerging, and Nokia also needed to embrace these players in order to stay on top of the converging mobility market.

This new trajectory, unexpected in the mid 1990s, is summarized graphically in Figure 8.1.

Such a drastic turn from what looked like a well-marked, straight development avenue obviously did not happen without much effort, nor was it easy to start.

Nokia's initial change in direction happened visibly only in the mid-2000s but was preceded by a long period, almost a decade, of exploration of new options and alternatives. Bringing in new cognition was difficult in an organization where a single product, a core standard, and a codependency with a handful of customers provided very strong blinders.

Blending old and new

New perspectives, insights, and understandings unavoidably face opposition within the company's core business(es). The value and usefulness of Nokia ventures, for instance, can be better seen today than in the late 1990s, with the benefit of hindsight.

At the time Nokia faced a dilemma: keep renewal activities too close to the core and renewal will be limited, stretch them too far and they will not gain relevance – at least not quickly. One key to renewal success is that the renewal activities – say new ventures – also educate senior management, and in particular lead them to sustain commitment to renewal options.

Maintaining bridges between the renewal and the established activities, but at the same time allowing the renewal activities to be differentiated, is key. One, perhaps most obvious, way to achieve this is to have both renewal and core activities report to "ambidextrous" executives who can see the value of both. In Nokia, the stepwise move to new business areas such as multimedia was driven by its core business group, NMP, and in the critical phase of the transition, all value domains (old and new) reported to one person, Anssi Vanjoki. Another approach, as seen with IBM, is to entrust responsibility for renewals activities to seasoned senior executives with no strong career ambitions or axes to grind. For younger people who come to play a leading role in renewal activities, it is essential to separate clearly the performance of these people from the results of the effort, to reflect that renewal efforts are experiments, and experiments fail but still provide useful learning. Blending new and old capabilities, and building new activities drawing on existing capabilities, allow one not only to decrease risks, but also to signal to the experienced holders of existing capabilities that they will still be relevant and valued in the future. This also paves the way for the possible reintegration of the new activities into the existing core businesses: the new may create a different activity system, and business model, but still have some activities with the preexisting core businesses.

Faced with these dilemmas, some companies decide to combine, to blend the old and the new. Henning Kagermann, the CEO of SAP, commented on the development of the company's new internet-based mid-market platform:

We needed a new approach to the volume business. We needed to simplify, but also to retain the strength of our product, so the question became "Is this just another version of the suite? Or an entirely new look at it?" We decided the new product needed to be entirely new but reusing existing resources where possible. Putting fresh people on top would have been too risky, we would not have leveraged the huge knowledge and experience in the suite we have. So we decoupled the platform of the new product – the project leadership was in the traditional development labs in Waldorf, and the user interface and workplace design piece was done mainly in India, with an entirely new team, and support from Palo Alto. We deliberately set up a mix of the new and the old, together, to limit conflicts and risks. Culture was less of an issue than you might think. The two teams were set up from scratch – India was mostly new hirees, there were no issues of precedence, no power conflicts, just a desire to get the job done.[18]

The critical point, no matter what approaches are taken, is to allow the new cognition to progressively permeate the old, in a credible way, which both subjects it to tough reality checks and relevance tests, as IBM's Emerging Business Opportunities review process does, and also makes the established businesses receptive to new learning and able to absorb new knowledge. In that way the growth trajectory of a core business can be loosened, to be less exposed to disruptions and discontinuities. On the contrary, it becomes possible to discover and exploit new growth options, over a wider market scope, as IBM, Nokia, and SAP are doing today.

Summary

Regaining strategic agility from a starting point of high momentum along a narrowly defined growth trajectory is primarily cognitive. It involves becoming strategically sensitive again, and overcoming the strategic myopia, tunnel vision, and dominance of the core business, such as mobile phones for Nokia, or enterprise integration platforms for SAP. This requires broadening the strategic perspective of the company, to consider and explore new growth possibilities that do not lie directly in the path of the core business growth, as well as being sensitive to threats and disruptions that may come unexpectedly from the side, such as the importance of the internet for Nokia and SAP. Both internal corporate ventures and acquisitions can play a role. Using ventures effectively, though, is difficult; it requires a careful balance between being too close to the core trajectory and not contributing to strategic agility, and going too far from the core business and being irrelevant. It also requires a paradoxical "backward fit", to gain support, and "forward misfit", to provide challenging perspectives. Too much ongoing top management scrutiny can also be detrimental, but by definition ventures are learning experiments: the strategic insights and the variety they bring keep changing.

References

[1] Tripsas, Mary and Gavetti, Giovanni, "Capabilities, Cognition and Inertia: Evidence from Digital Imaging", *Strategic Management Journal*, October/November 2000, Vol. 21 Issue 10/11.

[2] Authors' interview, Wolfgang Krips, Senior Vice President, Partner Care and Enablement Services, SAP, 6 June 2005.

[3] Huff, Anne S. and Huff, James O., and Barr, Pamela S., *When Firms Change Direction*, Oxford University Press, 2000.

[4] Ghoshal, Sumantra and Bartlett, Christopher, "Linking Organizational Context and Managerial Action: The Dimensions of Quality of Management", *Strategic Management Journal*, Summer 1994, Vol. 15 Issue 5.

[5] Berger, Peter and Luckmann, Thomas, *The Social Construction of Reality: A Treatise in the Sociology of Knowledge*, DoubleDay, 1966; Weick, Karl E., "Theory Construction as Disciplined Imagination", *Academy of Management Review*, October 1989, Vol. 14 Issue 4; and Giddens, Anthony, *The Constitution of Society: Outline of the Theory of Structuration*, Polity Press, University of California, 1984.

[6] Bourdieu, Pierre, *Outline of a Theory of Practice*, Cambridge University Press, 1977; and Bourdieu, Pierre, *Pascalian Meditations*, Polity Press, Cambridge 2000.

[7] Bartunek, Jean M., "Changing Interpretive Schemes and Organizational Restructuring: The Example of a Religious Order", *Administrative Science Quarterly*, 1984, Issue 29.

[8] For details see Doz, Yves and Hunter, Mark, "The Timken Company" (A) (A1) (B) INSEAD case study, 2003.

[9] O'Reilly III, Charles and Tushman, Michael, "The Ambidextrous Organization", *Harvard Business Review*, April 2004, Vol. 82 Issue 4.

[10] Authors' interview Pekka Ala-Pietilä, former President of Nokia, 19 September 2006.

[11] Some of the Nokia Ventures, such as mobile TV, started in 1999, became an important new growth opportunity for the Multimedia business group in 2004.

[12] For example, see Gawer, Annabelle and Cusumano, Michael A., *Platform Leadership: How Intel, Microsoft, and Cisco Drive Industry Innovation*, Harvard Business School Press, 2002.

[13] Investment banks and stock analysts started adopting the idea and writing reports explaining its importance. Since its heyday, Microsoft's approach to Windows also provided a distant but conceptually analog precedent.

[14] Hamel, Gary and Prahalad, C. K., *Competing for the Future*, Harvard Business School Press, 1996.

[15] Garvin, David and Levesque, Lynne, "Emerging Business Opportunities at IBM" (A), (B), Harvard Business School case study, 2004.

[16] Doz, Yves and Hunter, Mark, "Symbian Ltd and Nokia: Building The Smart Phone Industry", INSEAD case study, 2005.

[17] Roughly half of Nokia's global sales came from cellular operators, the other half from independent distributors.

[18] Authors' interview, Henning Kagermann, Chief Executive Officer, SAP, 6 May 2007.

9

Energizing hearts

A different challenge, faced from a different starting point, is stagnation rather than momentum. Chapter 8 described the challenge of redirecting the growth trajectory, and of widening the growth path of an organization still full of momentum. The number one challenge, when coming from that starting point, is to broaden cognition without losing energy. Here, for companies starting from stagnation, energy has already been lost. The company has suffered a growth stall, and found itself in a stagnation period. In some cases, stagnation has been reinforced by cost cutting and efficiency efforts. At best, as with Lou Gerstner at IBM, an ambidextrous organization has been built: rationalizing and streamlining the core business, and, on the side, building new businesses. The number one challenge here is to reinstil energy, drive, and commitment to the core businesses of a mature and disillusioned organization, whose members may have become skeptical of their leadership's skills and capabilities. The inflection point has been reached long ago, for everyone to see, with dire consequences, financial and operational.

Emotions as a source of energy or apathy

Emotions are a powerful source of energy for action – or of apathy and passivity – in organizations. Energy is more often driven by emotions than by mere calculated self-interest, contrary to what economists would like us to believe. Emotions can be a cause of inertia, of not being able to move forward, with cognition and emotional commitment being often closely intertwined. In periods of change, emotional uncertainty and disarray can be paralyzing. Conversely, going beyond the call of duty requires strong positive emotions.

Interestingly enough, though, both very positive and very negative emotional states undermine strategic agility. Positive emotions lead to self-satisfaction and peace, but also laziness, intellectually and practically. Unmitigated bliss seldom drives action. Momentum leaves little room for new commitments, but may lead to satisfied passivity. In Nokia, for instance, emotional commitment – and for many, fulfillment – came from riding the mobile communication storm. The more visionary but less concrete efforts started around intellectual leadership ideas in the mid-1990s did not elicit much additional emotional commitment, although they caught the imagination of many.

❝ even in very successful organizations, strategic renewal may call for a different skill mix ❞

Conversely, very negative emotions, fear for instance, may lead to anger, and to feelings of dejection and helplessness, which are seldom conducive to constructive action. Many people in stagnating organizations may become rebels without a cause, leading to passive-aggressive attitudes and behaviors. Even in very successful organizations, strategic renewal may call for a different skill mix, and question the identity and self-worth of key staff and experts. Take SAP. For SAP, reintegrating the company around a common product architecture (manifested in the SAP NetWeaver platform) was emotionally identity-confirming but also raised a formidable challenge to the company. Building the "applistructure" (the merger of enterprise application and infrastructure technology) concept around an open platform and external application developers raised a major emotional and cultural challenge to SAP rank and file workers. The technological change helped the management to change SAP from a product-focussed company to a customer-focussed one. Besides the complete transfer of the existing applications to the new platform, the broad entry into the mid-market with a new product and a new business model (and the attendant turning of services into products), and growing indirect sales channels, added additional challenges. The platform team now has to serve three "customers": the existing large customer applications, the new mid-market product, and an external group with resellers and partners. They have to balance the request from all three. The challenge for the entire organization is now to serve two business models sharing the same platform. Henning Kagermann describes the situation:

Yes, we had many discussions about the execution, but the strategy was always clear and remained the same. You have to see people are not only intellectually involved, but also emotionally. These discussions are good, because they allow

table 9.1	SAP 2010 vision requires transformation to new requirements and continued commitment to core values

Continuity of foundational values	
Customer focus	Integrity
Quality	Commitment
Engineering excellence	Passion
Change from	*to*
Protecting *status quo*	Agility
Complexity	Simplicity
Pockets of execution	High performance
"Not invented here"	Global collaboration
Employee management	Talent development

Source: SAP Corporate Strategy Group

people to get more deeply involved, but at a certain time you have to make clear as CEO what the direction is, even if the discussions have not fully come to an end.[1]

Changes for SAP ran deep, as captured by a summary outline of value transformation in Table 9.1.

What became apparent at SAP was the fact that there were conflicts on many different levels. For instance, perception of the chosen patch was inconsistent across the company. What was perceived as a very sensible thing at the top was seen as a discontinuity down below. The perception differed also from region to region. In the US, for instance, problems with the customer relationship model had surfaced earlier and thus the drive to a new approach was much higher. Also, the new approaches caused many disruptions, according to Ted Sapountzis and Timmo Sturm:

What was done around the internet and SAP NetWeaver did not initially reach the core business. But over time we saw product release cycles go from five years to two, and then to one! And development projects from years to a few weeks! The new concept is a cultural system, a disruptive innovation for the old SAP.[2]

Obviously, this was not an easy conflict to solve. The blending of the "old" and "new" people into development teams described in the previous chapter as a way for the "new" to constructively challenge and influence the "old", rather than clash, was not sufficient to avoid conflicts among SAP employees not directly involved in the renewal projects. In the end, Kagermann had to step in personally, clarify priorities (large enterprise customers' success first, making the new product successful second, everything else third), publicly announce the mid-market new product, and show his commitment by allocating $400 million to the new product deployment and sales, in addition to what was already committed.

In doing so Kagermann was carefully balancing and blending the attachment to SAP's core *raison d'être*, as a problem solver for large companies, and the need to broaden its market and find profitable formulae to reach a much wider customer base – fast. This included turning service and support into a product, and creating a much wider and flexible *à la carte* menu of applications, including many from development partners. This allowed him to balance the positive emotions attached to SAP's traditional approach, and the aspirations for growth and renewal. The negative emotions attached to "mass market" penetration by SAP developers and sales forces were balanced with the attractiveness of new growth prospects.

In other words, strategic agility is not about the "feel good" or "happiness" index, but neither is it about anxiety and anger. Corporate leaders who can combine positive and negative emotions, and build on the tensions between them, may be at an advantage.

Capitalizing on emotions

Other leaders capitalize on such tensions. Gerstner, at IBM, for instance, could turn the despair, anger, and humiliation felt by many IBMers, particularly in what used to be the IBM "heartland" in the Hudson Valley (north of New York), into positive energy and an ambition to regain pride. Frustration with decline, and shame, provided a good starting point for rebuilding pride, and people worked countless hours toward that change. More specifically, in the turnaround process, the sweet and the sour sides were combined. Laurence Guihard-Joly, one leading executive of IBM, recalls these days:

I was in France, in the process of selling or closing down a recently acquired application software company [a business Lou Gerstner decided IBM should exit]; it was hard. Yet, at the same time new initiatives were started, other people were hired. There was constantly a sense of vitality, a balance between the negative and the positive, a bright light at the end of the tunnel.[3]

Restoring feelings of control over actions leading to positive outcomes (*vs.* the feelings of powerlessness most crises bring) re-energizes members of the organization and feeds a virtuous circle of growing self-efficacy.

Emotions being a fact of organizational life – and of the human condition, using them as a lever of leadership, rather than pretending they have no role to play and attempting to ignore them, makes good sense. Emotions in corporate situations result from a two-stage, but largely unconscious, process:

■ an evaluation of the importance and significance of an event, a change, or an awareness, in relation to an individual's values, goals and concerns;

■ an assessment by the individual of their ability to deal constructively with consequences and develop an adaptive response.[4]

Obviously, though, and contrary to an excessively intellectual view of change and renewal, a lot of that individual processing is unconscious and therefore cannot be articulated. For instance, similar management actions (e.g., calling upon a relatively junior executive to participate in a strategy team) may lead to very different commitment to action depending on emotional states (e.g., pride of having been selected *vs.* anger of being asked to contribute actively to a process unlikely to have an impact).[5] Judgments, feelings, and impressions have their role to play. How impressions of change, and structuring of what change means, take shape is a function of emotions. Executives who would attempt to ignore them, or deny their importance, do so at their own risk.

❝ emotions can achieve faster change than other leadership levers ❞

Furthermore, emotions can achieve faster change than other leadership levers. Emotional states are contagious within organizations, when people work closely together. Management can thus see emotional changes as amplifying and accelerating renewal processes: emotions snowball. Emotions spread not only by tacit proximate contagion, but also through the power of collective interpretation. Individual behaviors and actions can become myths, or role models. In Nokia Networks, for instance, the longtime business group head, Sari Baldauf, clearly built the image of the lone Finnish engineer, on call to fly to the furthest corners of the world on no notice and fix a customer network, all by themselves, overnight. This was seen to contrast with the ponderous and slow bureaucracies of competitors. Individual prowess and self-sacrifice became emotional values.

Bringing emotions to contribute to strategic agility

The CEO can undertake a series of actions for emotions to contribute to strategic agility.

First, reconnecting to and rekindling sources of pride and self-efficacy are powerful levers. Gerstner quickly recognized that IBMers found pride in working together to solve complex integration problems. The move to client-server computing made these skills look unneeded, and devalued. Pride was hurt, competencies felt obsolete. By emphasizing IBM "staying together" as an integrator, Gerstner rekindled deeply felt pride. In doing this Gerstner enjoyed at least three advantages in influencing how IBMers perceived themselves and their relationship to the world. As a longtime customer of IBM (since he ran International Data Corporation, the IT and data system subsidiary of American Express), a seasoned consultant, and a CEO, he had already a different "gestalt" in mind: IBM as an integrator. IBM had already been going through years of decline and lay-offs: the situation was ripe for something new. Keeping the company together, rather than floating off product line after product line, was a much more compelling perspective to IBMers, a perspective that echoed IBM's heyday, as an integrator, with the IBM 360/370 mainframes.

Second, appealing to a more widely shared context and historical emotions provides energy. Jorma Ollila at Nokia, for instance, used such a lever, at multiple levels. He used the "logistics" crisis of 1995 (when the supply chain was falling apart for lack of process) as a way to emphasize teamwork, and gave a deeper and stronger meaning to Nokia's values. But beyond articulating the logistics crisis as a defining moment of Nokia's identity, he related teamwork to a deeper emotional context rooted in history. In the "Winter War", when in 1939 the Finns fought, alone, a full Soviet onslaught, they won through small teams (platoons) of highly mobile troops. Ollila linked Nokia's team spirit to the "save your buddy" spirit of the Winter War victory, a source of pride in Finnish history, recounted by parents and grandparents to many younger employees of Nokia. He also used the self-image of the Finns as proud underdogs, alternately invaded by the Swedes and the Russians, to mobilize all in Nokia, in a whispering mode, around the tacit "beat Motorola and Ericsson" pride, in the same way as Finland had bravely defended itself against the Soviets.

Third, a culture of care can go a long way in fostering positive emotions. Confidence that support will be provided against the potential adversities of life, and that individual needs for security, and for feeling valued and appreciated, won't be ignored, can bond people constructively to a caring organization.

Care, not just as insurance but as personalized concern and empathy, has an even more fundamental role to play. As stressed, in the context of creating a more interdependent organization, and a more united leadership team, care, in the sense of serious concern and interest in another person and their positions, is a precursor of trust. Effective care requires that emotions not be repressed, hidden, or frowned upon.[6] Beyond the obvious personal security against the hazards of life, useful care can only manifest itself through empathy. But unless one can let go, and express and share one's emotions openly, true empathy cannot be attained, and people do not connect emotionally. Care can only be an emotional connection between human beings. The need for quality of interactions within the top team, to elicit trust, understanding, and empathy, and to foster open genuine dialogue is also (and even more) needed within the organization, between peers, between subordinates and bosses, and even more generally between any organization members who also need to coordinate their actions. Care and empathy is the ability to consider a situation from someone else's perspective. They also play a major role in fair process, i.e. in being able to make legitimate and justified decisions that are not just a compromise between conflicting interests or between disparate perspectives and priorities. They are fundamental contributors to leadership unity, but also to the whole fabric of the organization.

Obviously, care and trust are fragile. In fact most organizations are remarkably good at destroying care! Fear, lack of fair process, perceived injustice, unfettered personal ambitions, and absurd "rules" forbidding the expression of emotions all play a role in making care and trust impossible. Reliance on "expertise" and punishing people for unsuccessful work done in good faith all play a further debilitating role.

" the importance of norms and values of reciprocity to foster collaboration must be emphasized "

Once again the importance of norms and values of reciprocity to foster collaboration must be emphasized, in particular norms (and soft incentives) that recognize and take into account, but do not attempt to measure precisely, mutual help beyond handling the usual interdependencies. According to Accenture:

The culture, core values and behaviors have sustained a global network and the long-term stewardship of the company. Asked for help, you respond no matter where you are, what you do.[7]

At a more day-to-day operational level, team-based incentives, explicit rewards for sharing expertise and mentoring others, and for assisting in problem solving, can all contribute to reciprocity. Beyond explicit transactional incentives, providing extrinsic rewards, strongly felt genuine values permeating the organization provide intrinsic rewards. This is all the more true when values have been developed in a participative, transparent, and legitimate process, rather than sent as edicts from above or developed in some "black-box" process. They provide a guiding beacon in terms of correct action. Training and coaching in emotional intelligence and adaptive leadership also helps. Care can also be expressed by adopting a morally meaningful lofty purpose, appealing to higher motives in human life.

Fourth, the purpose of the company itself can indeed appeal to higher meanings in human life. Jorma Ollila clearly articulated Nokia's role as a promoter of freedom, both economic and political. Bringing mobile phone services to the masses in Africa may help local farmers participate knowingly in world commodity markets, rather than be exploited by local traders. Mobile phones can also participate in grass-roots democracy and the expression of political dissent in countries suffering from repressive regimes. Pharmaceutical and IT companies obviously may have an easier time than others in reframing their purpose in humanitarian and liberating terms, but still, the ability to subsume the mission of a company under a wide ideal – not just shareholders' (or even employees') wealth – is critical.

Fifth, relying on and praising insiders for key roles in strategic renewal, *à la* the IBM strategy team, rather than relying on external consultants (no matter how sound and insightful their advice might be), also contributes strongly to emotional commitment. In fact, although they used expert advice extensively, all the companies studied used outside consultants sparingly and would rather build internal resources, *à la* SAP or Cisco, than engage in large projects with major consultancies. Relying on internal resources created pride of ownership and a sense of responsibility and self-efficacy.

Enabling conditions and limits to using the emotional lever

Not every CEO can use these approaches effectively, however. The use of the emotional lever requires trust, in particular in the CEO (or whoever purposefully attempts to elect and manage collective emotions in the organization). In the absence of a high level of personal trust, attempts at creating emotions will be perceived as manipulative, and suspect. Motives may be unclear, and efforts to handle emotions will be perceived as manipulative, and suspect. Even in good faith, capabilities to handle emotions responsibly are untested. A newcomer with a clean slate and no axe to grind, or a trusted incumbent whose motives and skills are not in doubt, can use the emotional lever effectively, but not every CEO can.

CEOs need to bring to using the emotional lever a style and an authenticity that are in tune, in terms of leadership and interpersonal charisma, with the deep "soul" of the organization they are trying to re-energize. Gerstner was in tune with IBM, in personal style and authenticity. Palmisano, having served as John Akers' executive assistant in the "near death" years and grown into a top executive under Gerstner, embodied both continuity and change, positive and negative emotions. To IBMers, he is very much "one of us". Carly Fiorina, in contrast, was perhaps too alien to the average HP engineer to be fully in tune with HP home-grown executives, and more importantly with the mass of HP professionals.

The reappropriation of the integration theme by Lou Gerstner immediately struck a chord with angry, ashamed, and disgruntled IBMers. Now focussed on services, rather than systems, the integration theme nonetheless credibly evoked memories of IBM's heyday. The articulation of the service theme also evolved in a stepwise development, from basic customer services to "On Demand" process outsourcing to addressing big complex societal problems such as healthcare, education, or disaster relief logistics. Each step was ambitious enough to be a stretch, yet each seemed achievable, ex-ante, and cumulatively built on prior steps.[8]

Following the growth stall of 1997, the retirement of Lew Platt and the appointment of Carly Fiorina in 1999, HP faced a tougher challenge. The heritage, the old identity of the company, did not fit the new reality, and could not be "recast" to make the future credibly look like a return to roots. Two contradictory priorities clashed. First, innovation: Fiorina and her team emphasized innovation, as a way to relaunch the growth of the company. The key internal mobilization and external communication theme of the "spirit of the garage" theme (referring to HP's roots in the garage of one of the founders) suggested an efflorescent organic growth into new areas, driven by innovations. In the HP culture a call for innovation was immediately interpreted as a license for autonomy, not inconsistent with the devolution of authority to business units practiced by Lew Platt in the 1990s. This interpretation quickly clashed with a second priority: integration. Carly Fiorina stressed the need for HP to be more integrated, declaring in an interview: "We have a lot of soloists in that company and what we need is an orchestra".[9]

Although the integrated approach did not face strong intellectual resistance, as people could see the cost of fragmentation, it was difficult to give it a strong meaning. An ambitious strategy dubbed "e-Services", which had been started in one business group in the 1990s as a way to respond to and exploit the internet, was taken up as a corporate theme, but implementation was left to each business group and division. So, except as a way to sensitize the whole organization to how the internet would disrupt existing indirect distribution channels, the content of the e-Services strategy, at the corporate level, remained hard to articulate.

Ann Livermore summarized HP's top management perspective on an integration strategy:

You don't necessarily need to tie together everything you have, just because you have it all, if not because of a true customer need or competitive advantage. Carly [Fiorina] tried to take too much advantage of the portfolio, to tie too many things together. In fact when you look across business groups, really valuable ties are a set of bilateral relationships, mostly. And most innovation, 70 to 80 percent, should really take place within a group. HP's strategic agility is better when innovation is contained within a group. So we need to carefully balance the narrow depth of expertise with the breadth of new growth opportunities.[10]

❝ HP's dominant culture remained a culture of engineers, with engineers' values ❞

HP's dominant culture, internally, also remained one of products, of devices, of hardware, not one of services. It also remained a culture of engineers, with engineers' values. The merger with Compaq, whilst strategically sensible and remarkably well planned and executed, did not add to innovation and integration except, in the latter, by making available to HP the outstanding service and system integration skills the DEC acquisition had brought to Compaq three years earlier.

At IBM, Gerstner first, and then Palmisano more recently, articulated a compelling future that was resonant with the past pride of the company, and provided a clear sense of direction.[11] At HP, reconciling the entrepreneurial and innovative past as the "spirit of the garage" with the search for an integrated value creation logic proved very difficult. The vision around which the integration strategy was built, and justified, was perhaps not compelling enough.

It was really only when HP's top team, under the leadership of Mark Hurd, redefined itself as "The World's Leading IT Infrastructure Company" that a balance between an integrative strategic framework and the decentralized management of individual businesses was struck. Shane Robison commented on this:

We have in here a pretty rich definition of information, data you can store in [a] data warehouse but not just that, rich digital media, audio, video, any combination of the above. It tells us what we do, and what we don't do. A hard copy is a form of information. Digital photography, TVs, home networking hubs, all this is for us IT infrastructure. At the other end of the spectrum, blade servers, super clones and the like are also part of our definition.[12]

Two additional difficulties may have contributed to the weak initial appeal of emotional levers at HP. In typical fashion, and in particular following a proxy battle which pitted the heirs of David Packard against Carly Fiorina, the merger with Compaq had to release substantial savings. Cost reduction measures, and the controls that go with them, undermined values oriented toward innovation. Second, as an outsider, with a very different personal style from that of an HP engineer, Carly Fiorina perhaps found it difficult to get her vision across to the company with sufficient credibility.

It is clear, though, that in both IBM and HP corporate management did not set specific strategies but stated identity, ambition, and boundaries (what we are *not* going to be), for instance, IBM recently stressing it did not want to build, or maintain, a significant consumer products franchise. HP's "The World's Leading IT Infrastructure Company" theme served a similar function. The value of corporate statements often lay more in their motivational value in the emotional realm than in the articulation of a particularly sharp vision in the cognitive realm. The "On Demand" concept represents a philosophy about how to engage the market but does not specify the particulars. Corporate vision was made specific through the interaction between corporate and subunit management (IBM's "deep dives" for established businesses and the EBO process for new ones, or HP's corporate reviews of individual businesses). Corporate management guided the emergence and articulation of business-group level renewal initiatives, and shaped the selection criteria and processes for the commitment to these initiatives.

Values as a key

In the early 2000s, rather than facing a crisis, Palmisano was starting to face complacency at IBM. There was no longer an immediate danger, but in the Gerstner's years the control arm had driven the ambidextrous organization, rather than the entrepreneurial arm. The company was not growing much. Palmisano no longer could exploit the shame of failure emotions that Gerstner had mobilized and turned into positive energy.

Palmisano enjoyed the advantage that IBM had for long been based on values, at least from Tom Watson Jr's days. The best customer service, the pursuit of excellence, and respect for the individual had been the corner-stones of IBM's values for decades. Yet Sam Palmisano and IBMers saw redefining values in the 2000s as an important requirement to re-establish the core of IBM's culture and brand, to expand the brand experience beyond products to integrated solutions and people, to enable and accelerate innovation across the company at all levels, to allow the management systems to leverage global and cross-unit integration, and to enable empowerment, speed, responsiveness, and consistency across the whole organization. Last but not least, the objective was also to get the employees' mandate for transformation, to create a "burning platform" for change, even when "the business is good".

❝the objective was also to get the employees' mandate for transformation❞

In part, recreating a sense of urgency was also built into the concentration of the values redefinition process, culminating in an intense three-day "Value Jam" in July 2003, to which all IBMers were invited to participate online, voicing concerns, issues, and contributing suggestions. All in all, nearly 50,000 employees participated, expressing over 10,000 comments and suggestions. A total of 1.2 million "views" (log-ins) were recorded in three days!

This led to a redefinition of IBM's values, in three major commitments, by a small team around Palmisano:

- dedication to every client's success
- innovation that matters, for our company and for the world
- trust and personal responsibility in all relationships.

A striking characteristic of these values is that they are very externally oriented, stressing client success, innovations for the world (very consistent with the Global Innovation Outlook approach described in chapter 3), and all relationships, including partners in the more open processes that IBM has entered for innovation and market development. In other words, they are articulated around providing guidance for each IBMer in relationships with others, inside and outside, in a way very consistent with what the company is striving to become. As such, they play a cornerstone role, as Palmisano stressed:

Values are the most important part of our whole management system, and the most important part of my job, as they keep our complex globally integrated company together.[13]

Immediate action followed the articulation of values, including, first, the identification of gaps between the newly articulated values and current practice. Reflecting on the experience, Palmisano commented:

You could say; "Oh my God, I've unleashed this incredible negative energy". Or you could say; "Oh, my God, I now have this incredible mandate to drive even more change in the company".[14]

Following the set of Value Jams, Palmisano concluded: "Well the values and the Jam were great inertia-busting vehicles".

Following the Jams, and the definition of new values, an intense communication effort to employees, executives, business partners, customers, and shareholders was undertaken to raise the awareness and the understanding of these values.

Linda Sanford, who headed the e-business of IBM, was put in charge of change. She commented:

This is a deep and complete change of culture. In the mid 1990s we had to ask permission for everything. The shift is really from asking permission to making decisions. As we do this, we have to rely on the values to achieve integration. People have objectives, but their behavior is not controlled. We shifted to start building a culture of trust. You are encouraged to always go beyond the scope of your job, to learn to self-balance your efforts, to stretch yourself, and help others. You get pride and motivation, and start to build reciprocity.[15]

Another on-line Jam – dubbed "Logjam" because its purpose was to identify barriers and blockages to the implementation of new values – took place in October 2004.

Palmisano captured the core of the values-based renewal: "People – rather than products – become your brand".[16]

He also stressed the link to strategic agility:

That's why the right set of values is so important. There is always going to be another strategy on the horizon, as the market changes, as technologies come and go. So we wanted values that would foster an organization able to execute a new strategy quickly. At the same time we wanted values that, like Watson's Basic Beliefs, would be enduring, that would guide the company through economics cycles and geopolitical shifts, and that would transcend changes in products, technologies and leaders.[17]

Laurence Guihard-Joly, who was implementing these actions, commented:

Awareness and understanding [of the new values] initially made people enthusiastic, but then we risk a "well-done" attitude, yet not living these values every day. So we needed a whole series of tangible actions. When we came to October 2004 we said, "We know what's not working, now we need suggestions to solve the problems". Of all that surfaced, there were around 200 suggestions that came back, one way or another, all the time. We selected them; then there were polls on, "What do you really want to implement?" It came to a few practical clusters:

■ *better managers (help us have a better manager)*

■ *client success (lower the center of gravity)*

■ *innovation and growth*

■ *improving the workplace environment.*

It was a way to get a collective "Let's do it" mandate, working up and down informally, to help the values take hold.[18]

A whole series of "scorecard" indicators were then put in place, with employees (values survey, "global pulse" survey, "exit" survey), with clients (experience and satisfaction with IBM), with strategic partners, and more broadly about the overall image of the IBM brand.

By involving all IBMers into painting the image of an ideal future IBM, as each saw it, and aggregating their contributions into a very ambitious and compelling intent, and to then ask all IBMers what current shortcomings were against that ideal painting, Palmisano was able to create a perceptual crisis. "Value Jam" exercises were a way to spread participation, involvement, and to provide a sense of joint outcome ownership.

Summary

This chapter has argued that emotions – positive and negative – are an inescapable fact of organizational life. As such, despite the reluctance of managers to tread on what they see as dangerous ground, they should not be ignored. To restore the strategic agility of stagnating companies, successful leaders capitalize on the tension between positive and negative emotions as a source of constructive energy rather than complacency or despondency. For a corporate leader to use the emotional levers effectively, however, requires great personal credibility and legitimacy – not just the authority and power of position and intellect – rooted in their identity. A sense of belonging "with" or belonging "to" the company is important, an advantage Kagermann at SAP, Palmisano at IBM, or Kallasvuo at Nokia could enjoy, but that most CEOs from the outside found difficult to elicit. Emotional commitment can be elicited in many ways, from the very specific – like rekindling pride or showing care – to the very broad – like appealing to aspiration-driven purposes in society. Collective involvement processes, like redefining values, can also contribute to provide an emotional energy to a company becoming strategically complacent, as IBM was described in the past few years.

References

[1] Authors' interview, Henning Kagermann, Chief Executive Officer, SAP, 6 May 2007.

[2] Authors' meeting, Ted Sapountzis, Vice President, Corporate Group, SAP, and Timmo Sturm, Corporate Strategy Management, Office of the CEO, 19 June 2006.

[3] Authors' interview, Laurence Guihard-Joly, General Manager, Global Electronics Industry, IBM, 13 January 2006.

[4] Lazarus, Richard, *Emotion and Adaptation*, Oxford University Press, 1993.

[5] Huy, Quy N., "How Contrasting Emotions Can Enhance Strategic Agility", paper presented at the Academy of Management, 2007.

[6] von Krogh, Georg, "Care in Knowledge Creation", *California Management Review*, Spring 1998, Vol. 40 Issue 3.

[7] Authors' meeting with Gill Rider, Chief Leadership Officer, Steve Rohleder, Chiel Operating Officer, Jill Smart, Chief Human Resources Officer, and Markko Silén, Chairman of the Nordic Geographic Council, Accenture, 13 February 2006.

[8] Hamel, Gary and Prahalad, C. K., "Strategic Intent", *Harvard Business Review*, May/June 1989, Vol. 67 Issue 3.

[9] Kehoe, Louise, "Fiorina moves to put Hewlett Packard back together", *Financial Times*, 7 December 1999.

[10] Authors' interview, Ann Livermore, Executive Vice President, Technology Solutions Group, HP, 6 February 2006.

[11] Of course, however, one could argue that this did not contribute much to strategic agility *per se*. One could make the point that services and solutions, reinforced with the consulting talent brought by the PwC acquisition, provide an intrinsically more agile business model than the development and manufacturing of computer hardware of operating systems. In other words, IBM both brought a more agile management to its business – as summarized in chapter 3 – but also migrated to a core business, making strategic agility easier to achieve.

[12] Authors' interview, Shane Robison, Executive Vice President and Chief Strategy and Technical Officer, HP, 31 January 2007.

[13] Authors' interview, Sam Palmisano, Chief Executive Officer, IBM, 6 October 2005.

[14] Hemp, Paul and Stewart, Thomas, interview with Sam Palmisano, "Leading Change When Business is Good", *Harvard Business Review*, December 2004, Vol. 82 Issue 12.

[15] Authors' interview, Linda Sanford, Senior Vice President, Enterprise On Demand Transformation and Information Technology, IBM, 13 January 2006.

[16] Hemp and Stewart, 2004.

[17] Ibid.

[18] Authors' interview, Laurence Guihard-Joly, 13 January 2006.

10

Flexing the organization

Organizational structures, and therefore organizational design, are often too much trusted as "the" lever of leadership *par excellence* for rebuilding strategic agility. Conventional wisdom suggests that wise leaders sit down together, once they have decided on a strategy, to design the organization needed to implement it. Organizational structure follows strategy, and is the main implementation tool. This leads to periods of stability, during which a strategy is consistently implemented through a stable structure, followed by moments of change, during which both strategy and structure change. Yet, this conventional model is a source of rigidity, not agility. In that approach, most of the time, structure rigidly drives strategy implementation. This is partly because structure guides managers' attention and interest, and thus influences cognition and commitments. Executives tend to develop strategic projects, plans, and proposals that somehow suit their existing organizational roles and responsibilities, and maximize their rewards in the current operating structure. Strategy also follows structure because structure constrains not just what strategies will be developed, but also what type of strategy can easily be implemented in a given organization. For instance, an agile integration strategy, based on a concept of corporate value creation logic, is hard to implement in a highly devolved organization with many autonomous product lines, each measured on its own results. Smart executives will develop and propose independent subunit commitments that fit well in the organizational structure rather than rock the boat. Thus, by defining "domains" and allocating responsibilities, structures constrain strategy.

While rational, to see structure as a tool of strategy execution is thus quite a restrictive perspective. Structure guides what strategies will be pursued and that, in itself, is a cause of strategic rigidity. Here too, the conventional wisdom of strategy formulation followed by implementation through a new structure and an "aligned" set of management systems fits with a one-time strategic redirection approach but not with the permanent development of strategic agility as a key organizational capability. What is needed here, as discussed in chapter 6, is structural indeterminacy, freeing strategy formulation and resource allocation from structural shackles.

New structures enable, and even generate new strategies. Hence, the organizational lever can be used in many different ways to gain an impact on strategic agility. This chapter first addresses the issue of how to free strategy from structure, i.e., how to build and lead flexible structures that can fast respond to a variety of strategic opportunities. Whether you start from momentum or stagnation, making the core business strategically more agile is an imperative. Multidimensional organizations are a possible answer, provided they are led actively and introduced progressively. Before a summary of how to do this, however, a further word of caution is needed on the limits of organizational design as a lever of leadership.

Beware of putting too much faith in reorganization

❝organizational change comes at the cost of some trauma❞

In the conventional wisdom expounded above, structure is a blunt tool. Periodic reorganizations realign priorities from one axis to another. Were conventional wisdom true, this would be a brutal and clumsy way to jolt the organization toward a different strategic direction. Organizational change comes at the cost of some trauma. Middle managers and staff fear reorganization for obvious reasons: personal adjustment costs are high, task routines and interaction patterns are disrupted, and many may be scared that they will come out a loser. Sparing the members of the organization these periodic realignments is a precondition for strategic agility: strategic change needs to be easier and faster to accomplish, with less trauma and disruption than allowed by reorganization.

Despite the painful realities of reorganization, senior executives sometimes still entertain the illusion that organizational structures can be changed at the stroke of a pen on an organization chart. This is not true. The underlying personal networks are remarkably resilient, perhaps as resilient as cognitive schemes. In many organizations social networks tend to survive –

and outlive – reorganizations. This has often been summarized as the importance of the informal organization. Although intuitively obvious, the importance of the informal organization is none the less often neglected, because it, too, belongs to the hidden part of organizational reality, like cognition and emotions. Turning organizational change into an effective lever for renewal therefore calls for attention to the complementary features of an organization's design, including informal networked relationships. No matter what, the informal multidimensional organization creeps back in. For instance, when Cisco reorganized itself from a product line organization to a global functional one, a series of countervailing mechanisms were introduced to represent other dimensions than the one favored by the formal organization, such as councils around customer groups and market segments, or human resource management policies and practices that emphasized cooperation along other dimensions. Therefore, no single dimension will remain dominant! Social networks, emergent relationships, and various management mechanisms will offset the impact of the structural dimension, and prevent it from gaining or maintaining dominance. The informal organization plays an extremely useful role in softening the impact of the formal organization and providing counterbalances.

Beyond ignoring the trauma often associated with reorganization and giving too much importance in the way they think about organization to the formal structure, executives are tempted to delude themselves about the strength of the organizational lever in yet another way: the search for organizational simplicity. Confronted with multiple strategic dimensions needing attention, no simple, one-dimensional structure can fit. Sam Palmisano, at IBM, captures the issues well:

When you think about it, there is no optimal way to organize IBM. We traditionally were viewed as a large, successful, "well-managed" company. That was a compliment. But in today's fast-changing environment, it's a problem. Think of our organizational matrix . . . Well, if you mapped out the entire 3D matrix, you would get more than 100,000 cells – cells in which you have to close out P/Ls [profit/loss statements] every day, make decisions, allocate resources, make trade-offs. You will drive people crazy trying to centrally manage every one of these interactions.

So, if there is no way to optimize IBM through organizational structure or by management dictate, you have to empower people while ensuring that they are making the right calls in the right way . . . I'm talking about decisions that support and give life to IBM's strategy and brands, decisions that shape a culture.[1]

Palmisano is not alone in formulating such observations. In fact, none of the companies researched could rebuild strategic agility and be organized in a simple way. When looked at close-up, those who professed simplicity, such as Cisco, showed a variety of integrating mechanisms and informal relationships along other dimensions as well. The combination of diverse activities, integration (corporate value-adding) strategies and multiple strategic perspectives and constituencies (customer groups, client industries, applications and connecting plat-forms, products and services, geographical *vs.* global accounts) made the search for true organizational simplicity futile. The possibility of a simple organizational solution was illusory. Organizational flexibility could not be achieved with a simple organization. So, a first way for an organization to contribute to strategic agility is to be multidimensional.

> **a first way for an organization to contribute to strategic agility is to be multidimensional**

The flexible multidimensional organization

The need for a multidimensional organization

In fact, it is the careful but sometimes fragile balancing of multiple dimensions and perspectives in the organization that provides for strategic agility. The companies researched were all trying to free strategy from structure. The more agile the organization, the less the power of organizational design, formal structures in particular. This means that, whatever name they were given by the executives leading them, the organizations studied all had matrix relationships. Roles, responsibilities, and measurements were simultaneously aligned to multiple dimensions. Individual executives whose roles, and performance criteria, were aligned with one particular dimension would obviously give priority to that dimension.

But they also had to engage in collaboration and negotiation with their colleagues representing other dimensions, controlling key interdependencies, in order to serve the dimension along which they were responsible for performance. For instance, client-facing account executive teams negotiate with resource holders – such as the professional or industry units in Accenture – to access the specialists needed to support their clients and to staff their projects adequately. In Accenture, as in all the other companies researched, a multidimensional organization carefully balancing various forces and perspectives was seen as a way to provide strategic agility,

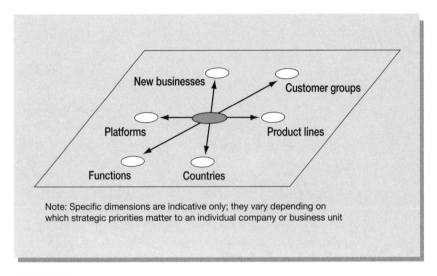

Note: Specific dimensions are indicative only; they vary depending on which strategic priorities matter to an individual company or business unit

figure 10.1 A multidimensional spiderweb organization

through multiple dimensions and priorities being represented in organizational decision-making and resource allocation.

Graphically, such an organization can be depicted as a spiderweb, responding to various priorities through temporary imbalance, but regaining balance afterwards, each of the spokes of the organizational web having both elasticity and resilience (*see* Figure 10.1).

In response to opportunities and threats, the center of gravity of the organization moves in one direction or another, or perhaps a totally different balance is reached temporarily for certain issues, but the organization regains its initial shape and balance, giving attention to multiple perspectives and priorities again, once the issue is dealt with. Organizational elasticity in reaching different balances for different issues is the central capability here.

Optimizing from the middle

Rather than being stably aligned to a single pyramidal organizational hierarchy, a multidimensional organization is by nature flexible and unstable within limits, provided its multiple dimensions are represented by executives who have a say in key decisions. Multidimensional organizations, therefore, require real investment in the quality of management processes and in the effectiveness of executives in developing collaborative behaviors

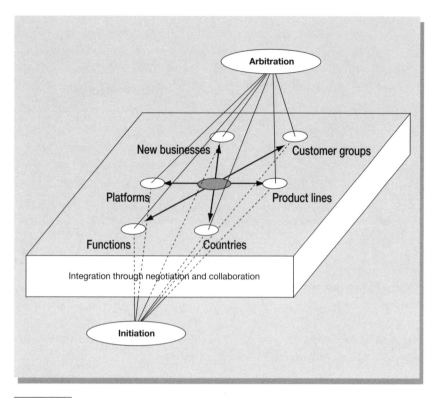

figure 10.2 The organizational diamond

and outcomes. In particular, such an organization requires constant ongoing negotiations and balancing among executives representing each of its dimensions, just as computers constantly adjust the controls of modern fighter planes on all axes. Ideally, such negotiations should take place at intermediate levels in the organization for successful integration between dimensions to be achieved.

Issues, though, have a tendency to float to the surface – i.e., top management – or to sink to the bottom – i.e., the lowest level of subunit management (*see* Figure 10.2).

Floating to the top results in obvious overloading of top management, and a jamming of the decision-making process and crammed agendas, with decisions being postponed or made without sufficient time or information. Sinking to the bottom leads to fragmented commitments by lower-level managers who may lack both the perspective and the self-confidence to make bold, adaptive decisions. It leads to compliance, to what has often been called by researchers "induced" decisions, another source of inertia and thus hardly a good vehicle to contribute to strategic agility, or it leads to fragmented initiatives, and devolved entrepreneurial process that lacks strategic integration.[2] This may provide agility, but not strategic strength.

Letting key decisions float to the top makes the needed negotiations at intermediate levels impossible. It also destroys collaborative capabilities at intermediate levels. Rather than genuinely seek agreement and issue resolution at their own level, middle managers engaged in negotiations at intermediate levels see it in their own interest to delegate upward. Rather than engage in constructive problem-solving, they camp on their own positions, and hope to score points with their own hierarchy by showing their firmness and defeating rivals in the eyes of top management. Positions and arguments become predictable, and discussions stale and sterile.[3] Determined push-back from the top, resisting the pressure for arbitration, is essential to the health of the process.

Guiding commitments

Even when key decisions stay where they need to be, negotiations at intermediate level may still go too well, or too badly. Negotiations going badly create obvious problems: delayed decisions, dissipated energy on internal fights, and ill will and suspicion in the organization. They are obviously debilitating. Strategic paralysis may follow. Negotiations going too well create other, perhaps less obvious but nonetheless real, problems: they reinforce *status quo*. For instance, in a product-geography interface – perhaps the most common interface in matrix organizations – the more easily sold products and the countries where the company is already the strongest will easily agree to joint commitments, to the detriment of smaller – but newer and probably more strategic – products and geographies. Both forms of negotiation are obviously harmful to strategic agility. This calls for a strategic framework within which negotiations can take place. Nokia, for instance, in its latest iteration of a multidimensional organization, has put in place a corporate roadmapping process which pulls together the various perspectives embedded in dimensions of its organization, products, services, and customer groups into a corporate-wide map of which products and services to offer to which types of customers. This provides a common context within which to make decisions and reach constructive future-oriented strategic trade-offs.

Obviously, the mechanisms described in chapter 6 which provide discipline and fluidity in resource allocation also have a role to play here. In sum, putting in place a multidimensional organization helps foster strategic agility, but also presents its own risk. Introducing such an organization on unprepared ground, and without strong complementary measures fostering lateral collaboration and guiding decisions at intermediate management levels in the organization, may actually be very detrimental to strategic agility.

Leading from the bottom

IBM, post-Gerstner, was putting emphasis, strategically, on global customers but had inherited the relatively heavy structure of a prosperous, traditional, multidomestic, multinational corporation. While Lou Gerstner had shifted the balance within that organization away from national responsiveness toward a partially more global approach, eliminating the national baronies of a multidomestic organization and "lightening" corporate and regional staffs, in Europe in particular, he had not fundamentally transformed the nature of the organization.

The account executives and their teams still found themselves dependent on the successful negotiation of their projects up a relatively complex geographic (territorial) hierarchy, and through a wide array of businesses and product lines. Whereas Gerstner had built an ambidextrous organization, with a lot of financial and operating discipline on existing activities (and the thorough "deep dive" review process), complemented after a few years by an entrepreneurial arm (the EBOs), Palmisano set to build a truly agile organization. To become real, though, this would require the organization to be "driven" by the account executives, as "front line" entrepreneurs, mobilizing and mustering support and resources from the rest of the organization. From other difficult attempts, such as those of ill-fated DEC a decade earlier, it is clear how difficult such a delegation and devolution process actually is. Liz Smith, a key executive at IBM describes the organization:

We have integrated market teams (IMTs), essentially as field organization entrepreneurial units. We have client-facing organizations by services, and by industries. Essentially, they have delegation on prices, technologies, and offer choices. They can operate their business locally. There is no more European organization per se, but two Integration Operations Teams (essentially Northern/Eastern Europe and Southern Europe and Africa) which support the IMTs with HR, finance, and marketing, manage the interface with global clients (served on a global basis, not via IMTs) and can also be centers of excellence.[4]

" the success of a multidimensional organization, in particular when led from the bottom, depends on the energy put into it "

To a very large extent, the success of a multidimensional organization, in particular when led from the bottom, depends on the energy put into it.[5] IBM could only make progress because account executives acted indeed as "front line entrepreneurs". This resulted partly from their strong profile (e.g., many were high-level ex-PwC consultants and IBM senior line managers), partly from extrinsic rewards (high-powered incentives), and partly from the thrill of the job. Managers in an emotionally toneless context, on the other hand, are not unlikely to be passive in a multidimensional organization: the weight of caring for all the interfaces and collaboration needed to get something done pulls them into inaction, into being reactive perhaps, but abandoning taking initiatives.

This may explain why: whereas top management at HP saw the potential of strategic integration to develop entirely new growth avenues, lower down in the organization such integration was sometimes perceived as the encouragement of bureaucratic interdependencies. Enthusiastic, highly emotionally-committed managers will "play" a multidimensional organization most effectively, less enthusiastic ones will shrink under the weight of interdependencies.

The recent experience of HP is revealing in this respect. According to Shane Robison:

If you get the foundations of a healthy business re-established, you get momentum, and there is no substitute for momentum. Momentum gives self-confidence, and self-confidence gives you the willingness to take risks, to experiment. We gave more autonomy to the businesses, dismantled some of the big integrated corporate groups, and they now work together much better than before.[6]

Indeed, more self-confident executives, who find the security of momentum in their own business, will more easily engage in wholehearted and voluntary, rather than imposed, collaboration.

Fostering normative control

A complementary lever of strategic agility, beyond adopting a multidimensional organization, is to shift from (bureaucratic) behavior control, i.e., rules and procedures to follow, to normative control, i.e., to integrate collective actions around common and shared norms and values to adhere to.

In other words, strategic agility calls for executives to make, on their own initiative and of their own choice, decentralized decisions in a way that expresses common norms and values, and a shared concern with the success of the whole organization. Of course, this does not eliminate the need for ex-ante planning and ex-post control (budgetary control, goal setting, measurements, and evaluation, etc.) nor does it make personal incentives unimportant, but these need to reflect collective success, not individual prowess. (For instance, in all the companies we saw try to rebuild strategic agility, incentives for senior executives were increasingly based on overall corporate success, and less and less on subunit success.)

So, how to accomplish real change?

To be effective, organizational levers need time to take hold, and time for their consequences to be felt. Normative control, of course, cannot just be decreed. It is rooted in values that need to be discovered and sincerely felt to become effective. The process of defining IBM's new values in the 2000s (described in chapter 9) shows how much effort and time this requires. There are many examples of botched reorganizations, where ignoring the need for changes in systems and processes (not just structure), and for being patient and thoughtful in letting new processes take hold, led to ineffective outcomes. Worse, such "incomplete" reorganization also breeds the typical cynicism of *plus ça change, plus c'est pareil* as the French bureaucrats say ("the more it changes, the more it stays the same").

Making the organization flexible

A new, more flexible organization in the mind

New dimensions of organization, when responding to a need for widening the trajectory of possible future development, not starting from a crisis, first need to gain intellectual justification. Interestingly, Nokia did not move directly to a multidimensional organization, but it evolved into it, the first step being the mapping of value domains as a way to think about business boundaries and market segments. The value domains started to map out and define, cognitively, potential new boundaries between activities. Their definition drew virtual boundaries in the mind of managers, who started developing market segmentation, marketing, strategy, and value creation logics based on them. It was only in 2004, two years later, that Nokia put in place a multidimensional organization consisting of four vertical businesses (stemming from the value domains) supported by two common horizontal units concentrating on sales and marketing, operations, logistics, and sourcing, as well as common technology platforms.

Starting with the more flexible parts of the activity system

Some elements of a business system may be intrinsically more plastic, more flexible than others. Reorganizing the "front end" (i.e., customer-facing) part of a company may be easier than refocussing major industrial investments. Focussing this more flexible part on redefined market creation opportunities allows one to trigger real change. That is essentially what NMP did as response to the market slowdown recognized in mid-2001. It redefined itself in spring 2002 as a set of nine value domains. Some of these were a mere relabeling of existing activities and organizational units in the mobile phones domain, but some were genuinely new. These new domains, together with ventures such as mobile TV in Nokia's Ventures Organization, provided the motivating stretch toward new areas, such as multimedia, entertainment, and enterprise. Interestingly, in Nokia, allocating camera phones – a runaway success as a product – to a new imaging domain, and later, in 2004, mobile TV from Nokia Ventures to a new business group, Nokia Multimedia, provided both a wider framing to camera phones and a substantive business "reality" to the multimedia group.

Redirection gathered momentum as NMP set up its nine different value domains in spring 2002. By focussing the organization on market opportunities, with shared logistics and technology platforms (on top of the corporate-wide business infrastructure) and support services, it provided for greater agility. This organizational change also successfully tested Nokia's common modular Business Infrastructure (BI) that improved both process and IT efficiency but also resource fluidity.

Rather than face a very rigid activity system, in which very little could be changed, new opportunities could now be placed in smaller units that could be freer to develop their own perspectives and priorities and make them evolve. These smaller units still benefited from shared logistics, technology platforms, and business infrastructure: the "plug and play" business processes and IT systems described in chapter 6. Interestingly, here too Nokia's experience was one of learning and action. The development of flexibility and fluidity was an iterative process over time.

Varying autonomy and interdependence

A complementary approach to putting in place a multidimensional organization and rebalancing control mechanisms in favor of normative control is to build ambiguity and change potential by related venturing, i.e., not falling into the usual trap of an unrelated corporate venturing process – from which little of relevance and importance comes – or of venturing too close to the core growth trajectory, at the expense of true renewal or, for that matter, of agility. What is needed is not just an ambidextrous organization, with separate arms doing very different things, in a different way, but an organization that can flexibly adjust its venturing further away or closer to the core, and manage individual ventures in a more or less differentiated way over time. IBM's EBO (Emerging Business Opportunities) venture process allows for such flexibility, but most companies have relatively more basic processes, which may not allow such flexibility.

What is important here is not just to be able to manage different ventures in a more or less differentiated way, closer or further from the core, but also to be able to vary such differentiation over time, for any given venture. Some ventures will become new businesses, and, in turn, new growth platforms spawning new businesses. Others will disappear or be spun-off. Others, still, will be merged back into existing businesses, like "SAP Portals" and "SAP Markets" for SAP.

To answer such uncertainty one needs to differentiate between mechanisms that allow substantive business-building differentiation – running an EBO is not the same as a core business group in IBM – and processes that foster ongoing interdependence and allow for reintegration, for instance rewards and incentives (collaboration is difficult between people subject to totally different incentives with very different personal risk and reward profiles).[7]

In the process of restoring strategic agility, the relationship between existing core businesses and new activities cannot be fully anticipated. Some new ventures may turn out to be springboards for new businesses, and better left to grow into a business division on their own. Some may give birth to new core technologies to be used in a plurality of businesses. Some may best be combined with a specific business unit. Strategically, their relationship may be such that there is no interdependence with existing core businesses, or that they become complements, or even, substitutes. As discussed earlier, their forward fit, or misfit, is hard to anticipate.

> **"forward fit, or misfit, is hard to anticipate"**

In Nokia, two mechanisms allowed for such flexibility. First, the combination of NVO, NMP's own business development efforts, and the focus on "value domains" as a series of strategic spaces – and later of organizing principles and boundaries – allowed for varied and changing differentiation – and greater or lesser distance – between core and renewal activities. So, as

Nokia cognitively moved from the well-marked "3G" trajectory to encompass a wider landscape over vast territories it was able to "populate" that newly discovered space with a plurality of ventures and exploration activities, closer or further from the existing core business. Second, once these activities turned into real businesses, the various platforms, starting with Business Infrastructure, allowed swift deployment – and potentially withdrawal too – in a way more or less related to the core businesses. New business domains and product units could be set relying on the shared infrastructure, either as strategically separate units or as part of wider groups.

Of course, putting in place these two capabilities did not happen overnight. In a way, as seen in chapter 8, the complementary nature of the various renewal efforts was to an extent serendipitous, from "intellectual leadership" theories and real worries about excessive focus on a single core business, to the burgeoning of a wide territory for mobile communication and entertainment multimedia applications. The emergence of organizational variety and flexibility both enabled and followed cognitive broadening, in an iterative way. Flexibility emerged almost as a side product of an emphasis on e-business, in the wake of the dotcom craze of the late 1990s.

Summary

In most traditional corporations, structure is a limit to strategic agility: new strategic directions require new structures, and reorganization is traumatic, takes time to be put in place, and often remains ineffective because key aspects of the informal organization are ignored rather than allowed to contribute. A flexible, multidimensional organization, as most companies in our research build and try to make work, provides a way to free strategic direction from structural rigidity. This is a key enabler to strategic agility.

References

[1] Hemp, Paul and Stewart, Thomas, interview with Sam Palmisano, "Leading Change When Business is Good", *Harvard Business Review*, December 2004, Vol. 82 Issue 12.

[2] Burgelman, Robert A., *Strategy is Destiny: How Strategy-Making Shapes a Company's Future*, Free Press, 2002.

[3]   The authors are grateful to Prof. Benjamin Phillips for helping articulate the insight.

[4]   Authors' interview, Liz Smith, General Manager, Infrastructure Access Services, IBM Global Technology Services, 13 January 2006.

[5]   Ghoshal, Sumantra and Bartlett, Christopher, *The Individualized Corporation: A Fundamentally New Approach to Management*, HarperBusiness, 1997.

[6]   Authors' interview, Shane Robison, Executive Vice President and Chief Strategy and Technology Officer, HP, 31 January 2007.

[7]   Doz, Yves, Angelmar, Reinhard, and Prahalad, C. K., "Technological Innovation and Interdependence: A Challenge for the Large, Complex Firm", *Technology in Society*, 1985, Vol. 7.

11

Depoliticizing top management

The political lever is key to unlocking stalemates. No amount of organizational tweaking and flexing will in itself re-energize an organization. Multidimensional organization, varying levels of entrepreneurial autonomy and strategic integration, and an emphasis on values as mechanisms for normative control (norms based on and driven by organizational culture) are preconditions to strategic agility but, by themselves, will not allow companies to restore strategic agility. Political levers are important in unlocking a situation, in ending an organizational stalemate – or bureaucratic paralysis. Political dysfunctions breed cynicism and undermine emotional commitment, they feed skepticism and apathy, the more it (the organization) changes, the more it stays the same. Like members of a public who feel their vote has lost significance, employees can become unengaged. The use of the political lever is perhaps most important not just to unblock a situation but also as early symbolic action of re-energizing an organization.

Indeed, strategic redirection can only seldom take place without changes in the distribution of power and influence in the organization. A typical organization, though, evolves into a very stable pyramid with decentralized, self-contained roles and responsibilities, and outcome control ("get your results or get out") prevailing, something not very different from baronies of yore. In that logic, the CEO deals with the head of each unit on a one-to-one basis, privately, face-to-face (or perhaps in a series of ongoing – often daily – separate phone conversations if they are geographically distant). What interdependencies there are, are handled in a mutual avoidance mode through a ritualized process. Executive board meetings, for instance, become highly structured events, with no time for any free-flowing exchange. The implicit ground rules of such meetings are of the

"Don't trundle on my turf and I won't on yours" or "Scratch my back and I scratch yours" variety. In other words they are built around avoidance or bilateral reciprocity behaviors (i.e., you don't challenge or embarrass your colleagues, nor do they, and you return help without asking questions). The juxtaposition of expert power, with each member of the top management group having their area of expertise (business domain, function, issue set, etc.) and deferring to others for other areas, kills any possibility of true dialogue, or even of open disagreement. Disagreement is expressed privately, or through passive-aggressive behavior, undermining the very possibility of making collective decisions. What interdependency there needs to be is handled not through the development of shared commitments in meetings, but through a series of "private" side-deals, negotiated one by one before a meeting. The meeting is then just a tightly scripted play to register publicly the set of pre-existing agreements.

Why are relationships among top management difficult to change?

❝patterns of leadership unity, or disunity, show remarkable resilience❞

Patterns of leadership unity, or disunity, show remarkable resilience. Roles, mutual perceptions and interactions change remarkably little. To an extent, of course, roles are defined by the cognitive and the organizational contexts, but once set they become anchored in social networks and interpersonal relationships, both of which typically transcend structural arrangements. This is obviously further reinforced in a winning team, the members of which know each other very well, as was true both at Nokia and SAP. A common past, and shared formative experiences, are therefore mixed blessings.

There is also in top teams an early "labeling" of people and roles, in other words, reputations of positions and individuals are established, or limited, all too quickly. Even in companies that have for long already practiced elaborate executive leadership development processes, 360-degree assessments and the like, beyond the formal process looms a more impressionistic "labeling" of individuals, often as the result of an early imprinting acquired in their first managerial roles. Whatever their careers, and the changes of organizational contexts, these labels tend to endure, and are difficult for an individual to shed.

Existing languages – the way executives express their own experiences and articulate how they think of their business – in companies that had built their industries, and whose cultures remain strongly imprinted by their home country origins, provide another challenge to changing interactions at the top. Resistance to the adoption of new language because it indirectly challenges old competencies, and attempts to remedy past "blind spots" in the competence development of the companies, may be strong. Bringing senior marketing executives from Nike or Coca Cola to Nokia, for instance, challenged the primacy of engineering, or even of product interface design (a strong point of Nokia) over other, less technical, dimensions of marketing. Giving content to appealing marketing slogans and terminology was difficult. Similarly at SAP, implanting the concept of ecosystems and the more subtle, partly collaborative partly competitive, relationship the "platform to an ecosystem" approach implies, required a significant mindset and culture evolution. This is not only a cognitive problem; it also highlights past limitations and deficiencies.

Personal fears of inadequacy, therefore, also limit change. To create collective commitment and energy, all the key executives who are going to drive renewal must know they are unambiguously in for the journey, unless they stumble or falter badly. Part of the challenge at HP a few years back was the fact that key old-time heroes were still around, pretty much as "sacred cows", and did not necessarily all support, or perhaps trust, an outside CEO. Some had earned their stripes by creating, in an act of autonomous entrepreneurship, some of HP's most successful businesses – printers first and foremost. Perhaps the most basic change Mark Hurd made early in his tenure was to renew the top team, essentially keeping only two very senior operating executives – Ann Livermore and Joshi Vyomesh – from the old team at the top. Shane Robison, the CTO, came to HP with the Compaq merger, and the new Chief Administrative Officer was a longtime controller. By the time Palmisano launched into making IBM a strategically agile company, he had a rather stable team, with a good mix of IBM old-timers and relatively new blood, and he could count on their support through the journey.

Given such resilience to patterns of roles, mutual perceptions, and relationships, it is illusory to expect political changes to be proactively undertaken in the absence of a crisis. At several times during Nokia's heyday, partial organizational changes – such as the introduction of regional management, or even the changes of roles among top executives in 1998 – had relatively little lasting impact. Only the deeper strategy work undertaken post-2001, both at business group and corporate level, and the progressive refocussing and reorganization of NMP into value domains and business subgroups, led to real organizational context transformation – the 2004 reorganization that, in turn, drove the changes in the composition of the top team.

Using the political levers: what can be done?

How can you break such a political system before it's too late? Essentially, you can reverse the drift towards politics by changing the stakes among key executives through reintroducing interdependencies between their action agendas, thereby calling for greater negotiation and integration skills in order to manage interdependences effectively.

Reintroduce interdependencies

It is obviously no coincidence that all the incumbent companies researched were articulating and implementing integrative strategies that strove for single, common, corporate value creation logic, not a portfolio approach. Obviously, convergence in the ICT industry drove these integrative strategies. This convergence, beyond "horizontal" disruptions such as the spread of the internet and all the threats and opportunities that offered, created the need to increase interdependencies between the action agendas of key leaders. Increasing interdependencies between them forced a re-engagement of members of the senior team into a collective process. Interdependencies can be reintroduced or increased in numerous ways, in particular:

- **Organizing by functions.** Distributing responsibilities at the top by functions, like Cisco, or by various steps in the value chain, like SAP.

- **Integrating via common activities and resources.** Combining horizontal "resource" units and "vertical" business units, like HP and Nokia, so commitments are made jointly between resource providers and resource users.

There are many other ways to achieve interdependencies, like the interdependent roles discussed in chapter 5. No matter what the specifics, they share a common underlying principle: to provide a shared, operational, and strategic agenda between members of the top group. That agenda requires substantive collaboration, very different from the stylized, financial-control-based, vertical relationships characteristic of a traditional organization by business units.

Manage interdependencies effectively

Interdependencies, however, are only as good as their management. What does it take to manage interdependencies effectively?

❛❛ General Electric's famed "Town Meetings" brought together multiple levels of management and all employees of a site ❜❜

First, it requires transparency and honesty. Transparency and honesty not only stem from "see through" accounting and performance assessments, although these are also essential building blocks. In addition, it requires a management that can "reach through", either formally (as in General Electric's famed "Town Meetings" which brought together multiple levels of management and all employees of a site, and other such processes) or informally (like Steve Jobs at Apple informally taking personal leadership of a product development team and delving into the specifics of the project). Rules and cultures of generalized reciprocity among middle managers also encourage transparency and honesty, but obviously the examples need to be set from the top!

"See through" and "reach through" capabilities can also be set up laterally, via overlaid organization and processes. Nissan's famed "Cross Company Teams" or "Cross Functional Teams", for instance, fostered transparency, honesty and discipline, by putting in place processes to challenge executives in the existing organization, leave them no room to hide, and put them under pressure.[1] These teams were set up at the initiative of Carlos Ghosn, the CEO, who selected members personally, and oversaw the teams' progress. Occasionally team members would have to challenge their own hierarchy, for instance on cost and performance issues. These teams forced a much higher level of interdependence in an otherwise bureaucratic organization, and provided the CEO with a powerful steering mechanism and a way to challenge ingrained patterns of interaction and build new relational networks.

Second, managing interdependencies effectively requires first-hand depth of understanding, and substantive mastery of key issues. In other words, the effective and timely handling of interdependencies needs to leave no room to hide and procrastinate. The leadership process is collective, substantive, and "real time". This may be formalized (as in Canon's "morning meetings" where time is set aside, every day, for the top team to meet without a preset agenda, including members who link up via teleconferencing) or kept informal (as in HP's executive suite where close physical co-location and layout ensures frequent encounters among top executives[2]). Such a process can work effectively only if executives share enough of a common understanding of each other's areas and issues, rather than take refuge in the comfort of their own expertise. Partly overlapping expertise, and careers that have spanned different areas and different managerial roles, obviously help here.

Third, and a natural corollary of the two points above, managing interdependencies effectively also requires interaction time as a top team. Crowded agendas and the almost exclusive focus on "review mode" business assessments that characterize the working of so many executive committees need to yield to more interactive dialogue time, as in Canon. This may require members of the executive groups to devote more and more time to corporate-wide matters, and also to adjust emotionally the balance between their subunit role and corporate role in favor of the latter.

Fourth, norms of interaction and engagements in meetings of the top team need to change to foster an open, in-depth dialogue. Norms can be made to change indirectly, by doing away with the "props" of formality, distance, and avoidance, such as Lou Gerstner banning "foils" (overhead transparencies and PowerPoint presentations) by removing projectors from all meeting rooms and excluding executive assistants from IBM's meetings. Norms can also be changed more directly by the power of example and the enforcement of discipline.

More open, less formal norms of interaction can take hold, however, only if there is enough mutual respect and mutual esteem among members on the team. In many companies, mutual respect comes from "having earned your stripes", and hence carrying credibility and loyalty.

At SAP and Nokia, for instance, most of the top team members had made it through the ranks – and earned their reputation and credibility on the way.

Informal interactions among top managers also stem from bringing value personally, i.e. from one's ability to contribute insight and deepen understanding in an open dialogue process. As Soichiro Honda, the car company's founder, used to say: "We are all equal in front of new knowledge." This became a principle of management embedded in the Honda culture, and a challenge to the culture of deference so characteristic of Japan.

Mutual understanding is also key. Not just some substantive understanding of each other's areas of responsibility and expertise, but a more personal understanding of individual motives, agendas, and ambitions. The more transparency in how each individual member keeps score, not just at the obvious level of title, compensation, and pride, but at the deeper one of private self-esteem, intrinsic rewards, and inner drives, the greater the ability to function as a team that fosters strategic agility rather than paralysis. Henning Kagermann at SAP, for instance, made it a point to invite his whole top management team for extended weekend retreats, so they could share more about what they truly valued and cared for.

Lastly, separating position from persona is a must. Recognizing individual value and contribution, independent from the particular position that person holds and the roles they currently play, allows more equality in team belonging, irrespective of who is "more equal" than others, operationally, at a given time. At IBM, for instance, sending some of the key "barons" from existing core businesses to head small embryonic EBO ventures contributed to this understanding. It also makes the flexibility to subsequently reallocate roles and responsibilities much greater.

Of course not everyone, senior executives in particular, can adapt to such a change of rules, so some will depart. This just needs to be handled gracefully by all. Although they seem to diffuse responsibility, the relational processes at the top discussed and suggested here are much more demanding on the quality of individuals than in a conventional hierarchy.

Aligning the top team

❛❛ the alignment of individual and collective interest is vital ❜❜

Beyond the maturity of a trusted team, the alignment of individual and collective interest is vital. Leadership unity, and the pre-eminence of corporate roles, are central issues here. In its 2002 reorganization, for instance, HP allocated to the same handful of executive committee members both subunit (business group) and corporate function/customer group roles, with a clear signal from CEO Carly Fiorina that the corporate roles were at least as important as the subunit ones. To emphasize the point, rewards for the members of HP's top team were 100 percent aligned with overall corporate, not subunit, performance. According to Shane Robison:

The businesses operate under a common set of goals and objectives, and teamwork is better than we have seen in many years. Incentives are aligned.[3]

Beyond alignment of formal rewards, clarity of intrinsic personal rewards (and personal concerns and fears) among top team members is key. Knowing what colleagues really draw satisfaction from, and what they most fear to see happen, is critically important. This may be easier among senior executives who have been "growing up" together and have had plenty of opportunities to see what made each other "tick", than within a newly appointed executive group.

Related to tenure and longevity, the buildup of a collective identity is also important. Beyond the Tower of Babel problem of newly composed executive teams – when the abstraction and context of individual members' languages vary greatly, making mutual understanding particularly difficult – motives of members, and ways in which they perceive reality and process information, remain ambiguous. Such ambiguity is only slowly renewed by interaction, observation, and reflection, over time.

Continuity *vs.* change in the top team

There are huge advantages to working with people you have known for years and you trust – but conversely too much familiarity can stifle renewal. The longer executive teams are in place and the less turnover there is, the more homogenous the team members' experiences and understanding become.[4] Predefined roles and personal loyalties, and maybe pecking order, easily grow too deep and overriding, and prevent true dialogue on alternative strategies and solutions. Over time, incremental learning processes, i.e., more of the same based on cumulative experience, overwhelm whatever diversity of experience and knowledge may have characterized the team earlier on.

As discussed earlier, the "lifecycle" of Nokia's top team was successfully extended by renewing the key members' roles and responsibilities in 1998. These actions brought new energy and perspective to top team players at the time when the organization's core business entered a new phase (Nokia took the number one position from Motorola in mid-1998). However, more drastic measures were needed in 2004 when the business paradigm changed. So, relational changes were needed and they were conducted in connection to a major organizational change. The organization put in place in early 2004 effectively created a matrix throughout the organization, between the four vertical subunits and three groups of horizontal activities.

The roles, skills, attitudes, and mindsets required of a senior executive in a matrix were fundamentally different from those required of the leader of a huge – self-standing – organization, as Nokia Mobile Phones had grown into. The same was true of Nokia Networks. The contrast was perhaps made even stronger, in Nokia, by the role specialization that had developed at the top in the late 1990s and early 2000s. Jorma Ollila, together with Pekka Ala-Pietilä, President, and Olli-Pekka Kallasvuo, CFO, were handling investor and other external relations, finance and other shared support services, corporate governance, new ventures, and corporate research. From a situation in which roles were self-standing, and autonomous, the reorganization brought a shift to a much more interdependent one, where resource allocation and key decisions had to be made collaboratively. This called for more leadership unity.

Alahuhta at NMP and Baldauf at NET were, *de facto*, acting as CEO/COO of their respective business groups. Post-2004, this changed. After a period as head of strategy and research, and overseeing of several shared corporate functions (such as business infrastructure and IPR) where he obviously did not find the same autonomy and full accountability he enjoyed as head of NMP, Alahuhta left Nokia when the opportunity to head another major Finnish company, KONE, presented itself. Baldauf, too, left the company in late 2004 to spend more time on non-profit activities and with both entrepreneurial and major corporations as a non-executive director. In late 2005 also, Pekka Ala-Pietilä chose to leave the company to pursue entrepreneurial opportunities. For key executives, doing what they have learned to like and what their experience has been built upon is of key importance. And experiences seldom repeat themselves in the same company.

Except for Anssi Vanjoki, who embodied the market-oriented entrepreneurial tradition, and Veli Sundbäck responsible for corporate relations, by mid-2006 the whole top team had changed, with of course the exception of Olli-Pekka Kallasvuo, who became CEO in mid-2006. Apart from one, all the new executive board members had worked for Nokia more than five years, many of them much longer. But they had not worked as a top team before and new patterns of relationship would develop among them.

Rather than changing the key leaders of its organization, SAP took a different approach in connection to a paradigm shift. It augmented the capacity of the top team, with selective additions, and much more extensive support. Shai Agassi was brought to SAP's executive board after SAP acquired his company; Leo Apotheker, from within, was the only other addition of recent years. Second, as seen in chapter 4, SAP built a strong internal corporate strategy team, reporting directly to the CEO, and working closely with him and the top team to provide analytical depth, intellectual insight, and political neutrality to the work of the executive board. So, by 2007, SAP was on a path to rebuild strategic agility – without having had to renew, or much change, the composition of its top team. But again, the change at SAP was a confirmation of SAP's entrepreneurial origins and identity: "Don't forget we are all German software writers," one

❝the change at SAP was a confirmation of SAP's entrepreneurial origins and identity❞

of SAP's executive board members told us. The danger was indeed to fall back to the very responsive and problem-solving oriented, but in a way "a-strategic", culture of the "old" SAP. The corporate strategy group team, as well as the selective use of new blood, provided ways to guard against that risk.

Summary

Perhaps the most obvious lever of leadership, changes in the composition and working of the top team – political changes at the top – are a powerful way to break set patterns of behaviors and relationships that stifle strategic agility. However, as should be abundantly clear, political changes do not suffice to rebuild strategic agility: a one-time jolt is not the same as permanently embedding capabilities. Hence, as will be shown in the concluding chapter, political changes at the top can only be part of a wider range of levers of leadership used together in a careful sequence.

References

[1] Huy, Quy, "Building Emotional Capital for Strategic Renewal: Nissan (1999–2002)", INSEAD case study, 2004.

[2] Authors' interviews, Ann Livermore (21 October 2004, 25 April 2005 and 7 February 2006) and Shane Robinson (7 February 2006), respectively Executive Vice-President Technology Solutions Group and Executive Vice-President and Chief Strategy and Technology Officer, HP.

[3] Authors' interview, Shane Robison, 31 January 2007.

[4] Keck Sara and Tushman, Michael, "Environmental and Organizational Context and Executive Team Structure", *Academy of Management Journal*, December 1993 Vol. 36 Issue 6.

12

Conclusion

Coming back to the challenges of complexity and speed of change with which this book opened, companies need strategic agility most when they face complex, interdependent, fast changes. Using the cognitive lever to increase strategic sensitivity of an organization is a key to improving its ability to handle complexity and emergent systemic change. Emotional commitment allows faster and more decentralized responses, so using the emotional lever enables fast strategies.

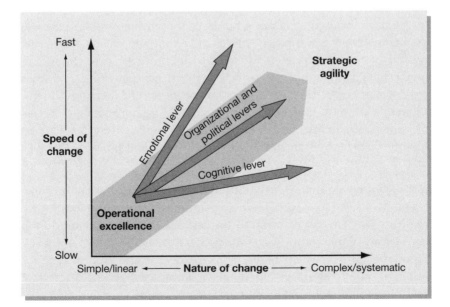

figure 12.1 Leadership levers as drivers of strategic agility

As Figure 12.1 illustrates, active use of cognitive and emotional levers of leadership are the key contributors to the fast strategy game and hence help companies thrive on change.

Contingencies

How can CEOs best use the four levers of leadership explored in the previous chapters: cognitive, emotional, organizational, and political?

Not all journeys toward strategic agility start in the same place. Among the many possible ways to describe and analyze the various starting positions, one stands out as particularly important in helping us think about the differences we observed in the sample of companies considered, both in the sequences of action taken by CEOs, and in their effectiveness. As argued in chapter 7, some companies started from a position of great success and strong momentum, but conditions were changing around them unexpectedly, mostly stemming from the internet disruption. Although threatened, both Nokia and SAP in the early 2000s were still successful. SAP was running out of room to grow with its traditional business model (well suited to Fortune 1000 companies and limited to enterprise integration platforms, a market SAP had essentially created and fully captured). Nokia was hostage to the unrealistic expectations that operators placed on 3G WAP-based (wireless access protocol) data applications, and to the huge commitments made by the European operators to purchase 3G licenses from governments. Although vibrant and outstandingly successful, both companies had to transform their core businesses fundamentally. They had exceedingly high momentum along a business development trajectory that would no longer secure their longer-term success. In contrast, IBM, and to some extent HP (the phenomenal success of printers was hiding weaknesses elsewhere), were starting from a position of stagnation. Both had faced growth stalls, and prolonged periods of slow growth.

Not all journeys to strategic agility aspire to the same destination. For some organizations, as seen with IBM, they are reaffirming the identity of a company that has lost its way, i.e., the destination evokes a return to the real identity of the company. For others, a journey is a voyage of discovery, the destination of which needs to be discovered and defined. HP, for instance, was trying to discover new opportunities that would integrate capabilities and skills from its various business groups.

Figure 12.2 sketches these basic distinctions.

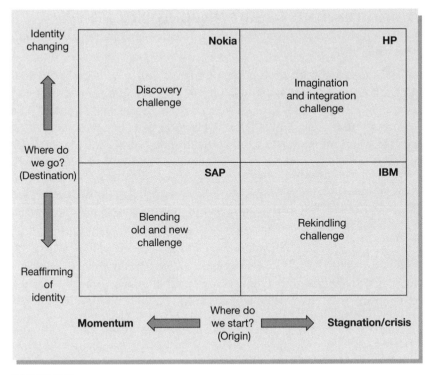

figure 12.2 Key contingencies in regaining strategic agility

A challenge of discovery from a position of momentum, as seen in the discussion of Nokia in chapter 8, calls mostly for new cognition to be made to grow and emerge. A challenge of transforming a business but reaffirming its underlying identity, also calls for new cognition, but such cognition can be accepted and made one's own more easily, as it evokes and reinforces the past identity of the company. The true challenge here is blending the new and the old so the transformation toward greater agility is progressive, and can capitalize on the past identity. Starting from stagnation calls for emotional recommitment and rekindling, as stressed in chapter 9, and is obviously easier when the change can be framed to reaffirm past cherished identity credibly (IBM) than when it has to discover new value creation logics (HP). This chapter starts with a capsule comparative summary of the four journeys – of Nokia, SAP, HP, and IBM.

From momentum to strategic agility

Nokia's journey

Nokia's journey toward strategic agility spans a decade, at least. In the mid-1990s, both a corporate effort to launch a corporate venturing activity and a business group renewal effort in Nokia Mobile Phones were launched. The corporate effort was a formal effort, Nokia Mobile Phones was more of an emergent and informal effort, supported discreetly from the top, both for business applications (the first "communicator") and for consumer application (the "Calypso" project leading to the first camera phone). Energies and emotions were mobilized around the core business, growing by about 50 percent every year, and gaining industry leadership – in sales volume – in 1998. So, as seen in chapter 8, the first phase of the journey was not driven by a sense of urgency, but perhaps more by a feeling of curiosity: what more could be done around mobile phones?

❝ Nokia's journey toward strategic agility spans a decade, at least ❞

This triggered a whole series of steps around Nokia ventures, new ventures, considerations of various business areas, false starts (too early in fact) in some areas like WLAN (wireless local area network). Beyond their own merits – leading in a few cases to major new growth opportunities such as mobile television – they cumulatively provided learning opportunities, and widened the perspective – among senior Nokia executives – about the future growth and renewal of the company. Perhaps most importantly, these efforts countered the loss of strategic sensitivity that would result from brilliant core business success and codependence on major operators.

In other words, the renewal process started with a rather prolonged period of cognitive learning. Nokia Mobile Phones' own efforts were closer to the growth path of the core business and, as they gathered momentum, led to a commitment to a greater range of growth opportunities. To make these growth opportunities more visible, more tangible, "value domains" (market segments) were defined, and strategic resource commitments began to be made according to these domain definitions. Although these domains did not organizationally turn into full business units, the customer-facing side of Nokia started to respond to the differentiation they implied. This contributed to the reorganization of the company into four businesses (networks, phones, multimedia, and enterprise solutions) and major "horizontal" platforms for R&D, standards and product architecture, logistics, and customer-facing sales organizations in various countries and regions.

Cognitive changes provided legitimacy to and were reflected in organizational changes. It was expected that over time the three businesses that emerged from Nokia Mobiles Phones (NMP) would develop increasingly different business models, customer bases, and activity systems, justifying their organization into separate business groups. For Nokia Networks the differentiation was even more obvious, leading to the search for a critical mass partner and the decision to join forces with Siemens in that business in 2007. The succession of Jorma Ollila at the head of the company, combined with the complex balance of integration and differentiation characteristic of the new organization, led to a renewal of the executive team between 2004 and 2006. In 2006 a new CEO, Olli-Pekka Kallasvuo, a closer collaboration process among top team members, and the reformulation of values all contributed to rekindled commitment among a new generation of senior executives.

In sum, Nokia was characterized by a relatively long period of cognitive change – broadening its strategic perspective and heightening its strategic sensitivity – followed by a faster sequence of organizational and political changes in the top team and, finally, emotional recommitment (*see* Figure 12.3, upper left quadrant).

SAP's journey

SAP's journey has both similarities and deep differences with Nokia's. Some of the organizational changes in the late 1990s and early 2000s triggered conflicts both internally and externally, to focus on specific industry segments and even more on specialized application areas, so SAP now looked to customers as the combination of a platform integrator and a series of quasi-independent application companies. Customers were unhappy about SAP relinquishing its integrator's attitude, and weary of seeing multiple SAP sales approaches for one application or another. Internally, senior executives, who had for so long worked as a team building a single core business, found themselves heading competing units. They competed externally for customer attention and market reach, and internally for resources. So, at the top, the executive team was ready to return to a more integrated way to work together, focussing on a common core platform, and to adopt open interfaces and invite independent application developers to work with SAP. In that sense the company was much more ready to change quickly than Nokia.

Otherwise, key SAP executives had followed a somewhat similar set of steps in widening their perspective on the business and its growth opportunities.

The internet was both a disruption and an opportunity, and as seen in earlier chapters, SAP responded quickly. The internet was regarded as a way to "productize" service – allowing SAP to develop a profitable business model to serve medium-sized enterprises – and as a channel to distribute services and products. This, together with a new, simpler, more modular platform, with greater variety of application portfolios, provided the key to creating a vast new growth opportunity.

Lower down in the organization, however, the shift to a mid/mass market growth focus faced emotional resistance. There were several reasons for this. Some were uncomfortable with a shift to open platform architecture and open innovation, and the loss of first-hand control over quality and product features this implied. Others were concerned with the shift from customized client problem-solving to what they perceived as "shrink-wrap" software product sales. Still others were worried about the implications of shifting to smaller, shorter, faster projects for their competence and on the nature and rhythm of their work. Finally, the lower quality and reliability standards of internet-based services belied the outstanding "German engineering" quality image of SAP.

Top management consensus, supported by the evolution of the NetWeaver platform (SAP's internet-based platform) led to a quick reintegration of the top team around specific steps and activities in value creation. In other words, organizational action followed two streams of changing cognition: the learning about the internet and the feasibility of internet-based platforms to serve the mid-market and, second, the faster and stronger market feedback that SAP should remain integrated and focus on platforms rather than applications. Personal adjustments came later, in particular with the promotion of Leo Apotheker as deputy CEO and the departure of Shai Agassi, the entrepreneur who had come with the internet portal acquisition of Top Tier. Overcoming potential emotional conflicts between Waldorf and Palo Alto, and between traditional and new activities in SAP, was accomplished via joint teams and shared projects, as well as Kagermann and other members of the top team signaling that strategic commitment to the mid-market was no longer discussable.

Sequencing the use of levers

Both at Nokia and SAP, a similar cognitive-organizational-political-emotional (COPE) sequence was followed, albeit at a faster pace in SAP, where the perceived urgency of change in the early 2000s was greater than at Nokia. In both companies the possibility of new wider growth avenues

❝development of new business models and cooperative ecosystems often took longer than expected❞

first had to be discovered and experimented with for the dependence on a highly-focused core business to be lessened. This required some considerable time, partly because new growth avenues were hard to discern early, and the pace of new venture development and corporate learning and commitment had to be kept in sync. Corporate ventures at Nokia were perhaps too early, whereas NMP's own efforts, for instance, failed to gather much support until a growth hiccup in 2001 cast some doubts on the long-term growth potential of core mobile phone devices. Although they were quickly assuaged, these doubts had triggered serious renewal and development efforts across a wider strategic field. These efforts continued in the mid-2000s, although market acceptance of new applications and the development of new business models and cooperative ecosystems often took longer than expected.

Once new growth options became credible, ensuring the existing organization would not stifle or quench them led the top managers of both Nokia and SAP to search for organizations that would allow higher levels of both integration and differentiation between market segments, and activity

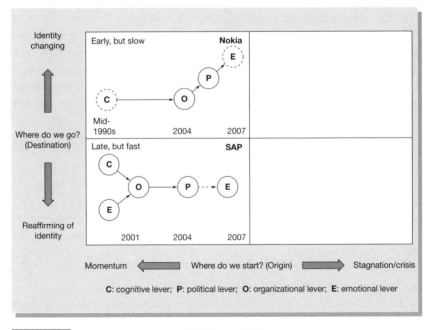

figure 12.3 Action sequences of SAP and Nokia

systems, and allow some flexibility to purposefully vary differentiation and integration over time. Organizational changes followed cognitive changes.

Although the reasons why senior executives leave companies are obviously varied, complex, and multiple, significant changes in the top teams of both companies followed. In part, these were linked to CEO succession issues, in part they stemmed from more personal aspirations on the part of the executives who left. In both cases, though, a new top team composition and configuration emerged. In both companies the emotional lever was somewhat less critical than other levers, because they were still vibrant organizations. A clear and stable top management team, following Ollila's moving to a non-executive chairman's role, and succession plans at SAP becoming clear, facilitated a soft "recommitment" of middle management. These changes are sketched in Figure 12.3.

Recovering from stagnation: HP and IBM

The companies we observed that started from stagnation faced a two-pronged challenge. First, typically, their corporate value creation logic had run out of steam and become obsolete, or it had spread itself too wide over too broad a market space, losing strength. Second, the extent to which, as a result, value creation at the corporate level could be defined any more, in addition to value creation at business unit level, became unclear, and often a matter for debate or conflict between corporate and subunit management. Hence, rebuilding strategic agility for an overextended multibusiness company recovering from a growth stall presented a very different challenge from that faced by more focussed companies with a still vibrant core growth business.

HP, for instance, had started as a focussed test and measurement instrument maker for the budding electronics and avionics industry in World War II and subsequent years. From putting printers into instruments to print test results and adding computing power to analyze measurements, it had evolved into calculators and computers, and their components (including semiconductors). The diversification of the company had been an evolving, mushrooming, entrepreneurial process. Indeed, in the 1980s HP was often cited and studied as an exemplar company that grew big and retained its entrepreneurial spirit, alongside other iconic examples such as 3M or Johnson & Johnson. In the 1990s, the phenomenal success of inkjet printers had taken HP into the home office and consumer electronics worlds. That success, to an extent, masked lack of strength in other areas, computers in particular, where HP found itself caught between IBM or Dell at the low end, and strong workstation makers such as Sun at the high end. The development of amateur digital photography and HP's strong position in consumer-oriented printing devices and cartridges was a mixed blessing: on the one hand it provided more than the company's total profits (other units making losses), on the other it allowed it to ignore weaknesses in other businesses. Furthermore, the printing business dwarfed other businesses and made the corporate value adding role at HP less clear. It was difficult for HP's CEO to find an integrated corporate value creation logic except by calling up appealing, but not always very substantive, convergence themes like "rich digital media", "the home of the future", or "the connected life". The very wide range of products HP made, and the diversity of the markets it served, made a strong integrated value creation logic impossible, even after the decision to spin-off instru-mentation and medical monitoring businesses into a separate company, Agilent.

Although less diverse than HP in products and markets, IBM, whose PC business had strategically played a role somewhat similar to printers for HP (moving it into consumer markets), but not financially (it consistently lost rather than made money), faced a somewhat similar problem. Open stan-dards and client server computing had made its integrated mainframe value creation logic overstretched, too broad, and obsolete. IBM, though, devel-oped a clear integrative logic: refocussing on service businesses to corporate customers. When it engaged in its "deep dive" reviews of business units, IBM considered both the market and competitive potential of each of these as a stand-alone business, but also, and even more importantly, the support each business unit could provide to the corporate services, "On Demand" problem-solving, and to business process outsourcing activities. Such selec-tion criteria, which led for instance most visibly to the sale of the PC business to Lenovo, allowed IBM to refocus itself toward implementing an integrated, but broadly defined, strategy. IBM's core competencies can be seen as complex problem-solving and solution development, implemen-tation, and administration for highly integrated domains, not only of businesses (e.g., P&G) but also of public issues (security, health, energy and environment, crisis management, and disaster relief, for example).

Following overextension (HP) or erosion of an integrative logic (IBM), stra-tegic agility becomes an issue both at the level of individual business units (for instance, IBM missing the transition from mainframe to client server computing, and from proprietary to open standards) and at the corporate level (increasingly ignoring service and customer care).

We observed that the roles of subunits and corporate leadership were therefore quite different. Confronted with a strategic agility challenge, business unit heads will naturally seek greater autonomy, and attempt to respond to it on their own. IBM, for instance, responded to the challenge of open standards and client server computing primarily at the business group level. Rod Adkins recalls:

A major factor [in helping IBM regain a high market share in client server computing] was a clear and decisive bet on open industry movements. This meant IBM had to introduce a new business model – a horizontal one – in addition to its vertical approach, and shift the emphasis between the two. Consistency and speed in approach were absolutely key. Each of the business models had to be consistent and have integrity. Horizontal platforms had to seek maximum economies of scale, from as many vertical manufacturers as possible, and vertical businesses had to become competitive, with or without the horizontal businesses.[1]

Yet, at the same time, IBM retained integrated sales and service forces, hence the need for the strategic agility challenge to be faced at the corporate level as well, to allow vertical and horizontal businesses to work together effectively. In addition to a series of business-group-level actions to rebuild strategic agility, in 2003 IBM engaged in a corporate-level action program – largely driven by management by values – to rebuild strategic agility in the whole company and counter the bureaucratization inherent in coordinating the interaction between numerous business units.

Strategic agility, as defined in this book, is more and more of a paradox, or even a conundrum, the greater the diversity of the corporation's activities. The simplest way to regain strategic agility, once stagnation has set in, is to break the organization into focussed single business (market) units and to demand high performance from them, both for returns and for growth. But, as stressed in chapter 1, such an approach – the one adopted by IBM pre-Gerstner – negates the benefits of an integrated strategy. Mark Hurd at HP took a more subtle approach: to demand higher performance of the business groups, to rekindle their momentum as if "stand-alone" (in line with a more hands-on control style than Fiorina's), and also to start to foster intergroup initiatives. Beginning in 2007, Hurd gave priority to new transverse initiatives, such as "managed homes" for consumer markets or integrated printing services for corporate customers. Strategic agility does not result from transforming the large company into a swarm of more or less well

❝integration across a wide range of businesses tends to slow things down❞

coordinated ventures, nor from "bringing Silicon Valley inside", i.e., from transforming the corporate role into that of a venture capitalist.[2]

Conversely, though, integration – strategic and operational – across a wide range of businesses tends to slow things down, to make collaboration complicated, slow and contentious, and to undermine strategic acuity by promoting hard to pin down (and make concrete) integration themes. Strategic agility and strategic integration don't easily go well together.

The challenge here is the emotional re-energizing of the organization. This calls for rekindling commitment. The sequencing in IBM was that Gerstner was able in 1993 to re-energize the organization by proposing a corporate value creation logic that was both consistent with the past of IBM and offered an avenue for profitable growth and renewal in services, as well as criteria to select which individual businesses to keep within the corporate portfolio. Essentially, Palmisano was confronted with a situation not fundamentally different from Nokia's Kallasvuo, i.e., the need to find a "second win" to accelerate the growth of the company, which then required the use of cognitive levers through the Emerging Business Opportunity (EBO) process and emotional recommitment through management by values.

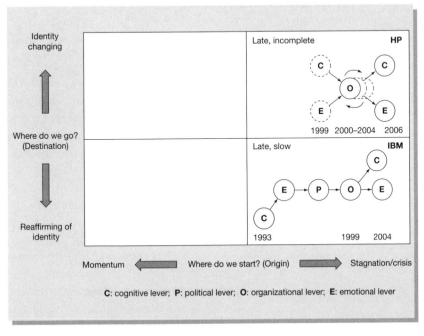

figure 12.4 Action sequences of IBM and HP

Conversely, as illustrated in Figure 12.4, HP's diversity made it more difficult to find a common integrated value creation logic, and such a search clashed with the entrepreneurial culture of HP's engineers. This led Carly Fiorina to work mostly on resource fluidity via a series of organizational integration efforts as an indirect way to promote strategic integration.

Summary: strategic agility is a never-ending quest

Despite their success in building strategic agility in their organization, management processes, and leadership behaviors, companies always face the risk of erosion, of being once more victims of their own success, running down a gaping dead end, or lost in stagnation. However, because strategic agility has such large behavioral and emotional dimensions, every year that organizations achieve and maintain strategic agility makes a fallback less likely. Strategic agility – and the ability for fast strategy – become embedded, institutional capabilities. They become the collective know-how

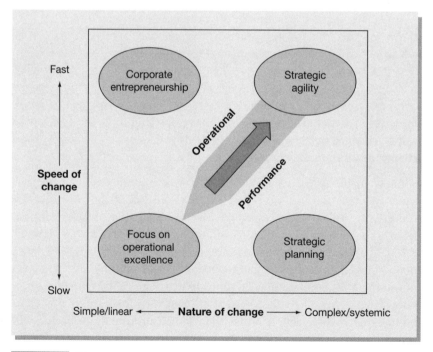

figure 12.5 The healthy tension between strategic agility and operational excellence

of the whole company rather than just the achievement of its leadership. Despite this increasing organizational capability, strategic agility is never obtained for good; it is a never-ending battle. Left to their own devices, most organizations and leadership teams are prone to becoming victims of their own success, as sketched in chapter 7, and to seeing their strategic agility erode over time.

Top management has constantly to balance the continuity and stability so essential to operational efficiency, with the need for evolution and change, and for greater flexibility and agility in strategic decisions, resource redeployment, and collective commitment.

One could indeed argue that most of the time strategic agility is unneeded and represents a costly investment. Of course, it is a bit like maintaining a large standing army in peacetime, a seemingly and hopefully useless expense, but one that can have enormous value. But different CEOs in different companies may make different choices and of course, as summarized in chapter 7, are quite unequally aware of both the need for strategic agility and the actual strategic agility profile (*see* appendix 2) of their company.

As noted, the speed at which specific capabilities underlying strategic agility can be restored, or not, varies between capabilities. Some can perhaps be left to decay, at least temporarily, and be recovered rapidly. Others can't. Opening the strategy process, our first recommendation, can be achieved relatively rapidly, but building trust, mutual understanding, and empathy among members of a top team is the result of years of patient, adaptive leadership practice. The same is true for resource fluidity. An organization can be changed quickly, but the underlying processes and activity systems change much more slowly.

Some elements of the capability profile are also more forward- and foresight-oriented, for instance, new ventures as scouts for core business trajectories. Their "yield" may be low but they may have enormous learning benefits and provide key real options. Obviously, forward-looking, foresight-creating capabilities cannot be left to wither, and need to be maintained attentively. Maintaining wide (in terms of diversity of sources of information) and far-flung (in terms of geographical speed) networks of knowledge-sensing activities is essential to sharpen foresight.[3] Other capabilities that involve action rather than anticipation and are likely to be faster to rebuild when needed, may not have to be given as much attention, on an on-going basis, as other (foresight-enhancing) capabilities.

We would like to conclude with a plea, and perhaps our most basic message: do not evaluate the underlying drivers of strategic agility by their immediate operational value. You could discover that you have lost strategic agility when you need it most. Keep on the strategic agility journey, keep the quest going, even when the immediate pay-offs are perhaps disappointing. You will be rewarded.

References

[1] Authors' interview, Rod Adkins, Senior Vice President, Development and Manufacturing, IBM Systems Technology Group, 4 April 2005.

[2] Hamel, Gary, "Bringing Silicon Valley Inside", *Harvard Business Review*, September/October 1999, Vol. 77 Issue 5.

[3] Doz, Yves, Santos, José, and Williamson, Peter, *From Global to Metanational*, Harvard Business School Press, 2001; and Doz, Yves, Williamson, Peter, and Wilson, Keeley, *Managing Global Innovation*, Harvard Business School Press, 2008.

Appendix 1

The curse of success

Appendix 1 takes a deeper look at the issues discussed at the beginning of chapter 7: the negative consequences of sustained success. The purpose of the analysis is to show how painfully natural the decline and even complete loss of strategic agility is under these circumstances. Without the "antidotes" presented in chapters 4, 5 and 6 in place, the very same sources of high performance that help companies endure successfully for years gradually turn into major obstacles for change and renewal.

The blurring of strategic sensitivity

Let's first focus on the negative consequences of single-minded attention to clear direction. Why and how do the sources of success gradually turn into toxic side-effects hindering strategic renewal? What causes the unnoticed deterioration and blurring of strategic sensitivity in companies?

Tunnel vision

People in companies suffering from tunnel vision can see sharply and far, but unfortunately only within a narrow angle. As mental models determine what information will receive attention, tight focus on successful core business leads companies gradually to narrow their attention to the core business trajectory – and see all new opportunities as a continuation of this familiar logic. As a result, a clear vision for the future of the core business easily turns into a counterproductive force. This problem is compounded because the new stimuli receiving attention tend to be interpreted through current mental models shaped by the past development trajectory. They limit the range of alternative solutions to the ones already known.

Continued growth and profitability may also confirm and strengthen out-dated mental models, delaying change until growth stops completely and the effects of inadequate mental models become painfully felt. For instance, the huge success of second generation (2G) mobile communications in the late 1990s led Nokia and the whole mobile communications industry to underestimate the time and effort needed to build up the mobile services market beyond voice communications.

Using a highly specialized, industry- and context-specific language rein-forces tunnel vision. Both SAP and Nokia were hostages to their highly contextual language in the 1990s, a language they had largely developed on their own as they created their industry. SAP's internal language was cen-tered around Enterprise Resource Planning (ERP) and Nokia's around the Global System for Mobile communications (GSM), originally from Groupe Spécial Mobile. Neither of those languages captured well the broader impli-cations of the internet. Suddenly, the highly context-specific language that had provided both companies with a speed advantage in building and leading an industry for years turned into a counterproductive force where external signals were interpreted in a familiar but misguided way, and not given their true meaning or importance. It took both companies several years and a few acquisitions to understand that the internet was not some-thing to be "just added" to their business but something that fundamentally changed their business.

Tyranny of the core business

Everything else starts to be seen "in light of" the core business as it grows, as if it becomes a prism coloring and selecting what can, or cannot be per-ceived. Growing a large core business easily dulls strategic acuity, because it captures so much top management attention. Even when the leaders of massive core businesses sincerely wish to cooperate, organizations where one business group is dominant, size- and cash-wise, come to look like Snow White and the Seven Dwarfs: the dominant business cannot but play a leading role. This is made more difficult when any other new opportunity, including the company's other businesses, can only look like poor siblings, unlikely to grow to the same size or deliver the same margins as the leading group.

Even more problematic is the fact that a dominant core business makes managers easily frame all new business opportunities only from the per-spective of what they bring to the core business. Executives consider opportunities only through the prism of their current beliefs and vested interests, largely shaped by their experience of growing and running the core business, so misperceptions not only persist, they accumulate. IBM, for instance, did not understand the full potential of services until a new prism was brought in by the new CEO, Lou Gerstner, in 1993. The company was in fact in services "big time" already in the early 1990s, since it had won major outsourcing deals with, for example, Kodak. But this was not seen as a business through the lens of the mainframe core business, only as a support function and as a way to retain engineers made redundant by the slowdown of mainframe.

Executives in a dominant core business also often consider new opportunities in a particularly conservative way. High external and internal performance pressures and the consequent tight management of risk further compound these problems, leading to additional resource allocation to the most familiar activities, to the detriment of renewal opportunities. Hence, it is very difficult to engage in new activities, the strategic framing of which may well be less fully understood and call for more frequent revisions, than that of the core business. Continuity and predictability come to be appreciated and rewarded more than renewal. Resources are committed to play it safe in the core business. A high emphasis on maximizing the growth of the core business leads easily to a cognitive and intellectual tyranny of the core business. New opportunities are not perceived on their own merits but only as potential extensions or threats to the core.

The tyranny of the core business is also one of the main reasons for many corporate ventures, or new business developments in general, not being allowed to develop to their full potential, either as independent businesses or new growth platforms. Instead, these new initiatives are either killed as non-relevant or low-potential ventures, or absorbed as features and functionalities into the core business. Both alternatives, although often justified based on financials, miss the opportunity to learn new business logics and models. The tyranny of the core business simply frames the thinking of management in such a way that seeing new opportunities on their own merits, and giving them enough incubation time, is difficult. This bias is compounded if the key criteria for evaluating the success of a new business follow the core business logic.

Strategic myopia

Like human beings, companies can also suffer from shortsightedness, myopia. They tend to become more shortsighted and inward-looking as they grow bigger, and especially the more successful they become.

Successful strategies, sometimes the product of historical accidents, fortuitous circumstances, or of a brilliant executive or thoughtful collective reflection, are all too easily turned into "winning principles" and procedures, so that often a few years later all that is left are implementation routines and heuristics, the justification of which has been forgotten. Ultimately, the actions taken become less and less consistent with any strategy. Rituals replace reflections, and success breeds failure. In a way, the strategic direction of the business is locked on a particular setting, like an airplane on autopilot. It can only go on a straight path.

This development is very natural in successful incumbents as they may run their business for years without really having to see very far. Once the right strategic path has been found, it makes sense to focus tightly on this track and just execute operations flawlessly. Efficiency improves as the organization practices basic skills. As the company establishes reliable and accountable relationships with external actors, uncertainties about flows of resources and revenues are reduced. The challenge comes only with time. The longer a company "just" executes operations, the more likely it is that it starts to suffer from strategic myopia, and lack of visibility beyond what is immediately ahead. Inertia associated with learning by doing anchors the organization to its past even in the face of environmental change. At this stage people in companies see what they believe rather than believe what they see!

The top team's strategic awareness also declines naturally over time. The longer executive teams are in place, the less turnover in the team and the more homogenous the team members' experiences and understanding become. "Groupthink" may also creep into a successful top team. Predefined roles and personal loyalties, and maybe pecking order, easily grow too deep and overriding, and prevent true dialogue on alternative strategies and solutions. Over time, incremental learning processes, i.e., more of the same based on cumulative experience, overwhelm whatever diversity of experience and knowledge may have characterized the team earlier on.

Active, open-minded communication with external actors also decreases over time. New information, which might alter established interpretative schemes, enters into play less and less frequently. Also, the longer a decision-making group is together, the less it experiments with new ways of doing things. The longer the period of incremental learning, the longer these processes of inertia operate, and the more top team history and precedent guide current behavior.

Set operational roles and overfamiliarity may also weaken the quality of dialogue among senior executives over time. It feels unnecessary to justify explicitly an argument or a point of view. Nobody cares to make checks, as they believe the person knows their stuff anyway, or simply because it feels "nasty" to challenge a friend. In addition, members of a top management team that see their company succeed are likely to become increasingly homogenous in their adherence to idiosyncratic traditions. "Our way of doing things" becomes an implicit unquestioned norm.

Dominance mindset

As companies grow and become successful they easily take dominance for granted. This was perhaps fine in the days of simple market leadership, where each company supplied its goods independently to customers. In the age of strategic alliances, networks, and ecosystem building, a company that strives for leadership in everything it does, and collaborates only if it can dominate its partners, is at a severe disadvantage. Nobody will play its game, and it can no longer succeed alone. This ecosystem perspective often comes intuitively to the resource-poor entrepreneur who knows they must leverage the strengths and resources of others.

Successful incumbents learn to expect that they can have a leading position in all their business endeavors, old and new. They start believing they deserve such a position and cannot accept having anything less. This mindset leads to a reluctance to tolerate uncertainty and a heightened desire for control. Trusting partners and entering into new domains together on an equal basis is very difficult under these conditions. Doing the work by oneself is often the most natural solution. As a result, many large incumbents fall into the trap of spending money on parallel external and internal product and technology development projects. In most cases, this only creates confusion, in addition to duplication of costs.

Snap judgments and intellectual laziness

Excessive self-confidence on the part of key managers resulting from a "been there, done that" attitude may also lead to hasty judgment and jumping to conclusions without proper groundwork. High-action orientation and self-confidence are strengths when dealing with familiar issues, but they easily turn into problems when dealing with new issues requiring thorough analysis and dialogue. Action-oriented people may not have the required patience for addressing complex, systemic problems requiring collective decision-making.

Companies and their top teams may also lack the competence for collective decision-making. Fast growth favors "action heroes" rather than conceptual thinkers. Action heroes question less, roll up their sleeves and get on with things, whereas thinkers appear not to do much. As a result, companies learn to value doing over thinking during high growth years – which over time leads to action bias in the top team. None of this is a problem until the company faces a need for strategic redirection calling for reflection and deep thinking. Suddenly, the company may be short of thinkers, and of respect for them.

The erosion of collective commitment

We now turn our attention to analysing the negative consequences of single-minded attention to quick decisions and commitment. Why and how do clear charters, strong experienced leaders, and specialized expertise so easily turn into inhibitors of collective commitment, paralyzing strategic renewal?

Management divergence

Here, the heart condition metaphor is all too apt. Management divergence sets in as an invisible "killer" of strategic agility, only to be revealed too late when important, difficult decisions can no longer be collectively made. Strategic paralysis follows.

Increasing subunit advocacy, a familiar consequence of growth and consequent divisional organization, and decreasing need for collective strategic decisions in periods of fast growth bring unseen divergence. Key executives who used to spend time brainstorming together and solving key common issues in intense dialogue now have their own interests, roles and responsibilities to attend to.

Complex operations need to run well day-to-day. As complexity grows, and perhaps their own personal ambitions inflate, executives find it more and more difficult to work as a team. The weight of their own responsibilities, high-powered incentives, and maybe personal hubris or anxiety all provide momentum, but separate and divide key executives. They no longer take time to have dialogues with the same depth, as they have the interests of their own units to cater for, the loyalty of their staff to keep earning. The bandwidth of discussable items gradually shrinks, leading at worst to decision stalemates. What used to be collective decision-making and cabinet responsibility becomes a contest among influential individuals for resource allocation, a series of border incidents about organizational turf, and perhaps tournaments for recognition and power. Success undermines the very leadership unity on which it was built.

Heady charm of fame and power

Strong leaders with proven track records easily succumb to the heady charm of fame and power. We know that self-confidence grows as a function of positive feedback in human life. Consequently, when exposed to extreme positive feedback for a long time, we develop inflated egos and hubris.

Successful executives easily ascribe success to their own merit, although their individual success, verified by measurable achievements, may be mostly based on favorable circumstances, often resulting from a positive combination of luck and the insights of a few individuals, and only marginally on their own personal contribution. This belief is often exemplified by the external praise coming from the press and social feedback.

The charm of fame and power also impacts risk-taking. People with inflated egos and hubris tend either to avoid risks, so as not to compromise their well-earned reputation or, on the contrary, to make overly bold commitments and bets. The risk of "losing face" and the ambition of "doing something really big for an encore" both bias decision-making. Both are harmful when evaluating new business opportunities and making respective decisions. Taking new but thoughtful steps with appropriate timing requires healthy self-esteem, deep thinking, and great humility.

Another consequence of continuous personal success is implicit pecking order. High-powered individuals tend to favor having people with similar values and behavior around them, as they need constant positive feedback to continue thriving at work. This leads gradually to internal politics where people avoid challenging each other, and particularly their superiors. And finally, people start losing faith in receiving fair evaluation. An implicit pecking order is also profoundly internally oriented by nature. An external, foreign input poses an unwelcome threat to the "system". As a result, a company's natural external orientation gradually turns to an internal one. A closed, small, "mutual admiration society" takes hold, increasingly disconnected from the real world.

An implicit pecking order also makes true dialogue at all levels, including the top team, difficult. In a setup where people's value and status depend on where they sit, and how strongly they impress others, it is difficult to have a constructive dialogue on an equal basis. The result is known before the discussion has started. And yet a team requires members who participate because they have something to contribute, not because they happen to represent the interests of a particular person.

Expert management

Expert management is another consequence of strong leaders with proven track record. Senior executives simply "know better"; in fact, in many companies this is why they got to top positions. Thus, when approached for advice or for commitment, capable senior executives make decisions on the basis of their best expert judgment.

The temptation for expert management is exemplified by high-action orientation and perceived time pressure on all decision matters. High emphasis on fast and firm decisions leads to expert management. Those who know best decide. Decision-making is delegated to the top, where choices are made quickly based on an individual's expertise, not on collective knowledge of the whole top team supported by a process of involvement of all the key stakeholders. Again, this is often an effective way to proceed in the middle of a high-growth period, but not when pondering difficult strategic questions.

Another problem with expert management is the high risk of non-constructive debate. We have observed strategically ineffective teams having too much or too little debate. Too little debate is easily explained: juxtaposed experts responsible for separate activities carefully avoid stepping on each other's toes, tolerate little challenge to their expertise, and maintain cordial but distant relationships. Leadership unity deteriorates and meetings adopt the format of successive separate, polite, and non-controversial "operations reviews" and mutual information-sharing sessions. Excessive debate may result from shared agendas, outcome interdependence, and process integration, but it will achieve little common ground and no agreed-upon language. Animated or even heated discussions take place, but no conclusions are reached or firm collective commitments made.

Emotional apathy

Gradually growing emotional apathy among experienced leaders is the last, but certainly not the least, significant toxic side-effect of deteriorating collective commitment. Even the highest paid and most dynamic executives can lose their energy after many battles won. People may just lose interest in what they have been doing or get tired. It is hard to avoid emotional apathy when future opportunities look less thrilling than past experiences. This is often the case in companies that have experienced extraordinary growth and sustained success. Finding new and grander challenges can be very difficult, if not impossible. Extrinsic rewards also become empty after a while, either because stock prices stall or simply because people already have enough money.

Fear can also lead to emotional apathy. This can easily happen under high external pressure – not typically because of the pressure itself but because of how people are treated. Fear creeps in only if people start feeling that their evaluation is not fair and if failure is not tolerated. Collective decision-making under fear easily becomes an arena where people try to impress the right individuals and avoid being exposed, undermining the integrity of the whole process.

The outcomes of emotional apathy are dramatic. First, the top employees gradually turn from an inspired team into a bunch of disenfranchised individuals trying to fulfill their responsibility without a "burning fire". The second problem relates to the spillover effects of the disenfranchised top team. The low energy level of top teams is directly reflected in the whole organization, which constantly senses the behavior and feelings of top team members. Lack of leadership unity and energy cannot be hidden. At worst, emotional apathy leads to leadership team paralysis, where big decisions are postponed, as no real will to take collective leadership can be found. This easily leads to middle-management cliques in the organization, as people try to compensate for their frustration by doing something. But without a mandate to decide, the frustration only increases.

The sclerosis of resource fluidity

Let us finally turn our attention to analysing the negative consequences of single-minded pursuit of high efficiency. Why does the drive for efficiency so easily result in increasingly resilient resource allocation patterns that lock the company on a given trajectory?

Resource imprisonment

Most successful companies lose their ability to move capital and human resources across the organization in a flexible manner in the face of fast growth. Continuous resource constraints, and creeping doubts about the magnitude of corporate-level resource allocation to growing their business, lead business-level executives to hoard resources within their units. The more successful and the more powerful and autonomous the business units grow, the more this becomes a problem. The heads of the biggest, fastest-growing and most successful groups end up virtually taking the top management hostage. As a result, resources are trapped into subunits, resulting in a risk of overfunding established legacy businesses and under-committing to new strategic opportunities.

As an example of the above, in a desire to enhance accountability and focus, decrease management complexity, impose tougher performance demands, and face lean, more specialized competition in a focussed way, John Akers, IBM's CEO until 1993, decentralized – and nearly devolved – management responsibility in IBM to a series of business division heads in the late 1980s. As a result, the autonomy of IBM's business groups grew and its resources were trapped in units fighting for the "limelight". Corporate-wide resource allocation to new promising opportunities, and dealing with IBM as an integrated supplier of IT systems and solutions, became increasingly difficult.

A conventional hierarchical organization often compounds this problem as it enables both conscious and, in many of cases, unconscious hiding of resources, as top executives do not always know how resources are being deployed beyond their immediate subordinates.

Transparency down in the organization is not always obvious and many budgetary "games" can be played all too easily. Even when caught, powerful business group heads can typically get away with it because of their huge financial contribution.

Ironically, conventional planning systems and budgeting practices only deepen resource imprisonment in many companies. Formal bureaucratic management processes leave little room for adjustment and change. Instead of challenging, they protect the interests of core businesses by seldom questioning the history and existence of the legacy, but rather asking: "What more do we need to do to continue being competitive in our 'home' domain?" New businesses are funded only after the legacy businesses interests have been served.

In addition to legacy budgeting, management systems are typically designed to support resource allocation within current businesses, not across them. This makes the evaluation of resource utilization efficiency across the company difficult. Many companies find out too late that they have been developing the same "wheel" in many places, with only slightly different "shapes".

Activity systems that become rigid

Riding the storm of fast growth encourages companies to develop "fit for purpose", highly specialized, and tightly integrated activity systems with proprietary architectures. Business-specific differentiation, speed, and initial cost efficiency simply call for this. The performance of these systems separates success from collapse. In the mobile phones industry, volume manufacturing and global logistics have been a key competitive differentiator for all companies for years. Many otherwise successful companies, such as Boeing, Motorola, and Nokia, suffered near supply chain "meltdown" in periods of fast growth. The risk is frighteningly real. Once systems are in place, the fear of changing elements of these partly tacit and complex activity systems, with sometimes less than fully known causalities, often accelerates this "convergence to fit" process.

Designing modular activity systems capable of changes and reconfiguration, and fostering collaboration, is difficult. The rush to shortcut rigorous business system design to meet exploding demand growth is tempting. Problems typically arise only when business matures and changes have to be implemented. Then the need for more flexible business systems is felt. Highly efficient business systems, well honed to one particular product and business model, for one purpose, do not support other purposes well. Instead, they turn into major rigidity and cost factors after a while. Proprietary activity systems, at the level of individual business groups or divisions, do not allow efficient resource sharing and people rotation. Different standards, processes, practices, and tools make it difficult for people to move from one to another.

Ties that bind

Enduring growth companies take great pride in their strong and lasting customer and partner relationships. Although they sometimes just reflect grudging customer dependence on a dominant supplier, these relationships are often the cornerstones of success. Strong customer and partner relationships also lead to ties that bind. Obviously, ties that confer strength on a given core business trajectory become a problem for strategic agility. Customer-responsive resource allocation processes in successful organizations provide impetus only for innovations demanded by current customers in existing markets, or seen by the company as anticipating their needs. In fact, the resource allocation processes of these companies typically deny resources to technologies and investments stemming from emerging new areas and customers. As a result, strong relationships with existing customers and partners place stringent limits on the strategies incumbent companies can and cannot pursue. Managing the expectations and fulfilling the promises and contractual obligations made for key customers and other primary stakeholders make agility very difficult for successful incumbents.

Ties that bind are obviously embedded also in proprietary product and solution architectures with strong backward and forward compatibility requirements across generations of products and solutions. Particularly in the business-to-business (B2B) environment, suppliers make long-term commitments to support older generation solutions. At best these ties can create favorable "customer lock-ins", but when the company wants to change course these ties become major obstacles for renewal. Breaking out from these ties calls for recreating the architecture for the whole solution and for expensive "migration" projects.

Finally, companies sometimes also become tied to their products and ongoing business via their CEO's public identity. This is typically the case in entrepreneurial companies with a longstanding owner-CEO. This close tie may serve a company well for a while, as the company's core product and strategy becomes better known, because of the personal touch and credibility related to them. However, over time this close association of the owner and the product/strategy becomes a burden. It is more difficult for these companies to change course, particularly as long as the "face" of the company is still onboard, unless the face itself is defined in a versatile fashion.

Management mediocrity and competence gaps

Resource fluidity can also be negatively affected by insufficient people development during fast growth. Learning by doing and building on experience are often the only possible people development paths for a long time in successful growth companies. As the business results continue to be good, these learning mechanisms easily become an accepted norm for competence development in these companies. The problem with these natural learning mechanisms is that they do not systematically build up people's leadership and general management competences. In this system, functionally trained experts can quickly find themselves as leaders of hundreds of people worldwide – with little or no general management training. Furthermore, these mechanisms do not encourage people to develop their professional skills on a broad basis, as moving horizontally across the company risks individual career development and their own unit's performance. Continuous performance pressures force these businesses to "play it safe" with those people that know the business best.

For a long time, fast growth and success in a core business may hide both professional and managerial competence shortcomings. Successful growth also makes it easier for the management to forgive these shortcomings when visible. Companies face difficulties only when growth levels off and competition intensifies. Learning-by-doing opportunities dry up, or no longer suffice to prepare people for new demands, and competence gaps become visible in people whose true managerial and leadership capabilities have not been tested in adversity.

Furthermore, global organization so typical of many of today's successful companies does not naturally provide many opportunities for general management development in a similar manner to the multidomestic organizations of the 1970s and 1980s, where smaller country subsidiaries provided natural training grounds at an affordable risk. If not rotated and actively developed, and in spite of fast growth, individuals may end up in top management positions without having had a proper chance to see and experience the corporation and its businesses from different perspectives.

Summary

This appendix described how and why strategic agility "naturally" turns into strategic paralysis over time – if companies do not put in place the preventative strategic agility enablers described in chapters 4, 5 and 6. The main toxic side-effects that cause deterioration in strategic agility are shown in Figure A1.1.

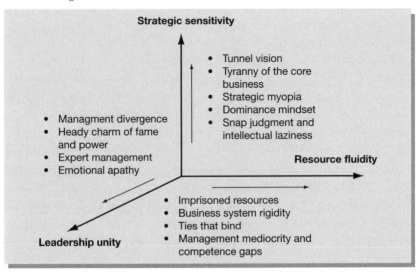

figure A1.1 Strategic agility easily turns into strategic paralysis over time

Appendix 2

Deciding on the path to take

Appendix 2 will help you, a corporate leader, to diagnose your company's current strategic agility profile and to get started with the required actions. After all, the lessons learned in this book are not worth much unless they help you rekindle energy and learn to thrive on change.

Where are you today?

The first thing you should do is to analyse your current strategic agility profile. A simple assessment in line with Table A2.1 of each of the toxic side-effects described in Appendix 1 will help you to get started. Evaluating with your management team, say on a scale from 1 to 7, how severely your company suffers from each toxic side-effect helps you get around issues that are not normally analysed in the course of daily business reviews. In addition to having a dialogue with your management team, you may want to invite a broad group of people in the company to contribute. Comparing the results of your own management team to the results of your key middle- and front-line managers gives you valuable additional insights. You may also want to extend the analysis in a slightly modified format to your key external stakeholders, to understand their perspective better.

You should be aware, however, of the caveats in direct evaluation. Rating the seriousness of each symptom is likely to introduce several kinds of bias among all levels of managers, as it easily allows people either to move into denial mode, or use the opportunity to vent all kinds of anger and frustration, and paint an exceedingly dark picture of the company's predicament.

Profiling your company against the array of toxic side-effects and making a systems analysis map of the interaction between several toxic effects are likely to help you identify high-leverage pressure points on which to exercise priority efforts (introduced in chapters 4 to 6) to prevent, or reverse, the decline of strategic agility. This obviously applies only if your profile is essentially to the left (healthy) side of Table A2.1, with only a few small spikes, or little bulges, toward the right side.

Arranging the results of your analysis of your strategic agility profile (from Table A2.1, or something equivalent) against the capabilities presented in chapters 4 to 6, and an assessment of how long it takes to rebuild them, may help you understand the nature and extent of the risks you, and your company, take in not investing in maintaining and developing strategic agility. Comparing the risks with the cost and complexity involved in specific capability development and maintenance gives you an idea of how much you need to invest in strategic agility. You may well conclude that for your company strategic agility is not required, or not quite valuable enough to justify its costs and complexity – organizationally, culturally, and otherwise – since the risks are not so high.

Conversely, should you see major discontinuity and disruption looming on the horizon, then investing explicitly in strategic agility becomes essential to survival.

Now, what if your strategic agility profile, emerging from an assessment such as suggested above, is actually disastrous? Then you need to get into a different action mode and take a leaf from the examples analysed in chapters 8 to 11, and think through the action spaces and leadership levers introduced in chapter 7. Concerted, CEO-led, intense action in all four spaces – cognitive, organizational, political, and emotional – is likely to be required.

Getting started

Let's conclude, practically, by reviewing how Nokia exploited the findings of our research. The authors met with Olli-Pekka Kallasvuo, then COO of Nokia in spring 2006, to share with him the key findings of this research as well as to discuss possible ways to use it. Kallasvuo found the findings interesting and relevant for Nokia's business situation. The company had been widening its core business trajectory already for years, and wanted to learn more about the enablers and mechanisms behind accelerating strategic agility. Kallasvuo also felt that the timing for sharing and discussing the implications of the research was good. Nokia had been undergoing a major top team transition and Kallasvuo himself was about to start as the new CEO of the company in June 2006. It was an ideal

table A2.1 Simple diagnostics for toxic side-effects

Toxic side-effects of fast growth and high performance	Source	Consequence	Not			Relevant		Highly	
			1	2	3	4	5	6	7

Destroyers of strategic sensitivity

	Source	Consequence
■ **Tunnel vision**	– Caused by tight focus on incremental improvements and consistency	– Internal short-term orientation
■ **Tyranny of core business**	– Caused by performance pressures and familiarity to core business	– Framing everything in the light of core business; committing resources through core businesses
■ **Strategic myopia**	– Caused by tight focus on core business trajectory	– Considering everything outside the core as non-relevant
■ **Dominance mindset**	– Caused by over-reliance on own experience and implicit assumptions	– Reluctance to open collaboration and experimentation
■ **Snap judgment and intellectual laziness**	– Caused by familiarity with core business details	– Risks of mistakes in unfamiliar territory

Destroyers of resource fluidity

	Source	Consequence
■ **Imprisoned resources**	– Caused by continuous resource constraints and growing doubts about corporate-level resource allocation	– Core business managers wanting to own their resources, lack of transparency
■ **Business system rigidity**	– Caused by increasingly tight fit between activities	– Highly differentiated and specialized activity systems
■ **Ties that bind**	– Caused by product compatibility needs and customer partner commitments	– Decreased strategic freedom
■ **Management mediocrity and competence gaps**	– Caused by hasty recruitment and insufficient people development	– Forgiven and hidden shortcomings, partly wrong competence

Toxic side-effects of fast growth and high performance

	Source	Consequence	Not			Relevant		Highly	
			1	2	3	4	5	6	7
Management divergence	– Caused by naturally increasing subunit advocacy and decreasing need for collective decisions	– Declining intensity of dialogue, stalemates, and politics							
Heady charm of fame and power	– Caused by the inflated egos and hubris of the key leaders	– "Action hero syndrome", implicit pecking order, risk aversion or overly bold commitments							
Expert management	– Caused by action orientation and perceived time pressure	– Decisions elevating to the top team where they are done quickly, based on individual expertise							
Emotional apathy	– Caused by future opportunities looking less thrilling than past	– "Tired hero syndrome"							

Destroyers of leadership unity

time to evaluate where the company was and where it should go in terms of strategic agility.

Consequently, Kallasvuo set up a two-day top team workshop we led in June 2006 to evaluate Nokia's strategic agility and to agree jointly on the action agenda going forward.

In preparing for the workshop we collaborated with Nokia's HR organization to conduct one-to-one interviews with each of the top team members. This was needed to familiarize the members with the strategic agility framework and key findings and to learn more about their expectations and individual opinions. At the same time, the workshop organizers gained a feeling about the key business challenges and dynamics between the top team members.

In addition, an indirect approach to the diagnostics of strategic agility was used. In a nutshell we surveyed – online – a large proportion of managers and staff, asking them to input short stories of specific incidents where the company had responded well, or failed to respond satisfactorily to major challenges, in the best of Nokia's spirit, or not. We also elicited a set of comments, freely written by all employees, on how they perceived the company and the behavior of its people. We then content-analysed and coded various contributions, using the categories of toxic side-effects of growth and success presented in Appendix 1. Obviously, some of these side-effects – management hubris, for instance – are perhaps more difficult to isolate and analyse than others, but we used text analysis and semiotics software tools to help in the process.[1] This provided a solid, and evocative, foundation on which to root a serious dialogue among executive board members.

We also elicited examples and comments about where the company had seriously "missed the boat", and why. Although we did not have time to pursue the analysis of these examples in detail, they provided additional insight. More generally, the experience of one of the contributors in helping other companies with these issues suggests that learning from analysing failure is important, all the more so when it comes to strategic agility. Obviously, losses of strategic agility are often progressive, hard to detect, and seldom clearly visible until it is too late.[2] But delays, mishaps in programs, in new product development, in understanding markets are good "warning signs" about the erosion of strategic agility.

Overall, the integrated survey provided Nokia's management a broader view on the company's strengths and weaknesses related to strategic agility.

The actual top team workshop was divided into two parts:

1 Sharing the results and evaluating Nokia's strategic agility in the light of top management interviews and the strategic agility survey.

2 Agreeing on the action agenda going forward.

The first part of the workshop included small group work:

■ evaluating Nokia's toxic side-effects and discussing the results of the broader survey;

■ identifying key areas for improvement.

The second part of the workshop concentrated on evaluating Nokia's strategy, strength of integrated value action logic, and corporate-level need for strategic agility. The key question in this analysis was: "How integrated a company do we want and need to have?" This was an important question, as it determined how much corporate-wide strategic agility was needed.

The workshop led to several focussed development activities during fall 2006, particularly in the area of management and governance processes. In this connection, for instance, the roles and responsibilities of each of the top team members were evaluated in the context of both corporate and subunit contributions. Each top team role was also opened up in relation to interdependencies: "What do I need, from whom, to succeed in my job?" was analysed in detail. This led to much deeper understanding of each other's challenges and much more balanced target-setting, as well as the beginning of a heightened awareness of a shared collective action agenda.

The governance mechanisms of key corporate-wide assets were also evaluated and new additional corporate-wide responsibilities were assigned to some of the key line managers. In addition to finding a good balance between corporate integration and business unit differentiation, this exercise helped Nokia further to improve collective commitment to a shared corporate agenda.

In spite of the usefulness of strategic agility as a concept and framework, Nokia's top team felt that it did not want to introduce yet another separate concept or change program. Nokia was performing well and it had been investing in many of the strategic agility enablers already for years, and therefore it did not require a transformative CEO-led change program in line with the cognitive-organizational-political-emotional (COPE) framework of this book. Instead, it agreed to embed strategic agility as a pervasive part of its overall leadership agenda, and of the management process of the company. This ensured that strategic agility was embraced as a permanent capability, not just treated as a one-time change initiative in the company.

Many of the strategic agility enablers had already been embedded in Nokia's planning process and organizational design (e.g., assumption-based continuous planning, multidimensional organization supported by shared business infrastructure), and values-based leadership approach. These well-established "management practices" provided a "home base" for the agreed additional strategic agility development efforts. For instance, it was agreed that improving external and internal collaboration should be addressed through all the key management process elements: planning process, organizational design, and values.

In June 2007 Nokia announced a new, highly interdependent organization, to be fully in place by 1 January 2008. In the new business, all mobile devices from the three previous business groups (Mobile Phones, Multimedia and Enterprise Solutions) were merged into one Devices Unit – and all the software and digital services activities from the business groups were put into a new Software and Services Unit. The go-to-market, manufacturing and logistics activities were organized into one Markets Unit. These units formed one highly interdependent company in which no major business decisions can be made without strong alignment and agreement between all units.

References

[1] We used a Finnish consultancy company, Fountainpark, as our partner in this analysis.

[2] For a very visible example of the loss or absence of strategic visibility, until it is too late, *see* Doz, Yves, "Airbus", INSEAD case study, forthcoming.

Abbreviations

3G – a third generation cellular mobile communication technology

CSG – Corporate Strategy Group, comprised of SAP's internal strategy development team

DCU – Digital Convergence Unit, a business unit of Nokia Mobile Phones business group, developing new applications beyond voice telephony

EBO – Emerging Business Opportunities

GPRS – General Packet Radio Service a "2.5" generation cellular mobile communication technology

GSM – Global System for Mobile communication, a cellular standard originally from Groupe Spécial Mobile

IP – internet protocol

NBDF – Nokia Business Developoment Forum

NET – Nokia Networks, a business group of NMP

NMP – Nokia Mobile Phones, the company's largest business group which was split into smaller groups in the 2004 reorganization

NVO – New Ventures Organization, one of Nokia's business groups from 1998 to 2004, which concentrated on developing new businesses beyond cellular communication

SAP – founded in 1972 as *Systemanalyse und Programmentwicklung* by five former IBM engineers in Mannheim, Germany

SKF – Timken's traditional European ball-bearing competitor

SMS – short messaging service, created by Tampere lab

WCDMA – Wideband Code Division Multiple Access

WIMAX – Worldwide Interoperability for Microwave Access

WLAN – wireless local area network

Index